Saulius Geniusas

Phenomenology of Productive Imagination
Embodiment, Language, Subjectivity

AF211790

BODY AND CONSCIOUSNESS

Editor: James Richard Mensch

Consulting Editor: Donald Phillip Verene

ISSN

Saulius Geniusas

PHENOMENOLOGY OF PRODUCTIVE IMAGINATION

Embodiment, Language, Subjectivity

Bibliografische Information der Deutschen Nationalbibliothek

Die Deutsche Nationalbibliothek verzeichnet diese Publikation in der Deutschen Nationalbibliografie; detaillierte bibliografische Daten sind im Internet über http://dnb.d-nb.de abrufbar.

Bibliographic information published by the Deutsche Nationalbibliothek

Die Deutsche Nationalbibliothek lists this publication in the Deutsche Nationalbibliografie; detailed bibliographic data are available in the Internet at http://dnb.d-nb.de.

Cover picture: ID 46316215 © Michael Kuelbel | Dreamstime.com

ISBN-13: 978-3-8382-1552-5

© *ibidem*-Verlag, Stuttgart 2022

Alle Rechte vorbehalten

Printed in the EU

For my mother,

Izolda G. Geniušienė

CONTENTS

ACKNOWLEDGMENTS

Some of the chapters in this study are reworked versions of previously published essays. Chapter I includes excerpts from the Editor's Introduction to *Stretching the Limits of Productive Imagination: Studies in Kantianism, Phenomenology and Hermeneutics* (ed. by S. Geniusas, London: Rowman & Littlefield, 2018). A shorter version of Chapter II was published under the title "What is Productive Imagination? The Hidden Resources of Husserl's Phenomenology of Phantasy," in *The Subject(s) of Phenomenology* (ed. by I. Apostolescu, Dordrecht: Springer, 2020, 135-153). Chapter III includes extracts from "The Stuff That Dreams Are Made Of: Max Scheler and Paul Ricœur on Productive Imagination," which was published as a chapter in *Hermeneutics and Phenomenology: Figures and Themes* (ed. by S. Geniusas and P. Fairfield, New York: Bloomsbury, 2018, 93-105). An earlier and shorter version of Chapter IV was published under the title "Productive Imagination and the Cassirer-Heidegger Disputation" in *Productive Imagination: Its History, Meaning and Significance* (ed. by S. Geniusas and D. Nikulin, London: Rowman & Littlefield, 2018, 135-155). A shorter version of Chapter V was published under the title "Miki Kiyoshi and the Logic of the Imagination" in *Stretching the Limits of Productive Imagination* (ed. by S. Geniusas, London: Rowman & Littlefield, 2018, 91-111). An abridged version of Chapter VII was published under the title "Between Phenomenology and Hermeneutics: Paul Ricœur's Philosophy of Imagination" in *Human Studies* 38/2, 2015, 223-241. Chapter VIII was published previously under the title "Against the Sartrean Background: Ricœur's Lectures on Imagination" in *Research in Phenomenology*, 46/1, 2016, 98-116.

In May 2016, I organized an international conference, *Productive Imagination: Its History, Meaning and Significance*, at the Chinese University of Hong Kong. The conference participants came from twelve different countries in Asia, Europe and North America. I have continued discussions with many of them to this day. I had all of their papers, which were subsequently published in various volumes, in mind while writing this book. A special word of thanks is due to Suzi Adams, Claudia Baracchi, Jagna Burdzinska, Nicolas de Warren, Annabelle Dufourcq, Alfredo Ferrarin, Gediminas Karoblis, Dalius Jonkus, Claudio Majolino, Eric S. Nelson, Kwok-ing Lau Dmitri Nikulin, Witold Plotka, Roger W.H. Savage, Michela Summa, George H. Taylor, Qingjie James Wang and Günther Zöller. I would like to extend my gratitude to George H. Taylor and Patrick Crosby for sharing with me Paul Ricœur's so-far unpublished lectures on productive imagination that were delivered at the University of Chicago in 1975. For some time now, George H. Taylor and Patrick Crosby had been preparing these lectures for publication together, and now, after Patrick Crosby passed away in 2020, it is to be expected that George H. Taylor will be the sole editor of the volume. I would also like to thank John Krummel for sharing his so-far unpublished translation of the second chapter of Miki Kiyoshi's "Institution" — the second chapter of Miki's *The Logic of the Imagination*. A special word of thanks is also due to James R. Mensch, the editor of the book series, *Body and Consciousness*, in which this study is being published, and to the two reviewers for their constructive feedback.

Furthermore, I would like to express my sincere gratitude to the Alexander von Humboldt Foundation for the Research Fellowship that made the preparation of this book possible. A significant part of this book was written in the Husserl Archive at the University of Cologne. A special word of thanks is also due to Dieter Lohmar, the Director of the Archive, for all of his hospitality and support.

INTRODUCTION

When Paul Ricœur delivered his lectures, *Imagination as a Philosophical Problem*, at the University of Chicago in 1975, he initiated his discussion with reflections on the reasons that had forced philosophers to disregard imagination in their investigations. At the very beginning of his Introductory Lecture, Ricœur lamented that imagination is a largely forgotten theme in philosophy in general. He spoke of the "eclipse of the problem" and of the reasons behind this eclipse. "At the present time," he bemoaned, "there is nearly nothing which could be called 'a philosophy of the imagination'" (Ricœur unpublished, 1:1).[1] Edward S. Casey expressed a similar sentiment a year later in his 1976 *Imagining: A Phenomenological Study*. In this outstanding investigation, Casey spoke of the "tradition of condemnation and neglect" of imagination, of philosophical attitudes that range "from distrust to disgust," and of the pompous assumption that thinking is, or at least should be, image-free. In light of this diagnosis, Casey set himself the task "to rectify the tendency on the part of many Western philosophers to belittle imagination — or, still worse, to neglect it altogether" (Casey 1976, ix).

The philosophical landscape has changed tremendously over the last decades. Since at least the beginning of the twenty-first century, there has been an explosion of interest in imagination in philosophy and its related fields, so much so that one can state without exaggeration that imagination now occupies a central place in contemporary philosophical and, more broadly, intellectual discussions. This view is strongly expressed in recently published handbooks on the philosophy of imagination (See Kind 2016) and in cross-disciplinary handbooks on imagination (See Abraham 2020). How are we to understand such a radical change of mindset across

---

[1]   Ricœur's lectures, "Imagination as a Philosophical Problem," which were delivered at the University of Chicago in 1975 and to which I am here referring, still remain unpublished. I am grateful to George H. Taylor and Patrick Crosby, who have been preparing the edition of these lectures for many years, for granting the permission to quote Ricœur's lectures. When citing this work, I will refer to it as unpublished and will indicate the lecture number before the manuscript page number.

the disciplines? In particular, what is it that motivates philosophers nowadays to reflect on imagination? Of course, the reasons are highly diverse. Some present their investigations in specific philosophical fields, such as aesthetics, epistemology, philosophy of mind or cognitive science, with the aim of disclosing the highly diverse ways in which imagination is implicated therein. Others see research on imagination as a fresh chance to open up cross-disciplinary discussions between different research fields. Others, still, are concerned with showing the rich variety of ways imagination has been addressed in the history of philosophy, indicating, precisely, the place it has been assigned in diverse philosophical frameworks and traditions. Yet others are concerned with concept clarification, that is, with the question: what does the concept of imagination mean and is it possible to provide a definition of it that would accommodate the different ways it has been employed in everyday use and in scholarly discussions? In these and other highly diverse ways, philosophical research corroborates the view that imagination lies at the very heart of our existence and that it constitutes an inextricable feature of our experience.

It should be stressed that the widespread interest in imagination in philosophy and related fields over the past decades has been largely triggered by recent technological developments. Since the mid-1990s, Internet and smartphone technology has had an enormous impact on the general culture. Whether in public or in private spheres, we are haunted by images, which are always there for our consumption, and which are channeled through our smartphones, iPads, laptops, TV screens, etc. This ubiquity of images has had a profound impact on human experience: manufactured and mass-produced images shape the way we see the world. This has led some postmodern thinkers to contend that, nowadays, the order between reality and the images of reality has become reversed; our everyday reality now imitates images, which were supposed to be imitations of it, but which now precede and shape the real world. In Jean Baudrillard's words, we live in a world of hyperreality, understood as the generation of models of reality without origin in reality: "the territory no longer precedes the map... it is nevertheless the map that precedes the territory—precession of simulacra—that engenders the territory" (Baudrillard 1994, 1).

Yet paradoxically, this ubiquity of images signals the retreat of imagination: insofar as they are everywhere, images rob us of the space that was previously reserved for autonomous imagination. As Richard Kearney insightfully remarked in the late 1980s, "one of the greatest paradoxes of contemporary culture is that at a time when the image reigns supreme the very notion of creative human imagination seems under mounting threat" (Kearney 1988, 3). This is not surprising; insofar as we are continuously haunted by images, we have no reason to shape them ourselves. To express this in phenomenological terms, the ubiquity of image consciousness renders phantasy-consciousness obsolete.[2]

Or so it would seem at first glance. And yet, before rushing to conclusions, we should ask ourselves the following questions: how can the cultural transformations I am here alluding to render imagination a thing of the past? Do these transformations really signal that images can no longer be understood in terms of their "subjectivity" or "phenomenality," but must, instead, be conceived as anonymous commodities? How can the image *precede* the reality

---

[2]   This tendency is born, not with the new technologies I have here mentioned, but with postmodernism in the arts. Consider Andy Warhol's observation: "I always think quantity is the best gauge on anything…When Picasso died I read in a magazine that he had made four thousand masterpieces in his lifetime and I thought, 'Gee, I could do that in a day.' So I started. And then I found out, 'Gee, it takes more than a day to do four thousand pictures.' You see, the way I do them, with my technique, I really thought I could do four thousand in a day. And they'd all be masterpieces because they'd all be the same painting. And I started and I got up to about five hundred and then I stopped. But it took more than a day, I think it took a month. So at five hundred a month, it would have taken me about eight months to do four thousand masterpieces… It was disillusioning for me, to realize it would take me that long." I am not the first one to suggest that postmodernism undermines the modernist commitment to the autonomy of creative imagination and that it signals the critical turn from production to reproduction by robbing artworks of what Walter Benjamin had called their "unique and irreplaceable aura." According to Warhol, an image is a "mechanically reproducible commodity" and it belongs to the "total communications package." In the present context, I wish to stress that over the last few decades, this proliferation of images and their transformation into a "mechanically reproducible commodity" is no longer a specific characteristic of the arts but a feature that characterizes our general culture.

that it represents? How can it infiltrate human experience and shape the appearance of phenomena? So, also, we should ask ourselves, what is this autonomous imagination that is now, supposedly, rendered obsolete by the ubiquity of images? Could it be the case that certain forms of imagination are irreducible from human experience, that although they can be covered up, they cannot be eliminated? In other words, is it, perhaps, impossible for a cultural transformation to emerge that would lead to their demise or replacement? Even with the uncertainty of all of these questions, one thing is uncontroversial: the widespread cultural transformations I am here alluding to give rise to numerous philosophical concerns.

The following study will focus on one particular form of imagination — productive imagination; it will address this from a phenomenological point of view, with the aim of showing how this figure of imagination has been conceptualized in the phenomenological tradition. One can only be surprised that, to this day, there are no book-length studies that have exclusively focused on the phenomenological analyses of productive imagination. The fundamental goal of this study is to show why such an investigation is needed and why, in its absence, our understanding of the phenomenology of imagination remains severely limited. My goal is to show that such an investigation can in significant ways enrich our understanding of subjectivity. More precisely, my goal is to disclose the fundamental ways that our world experience has been shaped by our *bodies, consciousness* and *language,* and also to uncover the central reasons why our embodied consciousness of the world, taken in its linguistic and pre-linguistic modalities, is soaked in imagination.

* * *

From the moment we are born, we exist in the flesh. Embodied existence is the only mode of existence we are familiar with. To what degree, and in what ways, is the power of imagination shaped by our embodied existence? At the same time, imagination is a feature of conscious life. Only insofar as we are conscious are we able to imagine. What must consciousness be like if it is to relate to the world, not only perceptually and conceptually, but also imaginatively? When we focus in on that specifically human form of life, we cannot help but admit that humans are speaking animals. To what degree, and in what ways, does language shape the powers of imagination? These are some of the central questions this book focuses on.

The following chapters will investigate the different ways that the concept of productive imagination has been conceptualized in phenomenology. The uncertainty about the meaning of productive imagination is strongly imbedded in this philosophical tradition. Some of the voices in this tradition have identified the narratives on productive imagination in post-Kantian philosophy (especially in German idealism and romanticism) as an "orgy of overestimation" (see Casey 1976, 1) – which must be replaced by dispassionate phenomenological descriptions. Others have argued that this concept still remains underdeveloped and that its further clarification constitutes one of the central tasks of the phenomenology of imagination.[3]

In phenomenology, Ricœur stands out as *the* philosopher of productive imagination. There is, however, one claim that we come across repeatedly in Ricœur's writings on the imagination that I find deeply problematic. According to Ricœur, the history of the phenomenology of imagination is the history of *reproductive* imagination. One of the goals of this study is to demonstrate that Ricœur's claim is unwarranted and that, in the classical phenomenological tradition, we come across both explicit and implicit investigations of productive imagination. These investigations should be viewed as either precursors, or as enrichers, or even as viable alternatives to Ricœur's own phenomenology of productive imagination.

Chapter I will provide an account of the Kantian conception of productive imagination. It will also sketch the history of productive imagination in post-Kantian philosophy, thereby exposing the

---

[3]   This view is expressed in a strong way in Paul Ricœur's lectures on imagination, to which I have already referred, and in a large number of articles that he wrote on imagination. His contribution to the phenomenology of productive imagination will be addressed in detail in Chapters VII and VIII.

historical framework within which specifically phenomenological analyses of productive imagination can be understood. In this chapter, I will also provide a preliminary conception of productive imagination that will guide my analysis throughout this study.

Chapter II will investigate the different senses in which we can speak of productive imagination in Husserl's phenomenology. Husserl provides us with the possibility of conceiving of productive imagination as a relative term, a term whose meaning is derived from its opposition to reproductive imagination. Such a methodological approach, which addresses Husserl's writings on phantasy and image consciousness (see Husserl 2005), is highly promising. Husserl's phenomenology is exceptionally fruitful when it comes to identifying the different ways we can speak of reproductive phantasy. Following such an approach, I will argue that there are three fundamental senses in which phantasy can be said to be productive in the framework of Husserlian phenomenology. First, phantasy is productive because it can intend "original" appearances — not in the sense of perceptual appearances, but in the sense that the phantasized appearances do not reproduce perceptual appearances. Second, phantasy is productive because it opens the field of pure possibilities and thereby provides consciousness with access to the field of the a priori as the field of essences. Third, and most interestingly, phantasy is productive because it intends configurations of sense, which consciousness can subsequently transfer from the field of phantasy to the field of actuality. In this third fundamental sense, phantasy is productive because it co-determines the meaning of perceptually given phenomena. Productive phantasy thereby proves to be a fundamental source that underlies the constitution of the lifeworld.

In Chapter III, I will turn to Max Scheler's contribution to phenomenological studies of imagination. Here, also, productive phantasy will be understood as a type of intentional experience, which does not merely produce non-existent objects called *fictions*, but also shapes the contours of the surrounding world. As we will see, Scheler conceives of productive phantasy as an ingredient of original perception (*Urperzeption*). Because of Scheler's work, we recognize that perceptual phenomena cannot be reduced to a configuration of sensations, but always already entail phantasmatic content. In my analysis, I will address the psychic, historical and cultural dimensions of productive phantasy, while focusing on the relation between phantasy, on the one hand, and drives, instincts and desires, on the other hand. In addition, I will also focus on the psychic and cultural developments of productive phantasy. It will also be important to see how Scheler's reflections on productive phantasy relate to his other established views, and especially to his thesis that the sense of reality is determined through resistance.

Chapter IV will revisit the Davos disputation between Ernst Cassirer and Martin Heidegger. This debate is commonly framed in terms of its political implications. However, such an approach suffers from a serious hermeneutical shortcoming in that it overlooks that the origin of this debate comes from a dispute over the meaning, nature and significance of productive imagination. Should we identify productive imagination as an original ground of human experience? Or should we identify it as a mediating power between the understanding and sensibility? Is productive imagination formative of reason? Or is it rooted in reason? These are some of the fundamental questions of the Cassirer-Heidegger debate. The thesis that everything that appears is always already shaped by productive imagination is the central point of agreement in Cassirer's and Heidegger's respective conceptions of productive imagination. For both thinkers, productive imagination produces the transcendental horizons of sense, that is, the operational fields or the modes of vision, which pre-determine human experience. There is, however, an important point-of-departure for Cassirer and Heidegger on the topic of productive imagination. The point-of-departure does not come from Heidegger's own thesis that Cassirer recoils from finitude, while Heidegger himself faces it head-on. It comes, instead, from the idea that Cassirer and Heidegger express two fundamentally different ways of conceptualizing finitude. In what sense, if in any way at all, can philosophy rise above finitude? The most important question here is whether philosophy should strive to rise above finitude, or whether it should commit itself, not just thematically, but also methodologically, directly to finitude? The Davos dispute leaves us, I will argue, with these fundamental philosophical questions.

Chapter V will focus on Miki Kiyoshi's contribution to the philosophy of imagination. In the West, Miki's work is severely underappreciated, which is understandable, since only parts of his *magnum opus*, *The Logic of the Imagination*, have been translated into English. Despite this limitation, one has to admit that Miki is an outstanding thinker whose contributions are largely shaped by phenomenological undercurrents, and who has developed his line of thinking far beyond classical phenomenology. In the present context, I will focus on the first two chapters of *The Logic of the Imagination*. These chapters address the significance of myth and institutions, conceived as figures of social imaginary. Within such a context, it will be important to see how productive imagination shapes our world-understanding. Building on Miki's investigations, I will contend that imagination shapes our world-understanding in three fundamental ways: by generating (1) collective representations, (2) symbols and (3) forms. I will further contend that, with these three different frameworks, we can identify the same logic of the imagination as it has been conceived in terms of *formation, reformation and transformation*. This threefold logic allows us to identify Miki's philosophy of imagination as a philosophy of absolute creativity, situated between pathos and logos, hope and despair, elation and disenchantment, cultural crisis and its overcoming.

Chapter VI will trace the developments of Merleau-Ponty's reflections on imagination, starting with his earliest work on this theme and ending with his final writings. In Chapter, I will show that even though Merleau-Ponty does not rely on the conceptual distinction between productive and reproductive imagination, this distinction is exceptionally well-suited to his philosophy of the imagination. As we will see, in his early period, Merleau-Ponty's conception of imagination was heavily influenced by Sartre's work on imagination. In his late period, Merleau-Ponty progressively distanced himself from Sartre with the result that a remarkably rich conception of productive imagination emerged – a conception that was at once transcendental and ontological, dialogical and dialectical. Here, we face a conception of productive imagination that is rooted in the body rather than in consciousness, but is rooted in the body in such a way that it becomes a necessary medium through which the visible can see itself. Productive imagination in this phenomenological framework manifests itself as a *sui generis* mode of intentionality that binds embodied subjectivity to the ontological and transcendental dimensions of the visible world, a bind which, in his late period, Merleau-Ponty identifies as the invisible dimensions of the visible.

In Chapter VII, I will turn to the most elaborate set of phenomenological resources, as far as philosophy of the imagination is concerned. Here, I will focus on Ricœur's published writings on imagination. My goal will be to interpret Ricœur's writings alongside the phenomenological tradition as a whole. Within such a framework, I will argue that imagination has an inherently paradoxical structure: it enables one to flee one's socio-cultural reality and to constitute one's sociocultural world. Most philosophical accounts of imagination leave this paradox unexplored; to the best of my knowledge, Ricœur is the only thinker to have addressed this paradox explicitly. According to Ricœur, to resolve this paradox, one needs to recognize language as the origin of productive imagination. Chapter VII will explore Ricœur's solution to this paradox by offering a detailed study of reproductive and productive imagination set within the framework of poetic imagination. In my analysis, I will subject Ricœur's distinction between reproductive and productive imagination to a critique that relies upon the principles of classical phenomenology. According to my central thesis in this chapter, the imaginative powers of language are themselves rooted in pre-predicative experience. This realization broadens the scope and significance of Ricœur's solution by enabling one to resolve the paradox of imagination not only at the level of language-based imagination (as is done by Ricœur), but also at the level of both dreams and daydreaming as well as at the level of non-language-based art.

In Chapter VIII, I will delve deeper into the foregoing analysis of Ricœur's philosophy of imagination by taking a closer look at

Ricœur's so-far unpublished lectures on imagination, which he delivered at the University of Chicago in 1975. Ricœur devoted most of his analysis in these lectures to different figures in the history of philosophy who addressed imagination in their reflections. Of all the figures he discusses, Ricœur's treatment of Sartre is unwavering: three of the seventeen lectures are devoted to the French phenomenologist. In this chapter, I will address Ricœur's critique of Sartre as it appears in these lectures. It will be important to see that Ricœur's critique is twofold: hermeneutical and phenomenological. The hermeneutical critique relies on two central claims, namely, that Sartre fails to distinguish between productive and reproductive imagination, and that this distinction is language-based. I will argue that neither claim is justified. By contrast, the phenomenological critique casts doubts on Sartre's sharp distinction between the real and the imaginary. It relies on Ricœur's phenomenology of painting, which offers an alternative way to distinguish between productive and reproductive imagination. One of my central goals in this chapter will be to address Ricœur's phenomenology of painting in some detail, a necessary task, I believe, given that Ricœur never developed his phenomenology of painting in his published writings.

In Chapter IX, I will directly focus on the issues I will have introduced at the very beginning of this study. Building on the basis of the analysis undertaken in the earlier chapters, I will contend that phenomenology of productive imagination is first and foremost concerned with enriching our understanding of subjectivity. It does this in three fundamental ways: (1) by binding imagination to consciousness, (2) with language, and (3) through the body. While the link that binds imagination to consciousness and to language has been addressed quite extensively in the literature, the same cannot be said about the embodied nature of productive imagination. In this concluding chapter, I will put forth the claim that the power of productive imagination is rooted in our bodies. Embodied subjectivity cannot help but shape its relation to the world imaginatively. There are two fundamental reasons why this happens: first, because to be embodied means to occupy "the zero point of orientation," and second, because to realize that we are embodied means to realize that our relation to the world is largely shaped by our drives, instincts and needs. In short, our embodied subjectivity always already necessarily relates to the world, and relates to the world not only perceptually and conceptually, but also imaginatively. To clarify the meaning of this seminal claim will lead me to conclude this chapter, and this study as a whole, with some reflections on social imaginaries and carnal hermeneutics.

CHAPTER I
What is Productive Imagination?
From Kant to Phenomenology

Introduction

As embodied beings, whose existence is largely shaped socioculturally and linguistically, humans relate to the world not only perceptually and conceptually, but also imaginatively, both at the individual and at collective levels. Such has been the view defended by a wide variety of thinkers from Aristotle onwards. Throughout the history of western philosophy, imagination has been commonly addressed as something deeply human, as a feature of experience without which we would not be human at all. Philosophers have been continuously perplexed by the highly diverse ways in which imagination infiltrates our experience, taken in its highly diverse modes, both personal and social. Yet, as so often happens with seemingly self-evident and commonplace concepts, our conception of imagination appears to be familiar whenever we are not asking about it, but becomes utterly strange whenever we do. This elusiveness of imagination, coupled with the suspicion that it shapes the basic modes of our relation to the world, has often given rise to philosophical wonder. Kant expresses this with force in the *Critique of Pure Reason*, when he famously speaks of the mysterious nature of imagination, characterizing it as a "blind and indispensable function of the soul … of which we are scarcely ever conscious" (Kant 2007, A78/B103) and as "an art concealed in the depths of the human soul, whose real modes of activity nature is hardly likely ever to allow us to discover, and to have open to our gaze" (Kant 2007, A141/B180).

In particular, the concept of productive imagination – which seems to be a specifically modern invention even though it, arguably, finds its origin in antiquity – has played a central role in modern philosophy (see Geniusas and Nikulin 2018, Geniusas 2018 and Geniusas 2019). However, despite its importance in the philosophical discussions of the last few hundred years (especially in Kant, German idealism, romanticism, phenomenology and hermeneutics), only a handful of studies have been dedicated to its analysis. It is therefore, not surprising that the meaning of this concept remains largely underdetermined, while its significance is all-too-often either exaggerated or underestimated. In this introductory chapter, I will be guided by a three-part goal: (1) to provide a brief clarification of the Kantian conception of productive imagination, (2) to sketch the history of productive imagination from Kant to phenomenology and (3) to provide a guiding definition for the phenomenological conception of productive imagination. I should stress that this chapter is meant to serve introductory goals. In other words, the reason why I address Kantian and post-Kantian conceptions of productive imagination is for the sake of clarifying the historical precursors of phenomenology. The purpose of this introductory chapter is to demonstrate that phenomenological analyses of productive imagination do not emerge in a historical vacuum. Such phenomenological analysis has, instead, grown out of a long history of philosophical struggle and proposed solutions, and should, therefore, be understood from within this historical framework.[4]

Methodological Considerations

What is productive imagination? It is not only exceptionally difficult to answer this question; it is not even clear where to look for an answer. In the history of philosophy, it is not uncommon to use this term without defining it clearly, and if we look closer into its implicit meanings, we soon recognize that it has often been employed in a large variety of ways, which not only complement but also conflict with each other. Looking at the history of this concept, one might wonder: to what degree is this concept *transcendental* and to what degree *empirical*? To what degree can one qualify its function in terms of *creativity* (as with Baumgarten and Wolff), or *reconciliation* (as with Kant, for whom it is meant to reconcile the antagonism

---

4   For more extensive treatments of Kantian and post-Kantian conceptions of productive imaginations, see Geniusas 2018 and Geniusas and Nikulin 2018.

between understanding and sensibility), or in terms of *origination* (as with Heidegger, who equates its meaning with that of original temporalization)? So also, is productive imagination grounded in poetic language (as the Romantics and, subsequently, Ricœur forcefully maintained)? Or is it rooted in deeper sources of human and, more broadly, animal existence (as argued by some contemporary phenomenologists)? Should productive imagination be understood as productive phantasy (as, among others, Dilthey, Scheler and Ricœur maintained)? Or is it a technical term meant to resolve a technical problem in transcendental philosophy, namely, to establish unity (*Ein-Bildung*) on the grounds of a more original disharmony and thereby delimit the domain of phenomenality (as Kant maintained)? Last but not least, does imagination have its seat in consciousness or in the body? The absence of straightforward answers to these questions clearly indicates that the concept of productive imagination is heavily overdetermined. In light of its diverse and contradictory qualifications, it appears senseless to ask straightforwardly – what is productive imagination? – for clearly, the answer to this question will have to rely on the same standpoint from within which one has engaged it. Before asking – what is productive imagination? – we need to confront the methodological issue of where we are to search for an answer to this question.

When the question is formulated in this way, we find ourselves at a crossroads, and in principle, there are two paths we can take. On the one hand, we can hold the view that the concept of productive imagination was defined by Kant, and that, therefore, when we use this notion, we have to use it in the Kantian sense; otherwise, we simply do not know what we are talking about. On the other hand, we can also maintain that nobody owns philosophical concepts, not even the thinkers who coined them or who drew out their philosophical significance. If the latter is the case, the meaning of the concept of productive imagination cannot be reduced to how it has been employed in any particular philosophical framework. Reflection on the meaning of this concept would call for historical sensitivity, and the meaning of this concept, no matter how broad and fluid it might be, would have to be derived from the multifaceted ways in which the concept has been employed through these various philosophical frameworks.

Kant on Productive Imagination

The Kantian approach has its distinct advantages, the chief of which lies in its promise to fix the meaning of this concept with some precision. Although Kant was not the first thinker to have used the concept of productive imagination (Christian Wolff and Alexander Baumgarten had already made use of it before him), he is the one who transformed it into a concept of central philosophical importance and who uncovered its genuinely transcendental problematic and significance. Disregarding Kant's precritical employment of this concept (see Ferrarin 2018), which largely consists of an uncritical appropriation of how this concept had already been employed by Wolff and Baumgarten, we come across three different frameworks in Kant's critical writings, through which this concept has been employed in its new, transcendental sense (see Lennon 2015). These three frameworks provide the textual basis that underlies the Kantian approach.

First, in the original version of the transcendental deduction of the pure concepts of understanding in the *Critique of Pure Reason* (the so-called A-Deduction, originally presented in 1781), Kant conceptualizes productive imagination as a faculty of synthesis, the function of which is to establish unity in the manifold. In the A-Deduction, Kant argues that experience as such necessarily relies upon the syntheses of apprehension, association (reproduction) and recognition (Kant 2007, A98-A110). This threefold synthesis is the work of productive imagination, by means of which the sensuous manifold of intuition is transformed into a perceptual image. According to Kant, it is only by means of the transcendental function of the imagination that experience as such becomes possible.

Second, the schematism of the pure concepts of understanding constitutes another framework, within which Kant addresses productive imagination (see Kant 2007, A137 / B176-A147 / B187). The problem Kant confronts here is that of explaining how intuitions are to be subsumed under the categories of the understanding and thus how categories are to be applied to appearances. In this framework, Kant draws a distinction between the empirical faculty of productive imagination and the pure a priori imagination. While the former produces images, the latter produces schemas of sensible concepts. In contrast to images, which are always concrete (for example, the number 5 is concrete, or an equilateral triangle of a specific size is concrete), schemas are general (for example, a number in general, or a triangle in general). Schemas are of two different kinds: there are schemas of sensible concepts (for example, the schema of a dog) and there are schemas of pure concepts of understanding (for example, the schema of substance or the schema of a cause). According to Kant, images cannot correspond to the schemas of pure concepts of understanding. Such schemas are to be conceived as determinations of the inner sense in general (time). Kant identifies productive imagination as the power that enables consciousness to subsume intuitions under the concepts of understanding. In the absence of such subsumption, no experience would be possible. In light of this, one could qualify productive imagination as the power that shapes the field of phenomenality.

Last but not least, third, we cannot ignore Kant's use of this concept in the *Critique of the Power of Judgment* (see esp. Kant 2000, First Section, First Book, §49 and §59). In his analysis of beauty, Kant provides us with an account of how productive imagination can function in a genuinely creative way, without subsuming the intuitive manifold under the pregiven categorial structure. In the third *Critique*, Kant conceptualizes the experience of beauty as a feeling of pleasure which arises from imagination's capacity to display the harmonious interplay between reason and sensibility.

What, then, is productive imagination as conceptualized from the framework of Kant's philosophy? First and foremost, it has an intermediary status and is meant to perform a reconciliatory function. In the first *Critique,* its central function is to harmonize two seemingly irreconcilable spheres — those of understanding and sensibility, which one could qualify as proto-structures of experience. In the third *Critique,* it once again performs a reconciliatory function, this time establishing harmony between reason and sensibility. In the first *Critique*, productive imagination realizes the reconciliatory function by means of schematization; in the third *Critique*, productive imagination realizes the reconciliatory function, in contrast, by means of symbolization (see Zöller 2018). Productive imagination establishes harmony between different faculties by means of generating both schemas (in the first *Critique*) and symbols (in the third *Critique*), which predelineate the look of things and make experience of them possible. In this regard, the function of productive imagination is fundamentally pro-creative. In contrast to reproductive imagination, which either replicates or re-shapes images out of pre-existent materials, productive imagination reconciles the antagonism between different faculties by rendering the intuitive manifold fit for experience. Still, even though productive imagination does not rely on anything empirical, for Kant, productive imagination is not original in that it relies on understanding and sensibility and serves the function of reconciling the tension between them.

The Kantian approach is not without its drawbacks. Oddly, insofar as we subscribe to the view that the meaning of productive imagination was fixed by Kant, we also need to contend that Kant was not only the first, but also the last philosopher to have spoken of productive imagination. Despite its rich meaning and profound significance, the Kantian conception is too thin to accommodate how this concept has been employed in post-Kantian philosophies of productive imagination. It is hard to maintain in full seriousness that only those who are committed to the fundamental principles of Kantianism have the right to employ the concept of productive imagination.[5] Moreover, one might further point out that even Kant himself does not employ the concept of productive imagination in a conceptually unified way and that his use of this term shifted from how he employed it in his precritical writings and how he

---

[5]   For those determined to hold on to the Kantian conception, a possible way out would be to stick to the Kantian definition while at the same time maintain that what post-Kantian thinkers refer to as productive imagination is in fact a different phenomenon, which one could call either creative imagination or practical imagination. See Ferrarin 2018.

employed it in the first and third *Critique* (See Nikulin 2018 and Lennon 2018).

Productive Imagination in Post-Kantian Philosophy

In light of these disadvantages, we are motivated to search for alternative approaches. As mentioned above, the chief alternative would suggest that to understand the meaning of philosophical concepts, it is not enough to fix their origins, but it is also necessary to trace their historical development. Sensitivity to the history of the concept of productive imagination invites one to qualify it as a register of Kantian heresies marked by a consistent effort to stretch the limits of productive imagination. It is a history that implodes the fundamental distinctions that we come across in Kant's account of this concept: transcendental vs. empirical; *Einbildungskraft* vs. *Phantasie*; sensibility vs. understanding. So also, it is a history that is marked by an attempt to extend the Kantian problematic in the frameworks that lie beyond its original reach.

Most post-Kantian thinkers do not subscribe to the conceptual dualisms that pervade Kant's philosophy: sensibility vs. understanding, phenomenon vs. noumenon, nature vs. freedom, theoretical vs. practical reason. Yet clearly, insofar as one does not subscribe to these dualisms, one must either give up the concept of productive imagination entirely, or, should one choose to retain it, infuse it with a new meaning. Thus, on the one hand, in thinkers such as Hegel we do not come across the concept of productive imagination. Hegel transforms productive imagination into one of the many aspects of the spirit's self-actualizations (see Nuzzo 2018). By contrast, a large variety of other post-Kantian thinkers — the other main representatives of German Idealism, the central spokespersons of Romanticism, as well as various figures representing phenomenology and hermeneutics — continue to employ the concept of productive imagination as they impart upon it a new life and meaning.

Reflecting on Kant's concept of productive imagination, one could single out two of its chief characteristics. First, this concept is meant to *reconcile* the antagonism between sensibility, on the one hand, and either understanding (in the first *Critique*) or reason (in the third *Critique*), on the other hand. Second, it is also meant to *constitute* the phenomenal field, conceived as the overall horizon of human experience. While in Kant, the *reconciliatory* and the *constitutive* functions are bound to each other, their fusion is brought into question in post-Kantian philosophical frameworks. Most post-Kantian thinkers do not retain the concept's first chief characteristic but consider it to be an artificial solution to an artificial problem created by the dualisms of Kant's philosophy. Yet even as they take their distance from Kant, post-Kantian thinkers simultaneously continue to follow him in that they continue to conceive of productive imagination as a power that constitutes the phenomenal field and that makes human experience possible. In short, post-Kantian philosophy of productive imagination is characterized by the effort to capitalize on its constitutive function and purify it from the reconciliatory function.

This general propensity to retain the constitutive function, while abandoning the reconciliatory dimension, has given rise to highly diverse accounts of productive imagination in the history of post-Kantian philosophy. This should come as small surprise, if only because in post-Kantian philosophy, the constitutive function of productive imagination is understood in highly diverse ways. For some (especially Heidegger or Cornelius Castoriadis), the purification of the constitutive function from the reconciliatory function comes with the demand to bolster the sharp distinction between transcendental and empirical fields and, by implication, to thereby bolster the distinction between productive imagination (*Einbildungskraft*) and phantasy (*Phantasie*). Heidegger, for his part, rethinks the distinction between the transcendental and the empirical as the distinction between the ontological and the ontic. For Heidegger, the power of imagination does not serve as an *intermediary mid-point* between sense and apperception, but is the *original ground* that underlies human cognition and knowledge. Heidegger understands Kant's power of imagination neither in the psychological sense, nor in terms of a "transcendental" power of imagination, conceived epistemologically. Rather, Heidegger conceives of productive imagination as distinctly ontological and he further interprets it as a primordial grounding that makes both experience, and objects of experience, possible (see Wang 2018). By contrast, Castoriadis reinterprets the distinction between the transcendental and the empirical as a distinction between the socio-historical and the psychological. Conceiving of the radical imaginary as a distinctly socio-historical force, he identifies it as an anonymous, trans-subjective and unmotivated power that creates *ex nihilo* figures and forms that make the world. Castoriadis stretches the limits of productive imagination to such a degree that it ends up being synonymous with the creative core of the human condition. Conceived as a radically instituting power, productive imagination procures figures and forms that make up the social world (see Adams 2011, 2014, 2019).

In the hands of the thinkers I have just mentioned, the purification of the constitutive function of productive imagination requires that one reinterpret (and, *mutatis mutandis*, reinforce) the Kantian distinction between the transcendental and the empirical. However, for a large group of other thinkers, the purification of the constitutive function carries the opposite demand, namely, that of imploding the distinction between the transcendental and the empirical. For Wilhelm Dilthey, productive imagination is poetic, historical, and scientific. Much like Max Scheler after him, whose contribution will be addressed in Chapter III, Dilthey conceives of productive imagination as productive phantasy. Besides playing a constitutive role in the aesthetic realm, Dilthey's imagination also co-determines the processes of understanding and interpretation in ordinary life by enabling humans to form a sense of the whole. One could say that Dilthey's central contribution to the philosophy of productive imagination is that of stretching its limits so as to render it capable of clarifying those fields that remain unexplored in Kant's philosophy. While in Kant, productive imagination served the function of clarifying how we make sense of the natural world, in Dilthey, its central function is to expound how we inhabit the human, socio-historical world. As Eric Nelson has recently argued (see Nelson 2018), Dilthey reinterprets productive imagination as the formative-generative imagination, thereby demonstrating that imagination is productive in the sense that it shapes the implicit, historically-embodied, orientational contexts, which are presupposed and utilized by human efforts to reach knowledge and truth.

The implosion of the distinction between the transcendental and the empirical imagination, or more precisely, the recognition that empirical imagination is itself productive insofar as it performs a constitutive function, is to be found in the thought of many other post-Kantian thinkers — in Sartre and Merleau-Ponty (insofar as one can speak of productive imagination in the framework of their respective philosophies), in Miki Kiyoshi, who more than anyone else has stressed the need to give up all dualisms in the framework of the philosophy of the imagination, and in Ricœur, who conceptualizes productive imagination as symbolic, oneiric, poetic and utopian (see Kearney 2018).

Our understanding of any concept, and especially the concept of productive imagination, cannot be reduced to the history of *explicit* analyses of its meaning and significance. We cannot overlook *implicit* reflections, which at first glance appear to be focused on different figures of the imagination, yet at a closer glance prove to be of great importance for our understanding of productive imagination. In some of her recent contributions, building primarily on the resources that we find in Merleau-Ponty's writings, Kathleen Lennon has interpreted productive imagination as a power that constitutes what Merleau-Ponty had called the "imaginary texture of the real" (see Lennon 2015 and 2018). By this we are to understand that productive imagination weaves together the present and the absent into gestalt-like formations, which the subjects of experience subsequently encounter in the surrounding world. These formations are neither imposed on the world nor discovered in it, but rather emerge from a creative interplay between subjects and the world. By interlacing the visible and the invisible, productive imagination provides the world with depth, affective character, salience and significance.

In a similar vein, taking Husserl's and Merleau-Ponty's phenomenologies of the imagination as her source of inspiration, Annabelle Dufourcq has explored the thesis that images and phantasies are made possible by the very being of things, rather than by the arbitrary activity of the subjective faculty that we identify as the imagination (see Dufourcq 2010, 2011, 2018). What is at stake here concerns an ontological account of the imaginary that relies upon Husserl's and Merleau-Ponty's writings. An inquiry into the ontological roots of productive imagination invites one to recognize the need to overcome the duality of the real and the imaginary as a necessary step towards the disclosure of being that would precede such a distinction. In this regard, Kristupas Sabolius has also developed a similar approach and has been led to similar conclusions in his research while focusing on a highly interesting yet largely overlooked thinker, Gilbert Simondon (Sabolius 2019).

To a large degree, productive imagination is an umbrella term that covers various forms and figures of imagination and the imaginary. In this regard, one cannot overlook Dieter Lohmar's various contributions, in which he focused on prelinguistic imagination. In many of his writings, Lohmar argued for the significance of pre-linguistic thinking in human consciousness. Pre-linguistic thinking, which is by no means only a human characteristic, is to be conceived in terms of the sudden occurrence of phantasmatic pictures in consciousness, which enable the subject of experience to resolve impasses as well as choose possibilities. Conceived as an "old mode of thinking," such reliance on the productivity of the imagination largely organizes decisions that underlie social relations (see, for instance, Lohmar 2008). So also, it is worthwhile mentioning Gediminas Karoblis's analyses of kinaesthetic imagination (see Karoblis 2018), which clearly demonstrates that in contrast to some recent views in phenomenology, productive imagination cannot be limited to its narrative forms alone.

Conclusion

What, then, is productive imagination, when conceptualized in such a large variety of frameworks? Since this concept has been provided not only with complementary, but also with contradictory determinations, it remains an open question whether it is transcendental or historical and socio-political; it also remains debatable whether productive imagination is grounded in language or rooted in more elementary levels of existence. In light of such a plurality of determinations, it is especially difficult to provide the concept with any kind of conceptual unity. Nonetheless, even as one reflects on this plurality, one could qualify productive imagination as *a basic modality of intentionality that indirectly shapes the human experience of the world by forming the contours of action, intuition, knowledge and understanding.*

I do not wish to suggest that this list of conceptual frameworks exhausts the ways that productive imagination has been conceptualized in the history of philosophy. I hold the view, however, that these conceptual frameworks act as a trailblazer for the analyses of productive imagination that we come across in other thinkers, as well as other movements, which I have here not commented on. Fortunately, the history of productive imagination is too rich to be comprehensively covered within any single introduction.

The goal of this short introductory chapter was to sketch the historical framework within which phenomenological analyses of productive imagination are to be understood and to offer a guiding answer to the question, how is productive imagination to be understood in the phenomenological tradition? Needless to say, a lot more can be said about how productive imagination has been conceptualized in the history of philosophy; however, given the goals of this study, the preliminary answers provided here will have to suffice. At this point, we are ready to turn to the phenomenological tradition, starting with Husserl, so as to see what this tradition has to offer to our understanding of the meaning and significance of productive imagination.

CHAPTER II
What is Productive about Reproductive Imagination? Edmund Husserl's Phenomenology of Phantasy and the Constitution of Cultural Worlds

Introduction

In this chapter, my goal is to open up a conceptual space for the analysis of productive phantasy in the general framework of Husserlian phenomenology. Such an undertaking calls for an exploratory investigation, which is primarily concerned with various hints, clues or intimations that we come across in Husserl's phenomenology. Building on these resources, I wish to explore the constitutive role of phantasy within the overall framework of constitutive phenomenology. In Chapter I, I already provided a preliminary clarification of the concept of productive phantasy. I suggested that this concept is to be understood as *a basic modality of intentionality that indirectly shapes the human experience of the actual world by forming the contours of action, intuition, knowledge and understanding.* Admittedly, Husserl never spoke of imagination in general, or of phantasy in particular, in such terms.[6] Rather, he consistently qualified both phantasy and image consciousness, conceived as the two fundamental forms of imagination, as essentially reproductive modes of intuitive consciousness, that is, as a kind of consciousness that

---

6   Here I am alluding to the distinction between image consciousness (*Bildbewußtsein*) and phantasy (*Phantasie*) that is of fundamental importance in Husserl's phenomenology of imagination. We can understand the difference between them as a difference between seeing an image of an object in a photograph or on a smartphone screen and having a direct phantasy of an object without the mediation of any material object whatsoever. In other words, image consciousness is a type of intentional consciousness that is founded in a perception of an object, which, apperceived as an image, refers to a different object. By contrast, phantasy is not founded in the perception of any object, but is a quasi-perception of an imagined object.

intends modified actualities, *actualities as if.* Nonetheless, in his writings we come across various clues, the elaboration and development of which can help us to recognize the constitutive function of phantasy within the overall framework of transcendental phenomenology.

It is not my goal in this chapter to offer a systematic account of Husserl's phenomenology of the imagination. Such an undertaking would be quite gratuitous in a study focused on productive imagination, if only because Husserl never described his phenomenology of phantasy as a phenomenology of productive imagination. Not only that: the rejection of Kant's psychology of faculties lies at the heart of Husserl's phenomenology of imagination, which, in turn, underlies Husserl's early conviction that Kant's concept of *Einbildungskraft* is outdated and hopelessly confused;[7] furthermore, it suggests that Husserl's phenomenology unfolds within a different conceptual framework from the one that is usually employed while discussing productive imagination.[8] This circumstance alone explains the common claim voiced in the literature on productive imagination, which is that classical phenomenology in general, and Husserlian phenomenology in particular, have nothing to contribute to our understanding of productive imagination (see, for instance, Ricœur 1975, Sallis 1992, and, more recently, De Santis 2019 and Doyon 2019). It should, therefore, not surprise us that very few critical studies of Husserl's phenomenology of imagination have provided an inquiry into productive imagination, even though, more generally, the critical literature on Husserl's phenomenology

---

[7]   Daniele de Santis is right to point out that a meaningful discussion of the intermediate position of *Einbildungskraft* presupposes a duality of *Sinnlichkeit* and *Verstand*. "Now, has not Husserl himself dismissed and abandoned that "duality" once and for all?" (De Santis 2019, 270) Already in his early work, Husserl replaces the opposition of *Sinnlichkeit* and *Verstand* with the distinction between meaning intentions and meaning fulfillment. Yet, when it comes to this duality, there is no need for a mediating term. It thus seems that in the framework of Husserl's phenomenology the concept of *Einbildungkraft* is superfluous.

[8]   As Natalie Depraz puts it, "for the phenomenologist, imagination is nothing like a faculty, a power of the mind, as it is for a classical and even a Kantian interpretation. Like perception and remembrance, imagination is an act of consciousness, but one which does not entail that the intended object would have to be posited as existent or as real" (Depraz 1998, 29).

of imagination is voluminous and has recently experienced a kind of efflorescence.[9] Thus, all appearances suggest that, to borrow James Morley's vivid metaphors, classical phenomenology pushes productive imagination into "the outer darkness of intellectual irrelevance" in that it treats productive imagination as a "Mischling" — a "bastard child," who has no place within the "image family" (see Morley 1998).

Still, a study on the phenomenology of productive imagination would remain incomplete and deficient if it overlooked the importance of various clues that we come across in Husserl's writings. The goal of this chapter is to focus on some of these clues and to develop them in a direction that Husserl himself did not explore and which he would, quite likely, not even wish to pursue. My goal is to show that Husserl's phenomenology can make a significant contribution to the philosophy of productive imagination, yet for quite a paradoxical reason: precisely because of its "obsession" with reproductive imagination, Husserlian phenomenology enables us to determine the concept of productive imagination with great precision. It is not so uncommon to suggest that only a paradigm shift

---

[9]   There are, however, some noteworthy exceptions. While discussing "how a passive synthesis can be a synthesis of the imagination" (Depraz 1998, 31), Natalie Depraz argues that an implicit phenomenology of productive phantasy runs through Husserl's writings and that the task of phenomenology is to render explicit what in Husserl is only implicit. So also, in his noteworthy analyses of phenomenology and psychoanalysis, Rudolf Bernet has presented a compelling way to speak of productive phantasy in phenomenology. His analysis leads to the realization that just as perception can be independent of a prior phantasy, so phantasy, too, can be independent of a prior perception; and just as perception can actualize a prior phantasy, so also, a phantasy can replicate a former perception. In short, both phantasy and perception are equiprimordial, which means that they can enter into an intimate relation, thereby replicating the content from one sphere to the other (see Bernet 2003, especially 209-210). See also Andreea Smaranda Aldea's recent article, where she presents her analysis of the subversive dimension of imagination and defends the compelling view that *"what presents itself in everyday intelligibility processes under the guise of metaphysical necessity is actually naturalized contingency"* (Aldea 2019, 209). See also the recent contribution by Augustin Dumont, where he argues that imagination gives the "impetus to a style in the actual perception of an object" (Dumont 2019, 302). Dumont goes on to suggest that "the entire world may be dependent on *Phantasie*, that is to say, on what Husserl calls a pure possibility" (Dumont 2019, 303). See also my recent contribution, which this chapter is based on (Geniusas 2020b).

in philosophy of imagination can lead to the recognition of the productive capacities of imagination.[10] Yet such a paradigm shift, conceived either as an ontological or as a hermeneutical turn in the phenomenology of imagination, constitutes only certain ways — and certainly not the only ways — to speak meaningfully about productive imagination. My goal here is to show that in no other philosophical framework than that of Husserlian phenomenology can one better develop an approach that takes its departure from the insight that *productive imagination is a relative term, whose meaning derives from its opposition to reproductive imagination*. To come to terms with what productive imagination is, we should first and foremost fix the meaning of reproductive imagination, and in this regard, it is exceptionally fruitful to turn to Husserlian phenomenology.

In what follows, I will take four steps. First, I will address the concept of reproduction in Husserl's phenomenology and fix the sense in which Husserl invites us to conceive of phantasy as an essentially reproductive consciousness. Second, I will address the relation between perception and phantasy and argue that once phantasy is determined as a reproductive mode of consciousness, it cannot be conceived as an ingredient of perception. In the third part, I will focus on the relation between memory and phantasy and will maintain that not only memory, but also phantasy can generate patterns of meaning, which can subsequently be transcribed into the field of positional experience. In the fourth part, I will further show how this outlined approach opens the possibility of interpreting the

---

10   As Paul Ricœur has argued in his studies of productive imagination, which will be addressed in detail in the later chapters of this study, insofar as one conceptualizes imagination alongside perception as a distinct type of intentional consciousness, one inevitably ends up limiting imagination to its reproductive function. Ricœur thus asks: "if an image is not derived from perception, how can it be derived from language?" (Ricœur 1991, 121) So also, in the framework of his analysis of Husserlian phenomenology of imagination, John Sallis speaks of a "reorientation prompted by several of Husserl's analyses ... despite the massive constraints that Husserl thus employs to restrict imagination to the horizon of perception. It is preeminently a matter of reorienting the analysis to the site of appearing .... It is, then, at this site, in the appearing of the image-object, that the hold of presence is broken and imagination is drawn to spacing" (Sallis 1992, 212-213).

plurality of cultural worlds as diverse configurations of meaning, whose constitution entails the accomplishments of productive phantasy.

What is Reproduction and What is Reproductive Imagination?

What is productive phantasy? Since phantasy has been commonly addressed in the history of philosophy as a reproductive mode of consciousness, let us begin by saying that *productive phantasy, if there is such a phantasy at all, must be a relative term whose meaning derives from its opposition to reproductive phantasy.* But if this is so, then we must first ask: what does it mean to qualify phantasy as a reproductive mode of consciousness?

In the opening paragraphs of Sartre's *The Imaginary* (Sartre 2004), which we will return to in later chapters of this study, we come across a good example of one rather natural way to understand the reproductive nature of phantasy. While writing his book on imagination in Paris, Sartre finds himself imagining his friend Peter walking through the streets of Berlin. Of course, when Sartre and Peter were physically present in the same city, Sartre could see Peter directly in the flesh and blood. However, once Peter leaves Paris and Sartre is merely imagining his friend, he can then only "see" Peter, that is, he can only intend his irreal presence. Commenting on Sartre's analysis, and his choice of this paradigmatic example, Ricœur remarks that when it comes to imagining, I relate to an image that is "more or less a picture of something that already existed" (Ricœur unpublished, 15:1). This suggests that imagination is reproductive in the sense that it, as a form of intentionality, intends copies, or replicas, of objects, which were previously given in actual experience.[11] As we will soon see, such a conception of

---

[11] Besides being merely reproductive, as in Peter's case, imagination can also be combinatory, as in the case of mermaids or unicorns. Yet combinatory imagination is essentially reducible to reproductive imagination: its fundamental elements (a horse and a horn, in the case of a unicorn, or a woman and a fish, in the case of a mermaid) are reproductive copies of pregiven reality.

reproductive phantasy, its widespread acceptance notwithstanding, is not only questionable, but also unjustifiable.

Few other philosophers have been as attentive to the reproductive nature of imagination as Husserl has, and few of others have been as sensitive to the equivocations that accompany the concept of reproduction (see, for instance, Husserl 2005, 692).[12] The collection of his manuscripts on phantasy, memory and image consciousness housed in Hua XXIII testify to the long path Husserl took to the realization that phantasy is an essentially reproductive mode of consciousness. At the beginning of this path, we come across Husserl's attempts to demonstrate that the structure of phantasy consciousness is in principle no different from the structure of image consciousness, that is, from the kind of consciousness that intends its object indirectly, as it is represented in pictures or portraits. In his early analysis, Husserl defends the view that just as image consciousness presupposes a split between image object and image subject, so phantasy consciousness, too, presupposes an analogous split: in both cases, we "see" something in something else. Yet, already in the second half of his 1904-1905 lectures on phantasy and image consciousness, Husserl rejects this view as lacking phenomenological justification: phantasy, he argues, is like perception in that it is a mode of consciousness that grasps its object straightforwardly, without the mediation of any kind of picture or image.[13] Here, it is not my goal to describe the details of the early Husserl's "picture theory." In the present context, I only wish to

---

[12]   Although Husserl himself rarely focused on the various accounts of phenomena that we come across in the history of philosophy, in Text No. 20 in Hua XXIII, after indicating that "'*phantasy*' is already related to the sphere of reproduction in *Aristotle*," Husserl further notes that the history of philosophy has not succeeded in clarifying the meaning of reproduction: "To be sure, the linguistic usage at present is not entirely univocal" (Husserl 2005, 692).

[13]   Thus, with regard to the manuscripts collected in Hua XXIII (for the English translation, see Husserl 2005), Eduard Marbach — the editor of the volume — writes: "In der Tat dokumentieren die Texte, die in vorliegendem Bande zur Veröffentlichung gelangen, eindringlich Husserls Weg von der Lehre der Phantasie bzw. Erinnerung als einer Form von Bildbewusstsein über die Kritik dieser am gewöhnlichen Sprachgebrauch sich orientierenden ,Bildtheorie' und den Ansatz der schlichten Vergegenwärtigung zur Theorie der intentional komplexen Reproduktion von Akten, die in Verbindung mit den Setzungsmodalitäten (Aktualität, *belief* – Inaktualität, Neutralität) zu studieren ist" (Hua XXIII, LI).

stress that it is Husserl's rejection of this theory that led to the realization that phantasy is a reproductive consciousness. With the aim
of clarifying the sense in which phantasy could be said to be essentially reproductive, let us turn to a manuscript that Husserl wrote
either in 1911 or 1912 and that was published as Text Nr. XIV in
Hua XXIII.[14] Arguably, no other text from Husserl provides as detailed a study of reproduction as this manuscript, whose central
goal is to fix the strict concept of reproduction.

Just as he does in many of his other manuscripts on time and
imagination, Husserl begins his analysis at the limits of language —
in this case, by focusing on the act for which "we do not have the
right word" (Husserl 2005, 363). Husserl qualifies such an act as
"the act of mere apparency" ("*der bloss* apparenziale *Akt*") and "the
act of appearing" ("*der Akt des Erscheinens*"). These expressions refer
to a merely perceptual act, yet taken in isolation from any positing
act of meaning. In other words, they are acts of consciousness conceived in the absence of what Husserl calls the apperceptive layer
of sense: they are simple, bare perceptions, which Husserl qualifies
as "schlichte Wahrnehmung" and "blosse Perzeption" (see Hua
XXIII 301/ Husserl 2005, 363). They refer to mere perceptions,
which entail a certain content of experience, although not yet apperceived in any determinate way. Consider what happens when,
after a long and sleepless trip to another continent, you wake up in
the middle of the night in a pitch-dark hotel room. As your hand is
searching for the light switch, it touches various objects on the bed-
side table. However, under the circumstances, you do not recognize
these tactually given objects for what they are. All you have are
mere appearances given in what Husserl in this manuscript calls
"the act of mere apparency." These acts, Husserl contends, are more
original than the acts of meaning, which Husserl views to be the act
of mere apparency insofar as it functions as "the substrate on which
the specifically theoretical act, the theoretical act of meaning, is
founded" (Husserl 2005, 363). Relying on the "apprehension — content of apprehension" schema, which plays a fundamental role in
Husserl's early account of intentionality and constitution, Text No.

---

14   For the English translation, see Husserl 2005.

14 presents the view that the constitution of full-fledged objects of experience is made possible by founding the acts of meaning upon the act of mere apparency. In other words, acts of mere apparency are independent and yet also insufficient, while acts of meaning are dependent and yet also indispensable for the constitution of full-fledged objectivities.[15]

In the manuscripts under consideration, Husserl employs such unusual concepts as "the act of mere apparency" with the aim of analyzing its re-presentational modifications (*Vergegenwärtigungsmodifikationen*). Moving within the sphere of actuality, Husserl suggests that "memory in the widest sense" is the re-presentational modification of the simple perceptual appearing.[16] By extension, once we move from the sphere of actuality to that of inactuality, phantasy can be qualified as the re-presentational modification of such simple perceptual appearing.

"The question to be asked first here is: What does *re-presentational modification* mean?" (Husserl 2005, 367) We face here an ambiguous concept, first and foremost because the modification can be

---

[15]   In another manuscript, published as Appendix XXXIII in Hua XXIII, Husserl further conceptualizes such an act of mere apparency as time-constituting consciousness. Husserl suggests that the act of mere apparency could be also qualified as an impression, yet only if we understand impressions in a broad sense. In the narrow sense, the concept of impression applies to those experiences which unfold in the abstract and formal now that lacks any kind of temporal extension. In this regard, Husserl distinguishes impressions from retentions and protentions. In a broad sense, the concept of impression marks the unity of the originary present, the originary just-having-been and the originary yet-to-come. In this broad sense, the concept of impression excludes reproductions, conceived as reiterations of impressions, retentions, and protentions. In this broad sense, the concept of impression signifies the act of mere apparency.

[16]   As Husserl famously puts it in §111 of *Ideas I*, "universally *phantasying* is the *neutrality modification of 'positing' presentification,* therefore of memory in the widest conceivable sense (Husserl 1983, 260). With this in mind, we can represent the Husserlian view of different forms of intuitive consciousness as follows: while impressional consciousness is original, retentional consciousness is a modification of impressional consciousness; a reproductive consciousness – which Husserl qualifies as a memory (*Erinnerung*), and which must be further conceived in its three modalities as a memory of the past (*Wiedererinnerung*), a memory of the present (*Miterinnerung*), and a memory of the future (*Vorerinnerung*) – is a further modification of retentional consciousness. Following this logic further, phantasy can be qualified as a neutralizing modification of memory (*Erinnerung*).

understood in both a noetic and noematic way. It is by clearing up this ambiguity that Husserl introduces the concept of *reproduction*. "Normally we say re-presentation with respect to *something objective*" (Husserl 2005, 367). Let us retain such a noematic conception of representation and let us supplement it with noetically conceived reproduction. Thus, in the case of a recollection of a perception, we should say that we represent what was previously perceived and that we reproduce the act of perceiving. In the case of phantasmatic perception ("seeing *as if*"), we can further say that we represent the perceptual objects intended phantasmatically while we reproduce the perceptual acts. In short, *acts are reproduced while objects intended in these acts are represented.* This means that phantasy consciousness is essentially reproductive, not because it reproduces perceptual objects, but because it reproduces perceptual consciousness. It thereby becomes understandable why in the section of the manuscript entitled "Definition of a Strict Concept of Reproduction," Husserl argues against the view that reproduction is a new production of the same objects that were once already given in experience, yet that now reappear as their pale echoes or afterimages. On the one hand, the representation of objects intended in experience should not be called a reproduction. On the other hand, "we still need a separate term for the separate re-presentation of internal consciousness, and this re-presentation may be called *reproduction*" (ibid).

Such a sharp distinction between reproduction and representation suggests that we draw a no less, sharp distinction between phantasy modification, on the one hand, and empty presentations, on the other hand.[17] We all know that a full-fledged perceptual act is not reducible to the act of mere apparency. When we turn to the front of a perceptual object, a determinate appearance awakens a series of non-given appearances that belong to the object's unseen sides. The question to be asked is whether or not these unseen sides

---

[17]   We are to understand "by empty intentions" those intentional rays that help consciousness intend the absent features of the intended object. The distinction between phantasy consciousness and empty consciousness is essential not only to Husserl's but also to Sartre's classical account of imagination in his *The Imaginary* (see Sartre 2004, 120-122).

are given through an act of phantasy. Husserl rejects such a view. Consciousness of the rear aspects belongs to perception, taken in its unity with the act of meaning that is founded upon it. To use Husserl's own neologisms, when I *prehend* a profile of the object, it is given to me within the horizon of *apprehension*: I intend the appearing object through a direct *act of apparency* and I also emptily co-intend the object's non-given sides through the acts of "co-meaning." Such founding of empty intentions upon the intuitive act of apparency is of fundamental importance, since, in its absence, consciousness would not be a consciousness *of objects*, conceived as noematic correlates of diverse intentional acts. In the present context, it must be stressed that while the consciousness of empty intentions is founded upon the intuitive consciousness of apparency, phantasy consciousness is, for Husserl, a reproductive modification of an original act of mere apparency, a reproduction which is essentially noetic, not noematic. Therefore, while the consciousness of empty intentions exists only as a companion of the "acts of mere apparency," phantasy consciousness cannot accompany, but can only modify perceptual consciousness, so much so that, as Rudolf Bernet has convincingly argued, perception and phantasy cannot exist contemporaneously: "phantasy 'represses' or 'covers' (*verdeckt*) perception, and the perception of the real world reacts allergically to every uncontrolled mixing with phantasy" (Bernet 2003, 213).[18]

Yet even such a noetic/noematic clarification of the concept of "re-presentational modification" does not clear up all of the ambiguity. In Appendix XXXV, Husserl distinguishes between three different senses of reproduction. By reproduction, one can either mean a reproduction of an object of experience (*der intentionale Gegenstand des Erlebnisses*), for example, a clearly or vaguely remembered object that had been previously given in original experience; or one can mean a reproduction of experience (*das Erlebnis*), for instance, a clear or vague memory of an actual experience; or one can mean a reproduction of an act of experiencing (*das Erleben*), such as a

---

[18]   As we will see in the later chapters of this study, many post-Husserlian phenomenologists question this view.

reproduction of an act of seeing, hearing, touching, thinking, loving, hating etc., taken in isolation from the concrete flow of experience and from the object of experience, to which it was previously intentionally related. This threefold distinction allows us to conceptualize the difference between memory and mere phantasy as two different forms of reproductive modification. "*Memory* is a reproductive modification of perception, but it has the remarkable peculiarity that it is also re-presentation of perception and not simply re-presentation of what was perceived" (Husserl 2005, 367). This means that memory is a reproductive form of consciousness in all three senses here distinguished. By contrast, mere phantasy can be (although, admittedly, it need not be) a reproductive form of consciousness only in the third sense: phantasy, in contrast to memory, can reproduce a certain kind of perceptual act (for example, the act of seeing, or the act of hearing) without simultaneously replicating the former act of experience or intending the object as it was given in past experience. In this regard, one can only concur with Bernet's observation that "phantasy as intuitive, reproductive presentification is best compared with a neutralized remembering which would not be related to a past perception of an object but to one that is both present and absent" (Bernet 2003, 208). As Bernet further notes, this renders phantasy a *productive* form of reproduction: phantasy is "a reproductive consciousness of presentation, that is to say, a reproductive modification that produces the modified in such a way that it modifies it" (Bernet 2003, 208).

Thus, if I phantasize that I "see" Pandora opening her box, I thereby reproduce an act of seeing, although without reproducing a former experience or a formerly given object of experience: I see her, yet it is only *as if* I see her. If I phantasize that I hear the sound of Pandora opening the box and hear the sound of the evils flying out of it, I thereby reproduce the act of hearing, although without reproducing a former experience or a formerly given object of experience: it is only *as if* I hear it. Despite all its powers, phantasy lacks the capacity to give us the objects of phantasy in flesh and blood. Whenever I phantasize, I can see, hear, touch, think, remember, anticipate, love or hate an object, yet this is always only *as if.*

Precisely because this *as if* is irreducible, phantasy is a reproductive mode of consciousness.

Husserl is fully justified to characterize phantasy as a reproductive mode of consciousness in the above-mentioned sense. It is hard to see how phantasy could produce an original (that is, unmodified) relation to the world at large in the sense of forming originally intuitive acts, such as seeing or hearing.[19] I contend that those critics who accuse Husserl of being blind to the productive powers of imagination (for example, see Castoriadis 1997, Drost 1990, Ricœur 1975, Sallis 1992) misunderstand the precise nature of Husserl's qualification of phantasy as an essentially reproductive mode of consciousness. Imagination is reproductive not because it can only intend copies, or replicas, of something that already exists, not because, supposedly, "there was always somewhere an original for the picture" (Ricœur unpublished, 15:1). Rather, phantasy is essentially reproductive because the acts of phantasy can only be reproductive acts.

As a response to the skeptic who worries that Husserl's conception of reproductive phantasy conceals phantasy's productive characteristics, I would suggest that precisely because phantasy can be said to be reproductive in many ways, Husserlian phenomenology leaves open the possibility for diverse determinations of phantasy's productive capacities. Phantasy cannot be productive in the sense that it cannot produce an unmodified relation to the world at large: whenever I phantasize, I can see *as if,* hear *as if,* or think *as if,* and this *as if* is irreducible. The consequence here is that phantasy is essentially reproductive in the noetic sense; however, this noetic sense does not exclude the possibility that phantasy might be productive noematically. Before uncovering in more detail the

---

[19]   Husserl's remarks in Text Nr. 1 in Hua XXIII thereby become more understandable: "[a] phantasy thing does not appear in perception's field of regard but instead appears, so to speak, in an entirely different world" (Husserl 2005, 62). Precisely because phantasy consciousness is a modified consciousness, consciousness necessarily forestalls positing its object as a real being. With this in mind, Bernet emphasizes that "knowledge of the phantasy *qua* phantasy obviously belongs to the performance of phantasy itself. Phantasy knows itself as phantasy because it is an inner reproductive consciousness of a (quasi)-perception" (Bernet 2003, 209).

different noematic senses in which phantasy can be said to be productive, let us now address some of the doubts that arise from what could be viewed as an excessively generous interpretation. The time is ripe to address the question of whether it is really true that the Husserlian phenomenology of phantasy so easily lends itself to be transformed into a phenomenology of productive phantasy?

Perception and Imagination

It is not by chance that virtually every theorist who has aimed to develop a model of productive imagination agrees with Kant's famous remark that "imagination is a necessary ingredient of perception itself" (Kant 2007, A120, fn). By qualifying phantasy as an essentially reproductive mode of consciousness, Husserl introduces an indissoluble breach between perception and phantasy, which excludes any possibility of identifying phantasy as an ingredient of perceptual consciousness, and *vice versa*. The question to be asked, then, is whether Husserl's phenomenology of phantasy necessarily proscribes the recognition and analysis of productive imagination.

In contrast to a large number of philosophers who argue that perception is "animated by," "infused with," "shot through with" or "soaked in" imagination (see Kant 2007, Wittgenstein 1986, Strawson 1974, Warnock 1978, Nanay 2010 and, as we will see, many post-Husserlian phenomenologists), scholars working within the Husserlian tradition retort that such a view presupposes a passive and static notion of perception, which lacks phenomenological justification. As Julia Jansen insightfully remarks, "there is no such passive and bare perception, which would require an infusion with imagination, in the first place" (Jansen 2015, 6). She argues elsewhere that "contributions [that] make use of the phenomenological evidence … highlight the differences between perception and imagination and thus reject the hypothesis of a 'grand illusion,' that is, of the view that imagination might be an ingredient of perception" (Jansen 2010, 152). The analysis I have offered above clarifies why, from a Husserlian standpoint, this hypothesis is superfluous and needs to be rejected.

Nonetheless, such a response does not clarify the relation between perception and phantasy. This is unfortunate, especially in light of recent neuroscientific findings. Consider a recent study by Christopher C. Berger and H. Henrik Ehrsson (Berger and Ehrsson 2013). In this investigation, qualified as "an unparalleled example of how imagination can change perception," Berger and Ehrsson (who work for the Karolinska Institute in Stockholm) argue that to imagine the act of hearing changes what one sees, just as to imagine the act of seeing changes what one hears. Their study relies heavily upon three classical examples in psychology, each of which demonstrate that sensory information in one perceptual modality affects one's perception in a different modality. First, let us consider the so-called *cross-bounce illusion*. This experiment, which has its roots in Gestalt psychology, demonstrates that the presentation of an unrelated sound at the moment when two objects coincide promotes the illusory perception that the objects collide (see Sekuler et al. 1997). In their study, Berger and Ehrsson modify this classical experiment by substituting the actually heard sound for a merely imagined sound. This modification results in the realization that not only actual sounds, but also imaginary sounds modify visual experience. Second, let us consider the *ventriloquist illusion*, which aims to prove that vision dominates the other senses in sensuous perception. In its classical presentation (see Alais and Burr 2004), this experiment demonstrates that conscious localization of sound largely depends on visual stimuli, so much so that with each and every shift in visual stimuli, sound localization shifts as well. In short, visual data affect the meaning of the auditory stimuli that one is exposed to. Berger and Ehrsson modify the ventriloquist illusion by replacing actually perceived visual shapes with merely imaginary ones. The results of this modification lead to the realization that the meaning of auditory stimuli is co-constituted, not only by actual visual perceptions, but also by imaginary visualizations. Finally, Berger and Ehrsson offer a third experiment in the form of a modified version of the "McGurk illusion" (see McGurk and MacDonald 1976). In one of its classical presentations, an auditory stimulus of the phoneme "ba" is paired with a visual stimulus of someone's lip movements articulating "ga," resulting in a fused illusory percept "da." Berger and Ehrsson modify this experiment by replacing an actually heard phoneme with an auditory imagery of the same phoneme. The participants in this experiment see the person's lips make the utterance "ga," while, at the same time, they imagine hearing "ba;" yet, because they synthesize "ga" and "ba," they end up hearing "da." This means that auditory imagery can be integrated with visual speech stimuli, thereby promoting illusory speech percept.

These neurological findings bring into question the view that, as Sartre famously puts it, "the image and the perception, far from being two elementary psychic factors of similar quality and that simply enter into different combinations, represent the two great irreducible attitudes of consciousness" (Sartre 2004, 120).[20] These findings suggest that, on the contrary, imagination can be productive in the sense that it can shape our perceptual relation to the world at large. In light of these findings, one can maintain that, at least under some circumstances, what we see and what we hear is largely shaped phantasmatically. Nonetheless, and this should not be overlooked, these findings do not corroborate the widespread view that "imagination is an ingredient of perception itself," for clearly, the participants in these experiments must have been conscious of the distinction between phantasy and perception, since otherwise they would simply not have been able to imagine sounds while being exposed to visual phenomena, or to imagine visual phenomena while being exposed to sounds. These participants must have at least implicitly been aware that, although perception marks their immediate access to actually existent phenomena, their ability to phantasize only allows them to see *as if* or hear *as if.* Thus, strangely, Berger's and Ehrsson's experiments contest the view that phantasy is a perceptual ingredient, even while these experiments nonetheless demonstrate that perceptual content can be shaped

---

[20]   I do not mean to suggest that Sartre's account of imagination is exclusively an account of reproductive imagination and that it is incompatible with any account of productive imagination. Such a view has been brought into question in recent literature. See especially Lau 2018 and Levy 2019. I will return to this issue in the later chapters of this study.

phantasmatically. How, then, is one to understand the intricate re-
lationship between phantasy and perception?

In such a framework, it is hard to overestimate the importance
of Husserl's passing remark: "perception as apperception is itself a
particular sort of 'memory'" (Husserl 2005, 700). At first glance, this
claim appears to be counterintuitive, since, as we saw in the last
section, memory is a reproductive consciousness, while perception
is original, unmodified, experience. Yet, Husserl here refers to perception *as apperception*,[21] which means that in this framework perception cannot be reduced to the act of mere apparency, since it also
incorporates *the act of meaning* that is founded in the act of apparency. This opens the further and highly promising possibility that
we can conceptualize the relation between phantasy and perception. Even though perception and phantasy are, as Sartre puts it,
irreconcilable attitudes of consciousness, phantasy can nonetheless
shape and reshape perceptual consciousness *indirectly*, namely, by
constituting those resources of sense from which the founded act of
meaning draws its sustenance. Thus, even though I cannot both
perceive and quasi-perceive the same object at the same time (see
Bernet 2003, 213), imagination can supply dimensions of sense,
which are subsequently transferred from the field of phantasy to
the field of actuality. In the case of Berger's and Ehrsson's modified
version of the cross-bounce illusion, the participants in the experiment do not conflate the imagined sound for a real sound; they are
fully conscious that the sound is irreal, since, otherwise, they would
not have been able to participate in the experiment. Nonetheless, as
they imagine the sound of a crash at the moment when one visual
body crosses the other, they transfer the meaning of the sound from
the field of phantasy into the perceptual field, and on this basis they
transform the meaning of the visual phenomenon. Ultimately, what
they *see* is a crash.

Imagination is not an ingredient of perception itself: I can either perceive or quasi-perceive an object, but I cannot do both

---

[21]   *Apperception is a matter of intending something that is not originally present as if it*
were originally present: this is the core meaning of the concept that we come
across in highly diverse contexts of analysis in Husserl's phenomenology. See
in this regard Geniusas 2020a.

simultaneously. Nonetheless, the foregoing analysis shows that the meaning of a perceptual object, which is constituted in the act of apprehension, can incorporate dimensions of sense that are derived from phantasy consciousness. Perception and imagination cooperate at the level of meaning-constituting consciousness. In this extended sense, perception is not only a particular sort of memory, but it can also be a particular sort of phantasy.

How, then, can we conceive productive phantasy from the terms of Husserlian phenomenology? As noted above, Husserlian phenomenology invites us to admit that phantasy is essentially reproductive in the noetic sense, and yet this admission does not force us to exclude the possibility that it might be productive noematically. Against such a background, we can single out three fundamental senses in which phantasy can be said to be productive in the framework of Husserlian phenomenology. First, one can qualify phantasy as productive in that it can intend "original" appearances — not in the sense of perceptual appearances, but in the sense that the phantasized appearances do not "reproduce" perceptual appearances. I can thus phantasize about unicorns, sirens, mermaids, dragons, and other fictional objects produced by my imagination. This is the minimal and most straightforward sense to speak of productive phantasy from the terms of Husserlian phenomenology. In this sense, the productivity of phantasy can be explained as an integrative activity. It suffices to say that perceptually given manifolds can be taken apart and reorganized in a novel way. In other words, besides reproducing perceptual experiences, phantasy can also compound perceptually given elements and thereby generate new objectivities, which cannot be encountered in our perceptual surroundings. As Bernet explains in his outstanding study, phantasy is a productive form of reproduction: "it is a modified form of perception which indicates the possibility of a perception without presupposing its factual givenness" (Bernet 2003, 209).

Second, phantasy is productive insofar as it opens the field of pure possibilities. For Husserl, this capacity on the part of consciousness to transition from the field of actuality to that of possibilities is fundamentally important, since the field of pure possibilities provides consciousness with a point of access to the a priori, conceived as the field of essences. The productivity of phantasy is of so much importance for Husserlian phenomenology that Husserl goes so far as to uphold fiction as the vital element of phenomenology and as the source "from which the cognition of 'eternal truths' is fed" (Husserl 1983, 160). Husserl scholars have paid special attention in the secondary literature to this aspect of Husserl's phenomenology of imagination. As Depraz remarks, if for Husserl "fiction is the essential element in phenomenological analysis, this is primarily due to the part eidetic variation plays in the constitution of phenomenological analysis" (Depraz 1998, 47). Or, as Jansen puts it, "a phenomenology of phantasy therefore truly is *first philosophy*" (Jansen 2005, 127) in that it enables phenomenology as an a priori science of pure possibilities and thereby prescribes a priori rules to reality.

Third, phantasy is productive insofar as it intends configurations of sense, which consciousness can subsequently transfer from the field of phantasy into the field of actuality. In other words, phantasy is productive insofar as it co-determines the meaning of perceptually given phenomena. This third sense of phantasy has hardly been explored in the framework of Husserlian phenomenology. This is understandable in light of Husserl's famous characterization of phantasy at §111 of *Ideas I* (see Husserl 1983, 260) as a neutrality modification. There are, however, noteworthy exceptions. First and foremost, Natalie Depraz' studies of imagination should be mentioned in this framework. Focusing on what she identified as "passive imagination" (Depraz 1998, 30) – which she understands as the implicit function of phantasy within the framework of Husserl's phenomenology of passive constitution, and which, in turn, paves the way for what she identifies as "transcendental empiricism" – Depraz maintains that neutralization provides us with a severely restricted conception of phantasy. According to Depraz, the conception of "passive imagination" must be fleshed out even if it goes against some of Husserl's own statements. "Imagination," Depraz writes, "is in fact constitutively related to spatiotemporality. By opening up possibilities of being which exceed our own limited belonging to space and to time, imagination makes possible an enlargement of our very notion of what is real" (Depraz 1998, 49). With such a function of imagination in mind, Depraz speaks of "the new 'principle' of imagination" (Depraz 1998, 50) as "highly phenomenological: it brings to the fore the *possibilities* of reality and not reality itself" (ibid). My goal in the remaining parts of this chapter is to analyze and develop this train of thought, while focusing in particular on the role that phantasy plays in the constitution of cultural worlds. Just as Depraz emphasizes it in her analysis, we will also need to explore this idea as it appears in Husserl's writings. We will endeavor to understand not only why the constitution of cultural worlds presupposes the constitution of other subjectivities, but also, and more importantly, why the constitution of other subjectivities relies upon phantasy acts, conceived as "acts of borrowing," that is, we will need to understand those kinds of acts that appropriate the configurations of sense from other subjectivities. However, before articulating how such acts should be understood, I would like to entertain some of the criticisms that such an unusual phenomenology of phantasy is bound to provoke.

Memory and Phantasy

One might object that, in my foregoing reflections, I was too quick to interpret the claim "perception as apperception is itself a particular sort of 'memory'" as the claim that perception is a particular sort of phantasy. Even though Husserl qualifies "memory in the widest sense" as the re-presentational modification of the simple perceptual appearing" (Husserl 2005, 363) and thus, in a broad sense, as phantasy, nonetheless, a closer look at Husserl's concept of apperception makes clear that the concept of memory is not interchangeable with the concept of phantasy.

In Husserl's phenomenology, "apperception usually refers to the co-present but unseen viewings of objects entering one's visual field" (Biceaga 2010, 104). In the course of experience, these implicit viewings can be either confirmed or disconfirmed, which means that these empty perceptual intendings can, in principle, be transformed into originary presentations.[22] The question from here is how and why the act of mere apparency is lived along with an apperceptive horizon of sense, or, in other words, how it is to be formulated in terms of another neologism that Husserl employs in his manuscripts on the imagination, that is, how and why the act of *prehension* can be given within the horizon of apprehension. Husserl's answer points to *motivation*[23]: it is the actual appearance itself, as it is given to consciousness, that motivates consciousness to apperceive it as an appearance of a certain type of objectivity. For example, what is actually given in the act of mere apparency when I see a person swimming in the sea? Although I see nothing more than the back of a human-like head as well as the movement of two human-like arms, what I see nonetheless *motivates* me to apperceive the given appearance as an appearance of a human body. Yet, why do these particular appearances in the sea motivate me to apperceive them as the movement of a human body and not, say, of a fish, a dog, or a mannequin? In light of this question, Husserl's passing remark that "perception as apperception is itself a particular sort of 'memory'" (Husserl 2005, 700) gains its significance.

Let us remind ourselves that, according to Kant, productive imagination produces schemata, while reproductive imagination produces images. In his noteworthy study of Husserl's type and Kant's schemata, Dieter Lohmar writes:

> Husserl did not take up Kant's concept of the schema productively, although it certainly could have been put to use in a phenomenological conception of object-constitution. In his later, genetic phenomenology, however, Husserl

---

[22]   Transformation of this nature can take place in the framework of perceptual consciousness; however, when it comes to analogical apperception, which is constitutive of the Other, such a transformation is in principle excluded. The constitution of intermonadic community will be the focus of the next section.

[23]   For a detailed analysis of the concept of motivation in phenomenology, see Husserl 1989. Also consider the following account from Husserl's *Lectures on Passive Synthesis*: "By viewing an object I am conscious of the position of my eyes and at the same time — in the form of a novel systematic empty horizon — I am conscious of the entire system of possible eye positions that rest at my disposal. And now, what is seen in the given eye position is so enmeshed with the entire system that I can say with certainty that if I were to move my eyes in this direction or in that, specific visual appearances would accordingly run their course in a determinate order." (Husserl 2001, 51)

> developed his notion of the pre-conceptual type, which plays the same role
> as the schema in Kant. (Lohmar 2003, 105)

According to Husserl, mere appearances motivate consciousness to apperceive them as appearances of particular *types* of objectivities. A type is an idea derived from experience that joins together, in a rather loosely associated way, various modes of appearances characteristic of a particular kind of objects of experience. Thus, I recognize what appears to me in the water as an object of a certain type, be it a human being, a fish, or a dog. Herein lies the answer to the question raised above: to claim that appearances awaken particular motivations is to suggest that they awaken the anticipation of particular types of experience. These types admit of various levels of generality: besides very general types such as "something in general" or "substrate of determinations," there are also more specific types of general objects of experience, such as human beings, dogs, and fish; last but not least, there are also types of singular objects, which characterize a particular person or a particular thing (see Lohmar 2003, 2005, 2008).

It is especially important to stress that types are not just passively pregiven structures of experience. Rather, "types come into being in concrete experience and they change constantly in further experience" (Lohmar 2005, 158). Husserl explains this when he writes, "with each new kind of object constituted for the first time (genetically speaking) a new type of object is permanently prescribed, in terms of which other objects similar to it will be apprehended in advance" (Husserl 1973, 38). It thereby becomes understandable in which sense perception, conceived as apperception, is a particular type of "memory": as apperception, perception reawakens the "memory" of the preconstituted types of experiences, which, in turn, determine the sense of appearing objectivities.

Husserl's phenomenology of typifying consciousness thereby corroborates the view that consciousness bridges the gaps that separate diverse fields of experience by means of *transference of sense*, which occurs not at the founding level of the acts of mere apparency, but at the founded level of the constitution of meaning. In the case of consciousness of typification, what is at stake is not a concrete memory of a particular event that took place in past experience, but the reawakening of a horizon of sense, whose origins derive from past experience. It is thus not by chance that when Husserl qualifies apperception as a type of "memory," he uses the term "memory" in quotation marks. What is reawakened is not a set of episodic recollections, but types, or schemas, that fit the currently given experience.

We can consider Husserl's account of typification as a further and much-needed clarification of the "apprehension – content of apprehension" schema, which Husserl employed in his early account of intentional consciousness and to which I have already referred above. Husserl's earlier reliance on this schema did not successfully clarify the constitutive function of the content of experience. Husserl's analysis of typification invites one to claim that the presently experienced content awakens in consciousness the "memory" of the past experience of similar contents, which, taken together with the forms of apprehension that enlivened them, motivate consciousness to apperceive the content in a similar way. It is crucial not to overlook this point: the awakening and motivation of which we speak here are given at the level of *passive* constitution. This allows us to say that the very functioning of typifying consciousness remains concealed in the framework of everyday experience. Here we can recall Kant's characterization of schematism as a secret art residing in the depths of the human soul (See Kant 2007, A141/B181). In this regard, one would be right to characterize typifying consciousness as a blindly functioning consciousness, that is, as a consciousness that in its daily functioning remains non-reflexive of its own passive accomplishments. It is a consciousness that shapes the objects it experiences, while at the same time remaining unaware of its own achievements. This, one could further remark, is the natural blindness of the natural attitude. As Andreea Smaranda Aldea so elegantly puts it,

> What presents itself in everyday intelligibility processes under the guise of metaphysical necessity is actually naturalized contingency. This is a claim Husserl himself does not make, but his analyses of typification clearly point to it: types understood as passively constituted, classifying, abstractive empirical generalities become sedimented through historical, communal

confirmation processes. Thus, what we come to deem "normal" through the guidance of types, what we deem "optimal" (satisfactory) for practical purposes, what we deem worthy of epistemic and/or ethical pursuit, is very much the product of historical, conceptual, discursive processes. (Aldea 2019, 209)

The foregoing analysis of typifying consciousness introduces some doubts about my claim that phantasy is productive in that it constitutes dimensions of sense, which are subsequently carried over into the field of actuality. Is it not obvious that consciousness of typification can only originate in positional and not in neutralized experiences? Clearly, the mere fact that I like to phantasize about mermaids or unicorns might affect how these magical creatures are given in my phantasy in the future. Nonetheless, these phantasies will not form a typifying consciousness, which will absorb my subsequent positional experiences. Small wonder that when I see the back of the head and the moving arms in the water, I will quite likely apperceive these appearances as the movement of a human body, yet I will not apperceive them as appearances of a mermaid. The world of phantasy is cut off from the world of actual experience. How, then, can phantasy be productive in the sense of co-constituting the world of actual experience?

We can answer this question in a twofold way. First, this objection presupposes a restricted conception of phantasy. It seems obvious that besides "seeing" mermaids or unicorns, I can also "see" Peter wandering through the streets of Berlin; besides "seeing" unicorns, I can also (as the modified version of the *ventriloquist illusion* demonstrates) "see" various shapes that will affect my apperception of actually heard sounds. Just as it is incontestable that phantasy can intend objectivities, which have never been and, most likely, never will be given in actual experience, so it is also undeniable that phantasy can intend appearances, which are, at least in principle, actualizable.[24] Second, the outlined objection is an instance of a misplaced criticism. I do not claim that phantasy is productive in the sense that it shapes phantasmatic appearances, which

---

[24]   As Bernet puts it, just as perception implies the possibility of a phantasy modification, so also, "phantasy implies the possibility of a perception" (Bernet 2003, 210).

can be subsequently transferred into the field of actuality. Rather, my claim is that phantasmatically formed unities of sense can be transferred from the field of phantasy into the field of actuality in that they can co-constitute the sense that absorbs actually appearing objectivities.

In this regard, Text No. 20 from Hua XXIII once again proves to be highly helpful. After drawing a sharp distinction between acts of phantasy, on the one hand, which are conceived as purely neutral acts, and perceptual acts, on the other hand, which are conceived as positional experiences, Husserl goes on to suggest that "there are, however, mixed experiences, and they are very common" (Husserl 2005, 696).[25] According to one type of these mixed experiences (*gemischte Erlebnisse*), "every phantasy consciousness, hence every pure phantasy consciousness as well, can be converted into a positional act…" (ibid). Conversions of this nature occur when one transforms a neutralized experience into a consciousness of pure possibility. Under such a scenario, what was initially given phantasmatically (as something neutral) is subsequently *converted* into a positional experience (as something possible). Moreover, while all phantasies can be transformed into pure possibilities, some of these possibilities are conceived as actualizable (as in the case of Peter wondering through the streets of Berlin), while others are conceived as non-actualizable (as in the case of mermaids swimming in the sea).

I should stress that such mixed experiences do not rely on a fusion of phantasy acts and perceptual acts. Rather, mixed experiences occur at the level of meaning-constituting consciousness. They are accomplishments of what I have called above *a transference of sense*. In the case under consideration, the sense of a phantasmatic object is transferred from the field of phantasy into the field of actuality. *Unities of sense, which are derived from meaning constituting acts, form the bridge that binds perception to phantasy, and vice versa.*

Yet, what can we make of Husserl's claim that such mixed experiences "are very common?" In the next section, I want to defend a perspective which Husserl does not explicitly endorse, but which can be conceived of as motivated by Husserlian phenomenology.

---

[25]   For a detailed discussion of such mixed experiences, see Ferencz-Flatz 2009.

Building on the basis of Husserl's writings, I would like to develop a position that such mixed experiences, which rely on the transference of sense from the field of phantasy into that of actuality, perform an essential and irreducible role in the constitution of cultural worlds, conceived both as homeworlds and alienworlds. In other words, in the absence of productive phantasy, consciousness cannot constitute intersubjective cultural worlds, within which we always already find ourselves. This suggests that it is not perception, conceived as a specific form of intuitive consciousness, but rather cultural worlds, conceived as specific configurations of meaning, that are shot through with dimensions of sense that in diverse ways are derived from productive phantasy.

The Role of Phantasy in the Constitution of Cultural Worlds

One might object that the proposed view is not only paradoxical, but also suspicious. How can phantasy, conceived as a capacity of consciousness to neutralize reality, perform a role (and not just any role, but a fundamental and irreducible role!) in the constitution of actual reality? Related to this, what exactly is actual reality, when conceptualized in the framework of Husserlian phenomenology? Husserlian phenomenology reduces all philosophical questions to questions of meaning and further clarifies these questions in terms of intentional accomplishments of consciousness(es). This means, among other things, that phenomenology conceptualizes actual reality as a particular configuration of meaning, and more precisely, as a configuration that derives from and finds its support in a peculiar unanimity of experience.[26] All claims to actual existence are grounded in evidence, and this evidence has as its basis transcendental subjectivity: "every imaginable adequation originates as our

---

[26]   As Husserl remarks in §26 in the Third Cartesian Meditation, "we can be sure something is *actual* only by virtue of a synthesis of evident verification, which presents rightful or true actuality itself" (Husserl 1960, 60). As he further remarks, "it is evidence alone by virtue of which an *'actually'* existing, true, rightly accepted object of whatever form or kind *has sense for us*" (ibid).

verification, is our synthesis, has in us its ultimate transcendental basis" (Husserl 1960, 60).

This passage brings to conclusion Husserl's all-too-brief analysis of actuality in the Third Cartesian Meditation. Here, actuality is conceived as the correlate of evident verification. One should not, however, overlook the fact that Husserl qualifies this verification as *ours* and not just as *my own*. As his further analysis in the Fifth Cartesian Meditation of the constitution of monadological intersubjectivity makes clear, the constitution of actuality cannot be carried through successfully within the boundaries of what Husserl identifies as *the sphere of ownness (Einheitssphäre)*. In §48 of the *Cartesian Meditations*, Husserl recognizes that actual being is originally constituted in the unanimity of experience. To this he adds that the unanimity in question embraces not only my own experience, but also the experience of other subjectivities. For Husserl, objectivities that come only from my own experience are not yet truly objective. They are objectivities that belong to what he identifies as "immanent transcendence" and "the primordial world." Only insofar as one's experience is presumed to be corroborated by the possible experience of other subjectivities can it be qualified as intending actual objectivities. This means that in order to constitute the objective world, consciousness must constitute not only an *alter ego*, but also itself as a member of a community of subjectivities. To put the matter in more familiar language, consciousness must apperceive itself as a member of a particular community. My hypothesis is that in order to enter a particular cultural world—be it that of my own or that of another—I must appropriate the way a particular community sees the world, and this act of appropriation calls for imagination.[27]

---

[27]   In the critical literature on the *Cartesian Meditations*, it was Ricœur who stressed the important role that the imagination plays in the constitution of the *alter ego* (see Ricœur 1967, 128-129). According to Ricœur, it is though the imagination that the ego coordinates the perspectives of the *alter ego*. This coordination is indispensable not only for the constitution of the *alter ego*, but also for the constitution of the common world. It is unfortunate that, in his commentary, Ricœur did not elaborate upon this insight in any great detail. My hope is that the following remarks will fill this gap in the literature.

To corroborate such a working hypothesis, it is crucial to recognize the fundamental function of embodiment in the overall framework of Husserl's account of the constitution of the *alter ego*. As Husserl makes clear in the Fifth Cartesian Meditation, the constitution of the *alter ego* has its basis in the givenness of the Other's body – a body which is like my own, but not my own. The Other's body emerges in the field of my own primordial experience as an object, which is simultaneously more than a mere object. I apperceive the Other's body through *analogizing apperception* (*analogische Apperzeption*): like my own body, so also the body of the Other is given both as *Körper* and *Leib* – both as a material object and as an organ of the will and free movement. Yet, the will in question is not my own will, just as the power of movement is not my own power. The Other is thus given as a subject of experiences, which, for principal reasons, cannot be transmuted into my own original experiences. To attempt to transform the Other's experiences into one's own is not only a futile task, but also proves to be the most narcissistic act imaginable, likenable to an act of "transcendental enslavement." It would equal the reduction of the Other's life to a moment of one's own existence. The Other's experiences cannot be lived through, but can only be appresented. These experiences are given in a manner that transcends the field of one's own givenness. The Other is thus accessible as originally inaccessible: the Other's physical givenness appresents a psychic life, which transcends the boundaries of my original experience. The Other is constituted not as a duplication, but as a modification of my own sphere of ownness: The Other is constituted precisely *as* Other.[28]

Insofar as any object is constituted in the unanimity of my own original experience, it cannot yet be qualified as an actual object existing in the actual world, since such a qualification would presuppose that the object's givenness appears not just for me, but also for other subjectivities. Every object, insofar as it actually exists, must transcend my sphere of ownness. The reason why this is the case is

---

[28]   As Tanja Stehler insightfully remarks, "no matter how hard I try to take the Other as a mere abstraction, that is, as a mere physical object, the Other will alert me that there is an alien sphere of ownness that is inaccessible to me, or accessible in the mode of inaccessibility" (Stehler 2008, 112)

because every object must entail a dimension of sense, derived from an appresentative level of constitution—in other words, that level which lies in the synthetic unity of synthesis between what is given to me in original primordiality and what is given to other subjectivities. Thus, to claim that an actual object exists in the actual world is to maintain that the object in question can be given intentionally, not just to me, but also to other subjectivities. At the same time, let us not forget that the Other's experiences are given as originally inaccessible. Despite its fundamental original inaccessibility, I must nonetheless presuppose some kind of access to these experiences of the Other if I am to qualify an object as an actually existing object in the actual world. *What, then, is this non-original access that is presupposed in the process of world-constitution?*

With regard to the constitution of a common nature (*Gemeinsamkeit der Natur*), which Husserl conceives as the first form of objectivity, one is right to maintain that *mere communication* suffices as a non-original point of access to the Other's experiences.[29] Here, mere communication refers to the *function of corroboration*. If this were absent, the constitution of a common nature would not be possible. The natural objects actually experienced by the Other are the same natural objects that are actually or potentially experienced by me: what is actually given to the Other is potentially given to me "as if I were standing over there, where the Other's body is" (Husserl 1960, 123). Moreover, as far as the constitution of mere nature is concerned, "the world belonging to their appearance-systems [i.e., the world of Others], must be experienced forthwith as the same as the world belonging to my appearance-systems; and this involves an identity of our appearance-systems" (Husserl 1960, 125). Thus, the constitution of a common nature is to be understood as the establishment of a sense of identity between my own primordial nature and that which is constituted in the Other's experience. Even though I cannot originally access the Other's experience, I can nonetheless establish a synthesis of identification on the basis of communication. In virtue of such a synthesis of identification, every

---

[29]   For Husserl's own discussion of the significance of communication in the constitution of a common world, see Husserl 1989, §51.

natural object, which is either actually or potentially experienceable by me in the lower stratum as "immanent transcendence," now receives an appresentational stratum, which is united in an identifying synthesis with the lower stratum. In short, the sense that belongs to common nature is derived from *harmonious intersubjective experience*, and is furthermore established through communication. While corrections might be required to preserve the harmony in question, these corrections only reinforce the congruence that guides the intersubjective experience of nature. Thus, as seen from a Husserlian standpoint, insofar as communication performs primarily a corroborative function, the constitution of common nature can be accomplished without any support of phantasy. Within such a constitutive framework, the role of phantasy appears to be superfluous: there is no specific function for it to perform.[30]

Yet the situation proves significantly different when we turn from the constitution of mere nature to the constitution of cultural worlds (see Husserl 1960, §55-§58). Although at this new constitutive level, communication continues to be the non-original point of access to the Other's experiences, its significance cannot be reduced to a corroborative function. I cannot enter into any cultural world if the Other only corroborates what I have already experienced, or what I know I would experience "if I were there," where the Other is. As mentioned above, the constitution of common nature presupposes that the Other's appearance-systems are the same as my own. By contrast, no matter how developed my own appearance-systems might be, I can only constitute myself as a member of a community if the appearance-systems of a particular community diverge from my own, and only if, despite this divergence, I find a way to

---

[30]   In "Phenomenology as Archeology vs. Contemporary Hermeneutics," Angela Ales Bello brings such a view into question, and for legitimate reasons. With references to anthropologically-oriented studies of primitive societies, she writes: "the primitive undoubtedly sees the tree, he is well aware of its remoteness or proximity, but what significance does the tree have for him? It may be that not all tress have a sacral-cultural significance for him, but one may well wonder whether the trees are then 'things' of a nature seen 'naturalistically' or even 'mechanistically'" (Bello 1991, 13). We will have good reasons to come back to this theme in Chapter III, when we turn to Scheler's account of productive imagination.

appropriate these extraneous appearance-systems. To enter into a cultural world, I not only need to be exposed to large depository of meaning, which is fundamentally not of my own making, but I also need to find a way to *appropriate* this meaning and to render it my own. In other words, only by learning to see and understand the world the way "they" see and understand it, can I transform the "they" into a "we."

We are not exposed to this depository of meaning when we turn away from objects given to us in our everyday experience. Instead, it is these very objects that are filled with dimensions of sense that transcend the boundaries of my own sphere of ownness. The objects I am exposed to in my daily experience are filled with axiological and practical characteristics: things are given as enjoyable, admirable, likeable, beautiful, venerable, etc. I can recognize these and other axiological and practical characteristics if and only if I appropriate the axiological and practical systems of appearance that are not of my own making. A phenomenological clarification of this kind of transcendental socialization, conceived as a type of cultural appropriation, is undoubtedly complex and no simplistic account can possibly do justice to it. That being said, it is not my goal in this present context to give a full-fledged account of this complexity. I only wish to suggest that, without productive phantasy, the process of transcendental socialization could not be carried out in full.

In phenomenology, it is not uncommon to observe that to be spellbound by the beauty of the sunset is not just a matter of seeing the sunset but rather a wholly new attitude of being captivated by the enjoyment of the scene. So also, to be burning with desire for x, or to have a strong aversion to y, or a strong admiration for z is not just a matter of intending x, y, or z. Building on Brentano's legacy, already in the *Logical Investigations* Husserl conceptualizes the structure of experiences that are concerned with a relation between founding and founded intentional acts. Our exposure to value characteristics, such as the beautiful, the desirable, the aversive or the admirable, is built upon two fundamentally different acts: the founding act, which is where the "natural" object is given to us, and the founded act, which is where the object obtains its value characteristics. Such a model of constitution invites one to maintain that we enter into cultural worlds when we apprehend the objects given in the founding acts as soaked in configurations of meaning, which are fundamentally not of our own making. We constitute ourselves as members of cultural communities when our founded acts project dimensions of sense, which are appropriated from other subjectivities. We all know that the axiological and practical values of the object differ significantly within diverse cultural worlds. This suggests that my elementary capacity to see objects as filled with axiological and practical qualities already presupposes my appropriation of particular systems of value, which guide my subsequent experience. Yet how exactly can these systems of value be appropriated?

Such an act of appropriation cannot be clarified on the basis of mere communication, although admittedly, communication can provide a foundation for it. While communication transcends the boundaries of intuition, the act of appropriation entails intuitive components, since it must culminate in one's capacity to *see* the world the way a particular community sees it. Communication must therefore be supplemented with a further point of access to the Other's experience, and this needs to be *intuitive*, even though it cannot be *originary*. What could such a non-original yet intuitive access be? There are only four possibilities to consider: such supplementary access can be provided either by perception, memory, anticipation or phantasy. As for the first of these, it is clear that perception cannot provide access to the Other's experience since it is an original form of consciousness. So also, then, neither memory nor anticipation can provide this access. Memory cannot fulfill such a function since it is bound to my own former experience; anticipation cannot fulfill such a function either, since, while the act of appropriation relates to the past and the present, the act of anticipation is linked only to the future. We have thus eliminated the others and are left with only one possibility: *imagination*, that is, *phantasy*. Phantasy is the only possibility that is able to offer this supplementary point of access to the Other's experience. Without this point of access, transcendental subjectivity would not be able to appropriate particular systems of value and thereby would not be able to constitute itself as a member of a particular community.

While communication exposes me to how Others see the world, when communication is supplemented with imagination, I am capable of intuitively reproducing their way of seeing it. Fundamentally, this capacity to reproduce the world of Others, even if it is done without much accuracy, already entails the capacity to apperceive intuitively given phenomena within a specific configuration of sense—that is, to apperceive phenomena so that it becomes suitable for this or that use or so that it is viewed to be beautiful, enjoyable, admirable, etc. So as to constitute higher levels of our intermonadic community, subjectivity must be able to recognize itself as a member of an intersubjective community, and this recognition must be understood as already resting upon one's capacity to transfer the reproduced configuration of sense from the field of phantasy to the field of one's actual experience. In other words, I am not only capable of understanding and of intuitively reproducing how Others see the world; I am also capable of *appropriating* this manner of seeing, that is, of *transferring* the apperceptive layers of sense from the field of Others (as it is given through my own imagination) to the field of my own experience.[31]

One possible objection to this is that, although this proposed conception of transcendental socialization clarifies how subjectivity appropriates the established systems of appearance, this analysis appears, on the face of it, to say nothing about the possibilities of

---

[31]   The view of imagination that I am here presenting finds further confirmation in the enactivist's account of imagination. The enactivist claims that imagination is not so much a matter of seeing, but of doing, a claim which emphasizes the embodied and social nature of imagination. Resisting the spectatorial view of the imagination, which depicts imagination as an inner theater, the enactivist's account emphasizes that, as Medina puts it, imagination is "something that we do, something that requires *active participation*" (See especially Medina 2013, 319). According to the enactivist, imaginings are not "in the head" but are "rehearsals of embodied and interactive explorations of the world" (Medina 2013, 320). According to the view I am here presenting, rehearsals of this nature underlie our transcendental socialization. The enactivist further corroborates this view by interpreting the expressive behavior of non-human animals as proto-enactive imagination.

modifying or transforming those sedimentations of meaning that make these systems into what they are. Yet, the very fact that the appropriation of these systems relies upon imagination provides support for the view that the appropriation in question should be conceived in a loose sense, and that this admits not only of variations, but also of modifications. With these variations and modifications in mind, one can say that cultural worlds must be historical through and through: the systems of appearance through which they are constituted admit of almost endless rectifications, transformations and variations.[32]

Conclusion

A common objection against Husserl's phenomenology of phantasy is that Husserl degrades phantasy to the point of being a frail replica of perception. Allegedly, his phenomenology can do no more than open up the inferior and incomplete presence, which is fundamentally secondary when compared to the full bodily presence, characteristic of perceptually given reality (see Ricœur unpublished; Drost 1990; Sallis 1992). Proponents of this objection claim that, in his reflections on phantasy, "Husserl has virtually reconstituted one of the oldest oppositions, that between image and original, reconstituted it precisely in its traditional role of serving for the differentiation of presence" (Sallis 1992, 203).

The foregoing analysis suggests that this widespread objection is an instance of a misplaced criticism. Admittedly, Husserl qualifies phantasy as an essentially reproductive mode of consciousness. However, the analysis here offered clearly shows that Husserl conceives of phantasy as essentially reproductive in the noetic sense of the term, a conception which, nonetheless, leaves open the possibility to conceptualize it as productive noematically. This happens in at least in three different ways: First, phantasy can intend objects

---

[32] In Husserl's own words, "that every such predicate of the world accrues from a *temporal* genesis and, indeed, one that is rooted in human undergoing and doing, needs no proof…. With this continual change in the human lifeworld, manifestly *the men themselves also change as persons*, since correlatively they must always be taking on new habitual properties" (Husserl 1960, 135).

and scenes, which do not copy perceived reality. Second, it opens a path for pure possibilities, which make up the field of phenomenology. Third, it proves to be indispensable for transcendental socialization and for the constitution of cultural reality.

Admittedly, in Husserl's published and unpublished writings, we do not come across a systematic analysis of the role that imagination plays in the constitution of cultural worlds. Nonetheless, I have tried to show in this chapter that Husserl does indeed leave us with a set of clues, and that these clues provide the basis to maintain a robust conception of imagination, a conception that performs a vital role in the process of world constitution. My goal here has been to follow these clues in a way that highlights the indispensable role reserved for phantasy in Husserlian phenomenology.

One of the great achievements of Husserlian phenomenology of imagination lies in its capacity to clarify the structure of productive phantasy. According to the structural interpretation I here offered, productive phantasy should not be conceived as a phantasmatic intending of sensuous objects within the perceptual field, but instead as a transference of meaning from the field of phantasy to the field of actuality. On such basis rests my claim that phantasy is productive, not because of its alleged capacity to permeate perceptual consciousness, but rather because it can generate patterns of meaning, which subsequently shape our subjective and intersubjective experiences of things and of the world at large. It is this transference of meaning from the field of phantasy to the field of actuality that justifies the Wittgensteinian insight that seeing always involves "seeing as." And yet, even though it justifies this Wittgensteinian insight, it does not abandon the Sartrean view that phantasy and perception represent two incompatible attitudes of consciousness.

In his early work, Husserl held the position that Kant's concept of productive imagination lacked phenomenological justification. While Kant conceived of imagination as a specific faculty, or as a power of the mind (*Einbildungskraft*), which is supposed to bridge the gap between the other two faculties, namely, between the understanding and sensibility, Husserl generally considered the theme of faculty psychology to be illegitimate for phenomenology. When viewed from a phenomenological standpoint, imagination is not a faculty, but is, rather, like perception and memory, a specific modality of intuitive consciousness, which has a distinct structure that calls for phenomenological clarification. Thus, in a recent essay on Husserl's and Kant's respective conceptions of imagination, Maxime Doyon argues that "in Husserl's phenomenology, and contrary to Kant's, the imagination does not assume a synthetic or transcendental function in perception" (Doyon 2019, 180). More precisely, "the result of Husserl's transformation of Kant's transcendental conception of perceptual intentionality is that there is no need to have recourse to the imagination to explain these experiences" (Doyon 2019, 184). These experiences concern the amodal character of perception (that is, the recognition that what we experience is not just a profile of a thing, but the thing itself), the identity of a perceptual object across time, and the subsumption of the manifold under a specific perceptual schema. But if Doyon is right, then the current ambition to inquire into the role that productive imagination plays in Husserl's phenomenology might appear anachronistic. In short, Husserl's phenomenology of imagination is a phenomenology of *Phantasie*, not a phenomenology of *Einbildungskraft*. However, by the time he turned to genetic phenomenology, Husserl explicitly spoke of Kant's great discovery of the "twofold operations of understanding" (see, for instance, Kern 1964, §22 and §23, Depraz 1998, 39, Jansen 2010, 145-146). In this context, we should not overlook one of the supplementary texts published in Hua XI (for the English translation, see Husserl 2001), which explicitly focuses on Kant's doctrine of productive imagination (see Husserl 2001, 410). In this text, written in 1920/21, Husserl speaks of "Kant's brilliant insights" from his "profound but obscure doctrine of the synthesis of productive imagination." Much like Heidegger after him, although for significantly different reasons, Husserl expresses his admiration for the First Edition of the *Critique of Pure Reason*: "but in our view, that is *nothing other than what we* call passive constitution..." (see Husserl 2001, 410). More precisely, Husserl calls the Deduction carried out in the First Edition of the *Critique of Pure*

Reason the "subjective deduction," while also identifying the Deduction carried out in the Second Edition as the "objective deduction." He stresses the importance that imagination plays in the subjective deduction and contends that the synthesis of imagination in the subjective deduction paves the way for what Husserl himself calls "genetic constitution." By contrast, objective deduction, Husserl contends, obscures the possibility of genetic constitution, since it confers the leading role not to imagination, but to understanding. However, as Natalie Depraz remarks, "Husserl never fully elucidated his own theory of imagination in the course of his analysis of passivity" (Depraz 1998, 30). Taking this into account, we can say that in the genetic framework, Husserl reinterpreted Kant's distinction between sensibility and understanding as the distinction between passive and active synthesis.[33] No less importantly, Husserl's reflections on the constitution of monadic intersubjectivity open the possibility to claim that, in the absence of productive imagination, transcendental subjectivity would remain largely enclosed within its sphere of ownness in the sense that it could not constitute higher level objectivities, conceived as unities of sense that arise in the unanimity of intersubjective experience.

The approach I have here presented opens the possibility to interpret the plurality of cultural worlds as diverse configurations of meaning. These diverse configurations of meaning are the constitutive accomplishments of productive phantasy, which are irreducibly social and historical. Despite Husserl's explicit concern that Kant's transcendental imagination cannot find phenomenological justification, his phenomenology provides a highly intriguing reinterpretation of Kant's view that imagination, when it takes the form

---

[33]   Consider in this regard Dieter Lohmar's telling remark: "For Kant, sensibility is a 'turmoil,' a 'chaos,' as long as the understanding does not intervene and regulate it through concepts. Husserl, however, departs from Kant at this point, for he believes that there are in sensibility so-called 'prominent features' (*Abgehobenheiten*), which stand out (*abheben*) in 'passive synthesis' in contrast to homogeneous and heterogenous realm in the field of intuition" (Lohmar 2003, 115). With this in mind, we can confirm Julia Jansen's insightful observation that "Kant's distinction between intellect and transcendental imagination is transformed by Husserl into the distinction between 'active synthesis' and passive synthesis'" (Jansen 210, 146).

of schematism, turns out to be "a secret art residing in the depths of the human soul, an art whose true stratagems we shall hardly ever divine from nature and lay bare before ourselves" (Kant 2007, A141/B181). When reinterpreted phenomenologically, productive imagination turns out to be "an art" hidden in the depths of the human body, whose true operations are to be divined from the cultural world itself. I speak of imagination being hidden in the body, rather than in the soul, because, as it has been demonstrated in this chapter, phantasy proves to be productive when it creatively appropriates configurations of sense from other subjectivities, whose constitution first and foremost relies upon their embodied presence. Yet this is not the only reason why we are able to characterize productive imagination as a secret power hidden in the body, rather than in the soul. As we will see in the next chapter, productive phantasy is strongly bound to drives, desires and instincts. This justifies the claim that productive imagination is bound to the body in a different sense from the one that was articulated in this chapter.

CHAPTER III
Between Phenomenology, Pragmatism and Metaphysics: Max Scheler's Concept of Productive Phantasy

Introduction

While nowhere near as extensive as Husserl's writings, Scheler's reflections on the imagination are of great importance in the present context, first and foremost because Scheler appears to be the first phenomenologist to have explicitly focused on productive phantasy in his writings. By rooting productive phantasy in what he identified as the vital soul, Scheler strongly emphasized the embodied nature of productive phantasy. However, Scheler's explicit analyses of productive phantasy have not received the attention that they deserve. In fact, I have not come across a single study that explicitly focuses on Scheler's philosophy of phantasy. Scheler's "Perception and Phantasy," published in *Cognition and Work* (1926) and "Metaphysics and Art" (1923) — a manuscript Scheler never published himself, but which appeared subsequently in Volume II of *Schriften aus dem Nachlass* — are the two most important texts where Scheler analyzes productive phantasy.[34] These two texts provide a highly important contribution to phenomenologically-oriented philosophy of productive imagination.

In this chapter, I will proceed by taking the following steps. First, I will clarify the context within which Scheler's concept of productive phantasy is to be understood. As we will see, this context mainly concerns Scheler's critique of pragmatism. Second, I will contend that phantasy is to be understood as a fundamentally productive activity in the *genetic* sense of the term, that is, as a

---

[34] Although both essays appeared in print in the mid 1920s, Scheler had been working on subjects of *Cognition and Work* since 1909 (see Frings 2001, 194 and 212). Some other helpful references to productive phantasy are also scattered throughout Scheler's last work, *Man's Place in Nature* (See Scheler 1961).

fundamental and irreducible component of what Scheler calls "original perception" (*Urperzeption*). My task will be to show that productive phantasy should be understood not only psychologically, but also sociologically, that is, as a component of psychic and social life. Third, I will show that Scheler's "vertical" thematization of productive phantasy can be supplemented with a "horizontal" analysis, which traces the workings of productive phantasy not only historically, but also cross-culturally. Fourth, while sticking to the genetic sense in which productive phantasy is to be understood in Scheler's writings, it will also be important to show that, even though productive phantasy undergoes significant restraint in the course of experience, nonetheless, it has not been extinguished. This realization will cause us to raise a question about whether anything could possibly resist the workings of productive phantasy. Fifth, I claim that the phenomenological reduction in Scheler's writings should be understood as a philosophical procedure meant to suspend the effects of productive phantasy. Sixth, this realization, in turn, will cause us to address the tension that arises between pragmatic and metaphysical conceptions of reality. This chapter will conclude with the analysis of questions that arise from the pragmatic-metaphysical debate.

Scheler's Critique of Pragmatism

The context of Scheler's reflections on productive phantasy is largely shaped by his critique of pragmatism and his drive- and motor-dependent theory of perception (*triebmotorische Wahrnehmungstheorie*). Scheler's central goal in *Cognition and Work* is to clarify the *relative* right of pragmatism—to curb its pretenses, divulge its philosophical errors, and fix the limits of its legitimacy. According to Scheler, the pathos of pragmatism threatens to diffuse a fundamental philosophical commitment—the view that a human being is *homo rationalis,* rather than *homo faber*. This commitment is threatened by the growing suspicion that modern technology is not merely a practical consequence, which derives from the otherwise purely theoretical cognition of nature, but that the will to master nature is the *primum movens* that fuels the cognition of nature itself.

Scheler's critique of pragmatism is a response to this very threat — to the spirit of the day, which pragmatism forcefully embodies. As a rejoinder, it is meant to demonstrate that the pathos in question, namely, the view that *all* human attitudes and activities are fundamentally practical, is not only philosophically illegitimate, but also practically dangerous, in that it instrumentalizes all values, thereby impoverishing the human relation to natural and cultural surroundings. Scheler's task is to find philosophical resources to resist such a form of reductionism, which tends to transfigure everything that can be encountered into a set of animate and inanimate resources.

According to Scheler, proponents of pragmatism are right to emphasize the primacy of the practical. They are wrong, however, to interpret this primacy not only genetically (that is, as the historical and psychological origin of human activities), but also conceptually, that is, as the ultimate framework of any kind of significance. Here, Scheler locates the blindness of pragmatism, namely, its incapacity to recognize the existence of other values besides instrumental. With this in mind, in his sociological interpretation of the historical shift that took place in Europe in the midst of the nineteenth century, Scheler remarks that pragmatism is "the counter-ideology of the new class of proletariats against the 'ideology' of the realistically and purely intellectually understood mechanistic naturalism" (Scheler 1977, 261). As a counter-ideology, it is no less biased and dangerous than the naturalistic ideology it was designed to replace.

In his epistemological reflections, Scheler conceptualizes the problem of cognition as a problem about the movement from ignorance to knowledge. He corroborates the pragmatic insight that cognition for the sake of cognition is just as empty as "l'art pour l'art" is for the aestheticians. However, against the pragmatists, Scheler contends that the purpose of cognition can be understood in significantly different ways. Scheler distinguishes between three fundamental purposes of cognition: (1) Cognition can serve the *practical* purpose of supporting domination, that is, it can serve the interests of the formation of the world in accordance with the prearranged goals and objectives. (2) It can serve the distinctly *ethical* purpose of personal development; in this case, knowledge concerns cultivation and formation of all that is personally relevant. (3) It can also serve the *metaphysical* purpose of understanding the principles that underlie the fundamental structures of the world and of understanding the logic that rules over the world's "becoming." Scheler maintains that while the practical purpose is subordinated to the ethical one, the ethical purpose is subordinated to the metaphysical. Moreover, he also holds that while the metaphysical teachings are especially prevalent in India, and while the ethical teachings are especially prevalent throughout Asia, the West (especially in recent history) has almost exclusively focused on the technical purposes of cognition. Thus, for Scheler, pragmatism (just as positivism) is a recent and one-sided philosophical expression of the current state of Western culture. The greatest limitation of pragmatism is that it recognizes only the first of these three purposes; it reduces what is distinctly ethical and metaphysical to what is merely practical. It is this very blindness that blocks the view of what Scheler calls *the absolute reality of things*, namely, that reality, which is only accessible to metaphysics, which, so he further contends, can only be established on the basis of the phenomenological reduction—that philosophical method, which suspends human interests and replaces the natural view of the world with the free vision of things. Thus, the fundamental limitation of pragmatism concerns not what it says, but what it does not say.

Despite these shortcomings, the pragmatist is within his or her rights to emphasize the genetic primacy of the practical. This primacy is not to be understood only in the epistemological sense, that is, only as a concern for the insight that genetically, human interest in knowledge is subservient to broader practical interests. Rather, the primacy of the practical manifests itself already at the level of the embodied relation to the world at large.[35] Our perceptual activities are dependent upon the involuntary and spontaneous performance of the body, which is largely regulated by drives and

---

[35]   In his defense of the drive- and motor-dependent theory of perception, Scheler writes: "the sensory functions and their accompanying organs are not instruments of an interested, theoretical knowledge of nature, but are regulatory and modifying procedures of our *actions* with them" (Scheler 2021, 92).

impulses.[36] Such a practical rootedness of perception in what Scheler identifies as the vital stratum of the soul should be further understood as an involuntary and spontaneous projection of sense upon one's perceptual surroundings. For Scheler, "our natural perception is *always* threefold: sensation + memory + phantasy" (Scheler 2012, 116) [emphasis added—SG]. The claim that sensation, memory and phantasy are inseparable moments of perceptual consciousness rests upon the insight that the involuntary spontaneity of perceptual consciousness expresses itself in terms of the projection of recollections and phantasma upon reality. According to Scheler, this projection of memories and phantasma is largely motivated impulsively and emotively.

How are we to understand perception's dependence upon and inseparability from phantasy? Clearly, it cannot be a matter of an arbitrary production of perceptual reference. The greater one's wishes or desires, the greater the feeling of limits that circumscribe the boundaries of perceptual experience. How, then, does Scheler's claim that phantasy is an irreducible perceptual ingredient fit with the common experience of a conflict between phantasy and perception, that is, with the recognition that the world of our experience does not live up to our deepest wishes and expectations? Let us recall Rudolf Bernet's observation that while phantasy represses perception, perception reacts allergically to all mixing with phantasy (See Bernet 2003, 213). In other words, phantasy and perception *cannot* coexist contemporaneously. Does Scheler's suggestion that productive phantasy is an ingredient of perceptual consciousness threaten to disrupt the distinctions between perception, recollection, anticipation and phantasy? Is it not these distinctions that enable us to define each of them? Only by looking more closely at Scheler's genetically-oriented phenomenology of productive phantasy will we be in a position to provide answers to these far from irrelevant objections.

---

[36]   Scheler goes on to suggest, "without some degree and some direction of *drive attention*, without *value*-grasping, and without the beginning of a *motor* process, a *perception*, no matter how simple it may be, *can in no way take place*" (Scheler 2021, 93).

Productive Phantasy and the Genesis of Experience

"All philosophers suffer from the same defect," Nietzsche remarks *Human, All-Too-Human*, "in that they start with present-day man and think they can arrive at their goal by analyzing him...a lack of historical sense is the congenital defect of all philosophers" (Nietzsche 1984, 14). Scheler, who in many ways was influenced by Nietzsche in his writings, expresses the same insight in his account of the genesis of experience. As seen from Scheler's standpoint, precisely such a "congenital defect" underlies the common partition of experiences into perceptions, phantasies, recollections and anticipations. This seemingly obvious classification is itself a historical and psychological accomplishment: it does not lie at the origins of experience, but emerges in the course of psychic and historical development.

A statically-oriented phenomenological approach, such as the one that guides Husserl's analysis in most of the manuscripts collected in Hua XXIII, begins with a clear-cut distinction between the essential types of intentional presentations (perception, memory, anticipation and phantasy). Scheler's alternative approach relies upon insights from child psychology, cultural anthropology and clinical experience. We can call this approach the *genetic* alternative, since the distinction we draw between perception, recollection, anticipation and phantasy is not to be found at the origins of experience, but rather emerges in the course of experience. This genetic alternative invites us to admit that there is a more original level of psychic and historical development, a level which precedes the above-mentioned differentiations of intentional presentations. Scheler qualifies this genetically basic level of experience in terms of *original perception* (*Urperzeption*) and argues that productive phantasy is its fundamental and irreducible component. So as to emphasize that, genetically, productive phantasy is more original than reproductive phantasy, Scheler identifies productive phantasy as primary and identifies reproductive phantasy as secondary. It thereby becomes understandable why the above-mentioned partition of intentional presentations into perceptions, recollections, anticipations and phantasies takes into account only reproductive phantasies and discounts the genetically prior manifestation of productive phantasy.

In the present context, it is important not to overlook the etymology of the German term *Wahrnehmung* (perception). The connotation in German is "to take something to be true." To claim that at the basic levels of psychic and historical development the distinction between different types of intentional presentations is not to be found, is to suggest that at this original level of experience, each presentation, be it a phantasy-presentation, recollection or anticipation, is "taken as true," that is, is apperceived as an actual perception. Only on the basis of *dissociation* (and not association, as the empiricists suggest) do we learn how to distinguish genuine perceptual objects from phantasy formations. Just as, for me to become conscious of the distinction between wakefulness and dreams, my dreams have to be recognized as dreams, so also, and more generally, both phantasy and other forms of conscious presentations need to *become self-conscious* (that is, apperceived as what they are) for us to be able to categorize and differentiate them. The kind of self-consciousness I am here referring to is not an inherent quality of conscious presentations, but a conscious feature that emerges in the course of psychic and historical development. In the early stages of this development, conscious presentations are undifferentiated and are all experienced as types of original perception (*Urperzeption*). Only at more advanced levels of psychic and historical development consciousness learns how to differentiate between different conscious presentations.[37]

---

[37] In this regard, Scheler's analysis comes close to Husserl's later and distinctly genetically-oriented reflections in *Experience and Judgment*. Here, Husserl writes: "*In the natural attitude, there is at first (prior to reflection) no predicate 'actual,' no genus 'actuality.'* It is only when we imagine and, taking a position beyond the attitude which characterizes life, we pass to actualities given in the attitude of imagination (…), and when, in addition, going beyond the occasional isolated act of imagination and its objects, we take them as examples of possible imagination in general and of fictions in general that there arises for us the concept of fiction (or of imagination) and, on the other hand, the concepts of 'possible experience in general' and 'actuality'" (Husserl 1973, 298). On this point, Scheler's analysis is more elaborate than Husserl's.

Scheler calls this genetically primary and undifferentiated level of experience "original perception" (*Urperzeption*), further noting that productive phantasy is "the original form of the perceiving (perzipierenden) life itself" (Scheler 2021, 154). At this basic developmental level, productive phantasy still lacks self-consciousness, although not in the sense of lacking what in contemporary philosophical discussions is called "prereflective self-awareness," but in the sense that it does not thematically recognize itself as mere phantasy and therefore does not conceive of itself as a specific type of intentional presentation that is opposed to others. By contrast, reproductive phantasy is by its very nature self-conscious, or self-translucent, in that it knows that its intended object is irreal and has no place in its actual surroundings.

Scheler maintains that the genetic analyses of productive phantasy have much to gain from research undertaken in child psychology, cultural anthropology and psychoanalysis. We cannot understand the magical world of a child, the enchanted world of an indigenous society, or the whimsical world of psychic illness without recognizing that these worlds are largely formations of productive phantasy. To be sure, one could retort that the child crawling like a cat *reproduces* the familiar movements of the animal, just as the physic patient engaged in a conversation with himself *reproduces* discussions he either has or could have held with others. In a similar vein, one could further retort that a member of an indigenous society who finds herself in a world inhabited by spirits, also *reproduces* in her natural surroundings what is human, all-too-human.[38] Yet, no matter how undeniable this reproductive dimension of imagination might be, one cannot account for the emergence of

---

[38]   In Chapter II, I suggested that what is nowadays called the "enactivist account of imagination" (see Medina 2013) can be understood as a corroboration of those insights that we come across in classical phenomenology. In the present context, I should stress that this is the case not only with regards to Husserl's, but also with regards to Scheler's phenomenology of phantasy. This capacity to reproduce what I discuss here as the movements of others is a type of doing, which calls for our active participation and for "rehearsals of embodied and interactive explorations of the world" (ibid, 320). The enactivists take this one step further by suggesting that it characterizes not only the human world, but also the world of non-human animals.

these different worlds on the basis of mere reproduction. That view that focuses exclusively on the reproductive function of the imagination remains blind to the *motivation* that underlies the genesis of these worlds. Scheler maintains that all these imaginary worlds spring from the *vital* form of psychophysical life, which in his final work, *Man's Place in Nature*, becomes the lowest stage of psychophysical development. We are confronted here with a form of psychophysical life comprised of drives and urges, which fall under Scheler's general category of impulsion (*Drang*). For Scheler, impulsion always has a specific direction, which can be understood as a pre-conscious goal-orientation. This allows one to qualify this stage of psychophysical development in terms of a pre-conscious movement toward something, or away from something. For Scheler, productive phantasy springs from such drives as hunger, thirst, sexual appetite, honor, struggle, etc. Precisely because it is nested in the vital sphere, productive phantasy is not only representational, but is also emotive. In the case of the child, the native, and the psychic patient, phantasy springs from the vital stratum and projects a layer of sense upon the actual world. The capacity to augment and transfigure our surrounding world is what renders phantasy genuinely productive. In virtue of productive phantasy, "we can feel what we never experienced, and wish what we never encountered" (Scheler 2012, 118).[39]

---

[39]   Scheler ascribes an overwhelming significance to drives. For Scheler, not only our perceptual relation to our surrounding world, but our history also is largely determined by drives. In his *Problems of a Sociology of Knowledge*, which, along with *Cognition and Work*, is another major essay included in Vol. VIII of his *Collected Works*, Scheler distinguishes between three essential stages of human development and argues that each of these stages is determined by a different drive. Thus, the first phase of this development is determined by the drive of propagation and preservation; the second — by the power drive; and the third — by the nutritive drive. Moreover, Scheler maintains that besides human history, the development of each personal life goes through the same three stages: in youth, the drive for propagation is most forceful; in adulthood the power drive gains significance; finally, in old age, the nutritive drive becomes the most potent. In addition to ascribing perceptual, historical and psychological significance to these drives, Scheler also speaks of their epistemological relevance. He distinguishes between three types of knowledge — religious, metaphysical and scientific — and argues that different urges underlie each of them. Religious

Sensation, Perception and Phantasy

What I have addressed so far constitutes only the first and by no means the decisive step in Scheler's analysis. According to Scheler, these different worlds—of the child, the native and the mentally ill—tell us something highly important about our own world. They reveal our common worldviews, which are shaped by an established, accepted and relatively stable set of shared beliefs that characterize our daily engagement with things and other human beings. They are themselves based upon a psychic and historical development, a development which should be conceived not in terms of fulfillment, but disappointment. Even limited exposure to these strange and seemingly inaccessible worlds allows us to identify the significance of those vital forces, whose presence is either unrecognized or denied. To paraphrase Aeschylus, the course of experience is characterized by *learning through suffering*.

To clarify this issue, let us turn to Scheler's distinction between sensations and perceptions. This is certainly a common distinction in phenomenological literature, yet precisely because the terms of this distinction are overdetermined, it is easy to misunderstand the exact meaning in the framework of Scheler's writings. For Scheler, this distinction is meant to reconcile the differences between causal and intentional accounts of perceptual experiences. As he says in *Man's Place in Nature*, these two processes are strictly identical ontologically, and yet they differ as phenomena (see Scheler 1961, 74). More precisely, sensations are lived through as changes that affect our bodies. They are physiological phenomena, and anything else that is said of them is a philosophical invention. By contrast, perceptions are not physiological, but psychological. Thus, when it comes to sound, we need to distinguish between sound waves that hit the eardrums and the sounds that we actually hear. Even though we sense the former, we actually perceive the latter. While the former call for a causal explanation, the latter should be accounted for intentionally. Just as sensations are not part of perceptions, so also,

---

knowledge derives from the urge for preservation and salvation; metaphysical knowledge—from the "Greek" astonishment; the root of scientific knowledge lies in the urge to gain knowledge so as to increase control over nature.

perceptions are not part of sensations. While at the sensory level, there are no phenomenal sounds, at the perceptual level there are no physiological sound waves (See Frings 2001, 240).

Thus, for principal reasons, perceptual phenomena cannot be reduced to a configuration of sensations, just as sensations cannot be reduced to perceptions. According to Scheler, perceptions are always shot through with the phantasmic transfigurations of sensory givens and their augmentation is established from what is not given sensuously, for it is precisely phantasy, triggered by drives and impulses, that transforms the sensed content into perceptual phenomena. Nonetheless, every living form – starting from cells, passing through tissues and organs, until we reach the organism itself – is continuously formed and transformed in the process of life. This compels us to return to the Heracleitean insight that one can never have the same perception or the same sensation more than once. Such sensuous and perceptual transformations affect not only the subject of experience, but the content of experience as well. It is these transformations that make things into the phantasmic images that they are. In this regard, Scheler's reflections on the phantasmic "image" in his posthumous *Metaphysics* are quite telling:

> I understand a phantasmic "image" to be the quintessence of *all* possible visual, tactile, etc. segments of a thing … in their concrete interwoveness. *This image we never have* but it is intended in every sensory intuition. It is a product of phantasy…. These images are 'ideal' — yet transcendent to consciousness, and objective — they are objective appearances, manifestations of the forces residual in impulsion which 'express' and 'represent' themselves in them. (Scheler 1979, 132)[40]

Scheler calls such phantasmic images *Körperbilder* and argues that they are not immanent, but are, instead, transcendent, and that they are not individual, but are, instead, social. In this regard, Scheler's reference to the role that productive phantasy plays in primitive societies gives us pause for thought. This reference rests on a direct acknowledgment that productive phantasy is not locked within the narrow confines of an individual life, but is also social. Scheler emphasizes this especially in "Metaphysics and Art," where he argues

---

[40]   Here, I rely on Manfred S. Frings' translation, as it appears in Frings 2001, 239.

that even though phantasy formations do not exist as separated from consciousness, they nonetheless cannot be reduced to individual consciousness. Phantasy formations are relative to experience, yet not necessarily to individual experience; they can be shared, even though they are irreal; they are *trans-conscious*.[41] The three guiding examples that Scheler uses in this essay—the number 3, Sleeping Beauty, and God Apollo—are phantasy formations of this kind.

These are not, arguably, the best choices for examples that illustrate the intersubjective nature of productive phantasy, since in all three cases, we are dealing with non-existent objects. Scheler's decision to use these examples overshadows the insight that productive phantasy is not reducible to the creation of fictive objects. Rather, our surrounding world is itself largely shaped by productive phantasy. We can derive a much more telling illustration of the social nature of productive phantasy from Scheler's contention that "history, too, is, in part, realized 'utopias'" (Scheler 2012, 117). Keeping Ricœur's phenomenological analyses of the social imaginary in mind, which he undertook half a century afterwards and which will be addressed in later chapters, one can further argue that besides utopia, ideology constitutes another form of productive phantasy, which transfigures social reality. What we face here are two fundamental forms of social imaginary, which determine the way we conceive of our surrounding world on the basis of the resources that productive phantasy provides.

---

[41]   In Scheler's words, phantasy formations "can separate from the momentary consciousness in which they first come up, and even separate from individual consciousness to become identifiable through several acts of consciousness and, what is more, they can be shared by a group of individuals" (Scheler 2012, 115). Or, as Manfred S. Frings puts it, "phantasmic images are: (1) transcendent, in which case they stem from physical force centers, and (2) in given consciousness, but only inadequately" (Frings 2001, 239).

The Psychic, Historical and Cultural Dimensions of Productive Phantasy

In his genetically-oriented account of productive phantasy, Scheler in one breath speaks of its *psychic* and *historical* development. While psychic development concerns the role that phantasy plays in the confines of an individual life, historical development refers to the social dimensions of productive phantasy. Just as within the development of an individual psychic life, phantasy is most pronounced in childhood and youth, and then becomes consistently more and more restrained in the course of experience, so also in human history phantasy plays a more prominent role in ancient civilizations than in the modern positivistic age (See also Scheler 1961, 25). Scheler contends that there has been a progressive decline of the role of productive phantasy in human history. He emphasizes the "glaring fact" that "all psychic and historical development of the human being is a long process of *disillusionment* and *disappointment* regarding primary phantasy images posited as real" (Scheler 2021, 150).

Following Scheler's lead, one could complement the account of social phantasy across the "vertical line" with a "horizontal investigation." Such an investigation would schematize different phantasy formations not only historically, but also cross-culturally. If it is indeed true that our surrounding worlds are constituted by productive phantasy, then it must also be true that the differences between cultural worlds largely rest upon different phantasy formations. It is to a large degree productive phantasy that renders the worlds we live in as diverse as they are. From a naturalistic standpoint, the different surroundings we inhabit are not different enough to explain the cultural differences characteristic of human existence. Philosophy in general, and phenomenology in particular, must find other resources to account for them. Although Scheler does not explore this issue explicitly, the metaphysical implications that he draws from his phenomenology of productive phantasy provide the basis to maintain these differences as different social formations of productive phantasy.

In the concluding sections of *Cognition and Work*, Scheler asks: if our perspective on reality is triggered by our drives and impulses and if reality itself is to a large degree constituted phantasmically, how can the intuitive content of our perspectives overlap with the presumed reality of the things themselves? In other words, how are we to distinguish between reality-constituting phantasy presentations and "mere phantasy?" According to Scheler, we can answer this question successfully if and only if we admit that reality itself is correlated with a single universal life, which Scheler calls *Alleben* (*all-life*), and which Scheler further qualifies as *"more than singular life"* ("*überindividuelles einziges Leben*") (Scheler 2021, 166). Following Manfred Frings, one could argue that this universal life of spirit, conceived as the constitutive origin of reality, is nothing other than what Scheler calls *impulsion*.[42] Impulsion, which Scheler at one point qualifies as the unity of highly differentiated drives (see Scheler 1961, 13), constitutes phantasmic images as a response to the stimulation of forces. If our individual drives and impulses overlap with those of the universal life, and if our individual phantasies that these drives and impulses give rise to coincide with the phantasies of the universal life, the intuitive content of our phantasies turns out to be partially identical with the content of reality; then, and only then, does the intuitive content of one's perspective overlap with the reality of the things themselves.

One could argue that Scheler's metaphysical considerations lack intuitive support and, for this reason, cannot be phenomenologically legitimated. However, it is much more fruitful to offer a more generous interpretation, that is, the interpretation that Scheler's concept of *Alleben* points in the direction of the historical manifestation of diverse reality-constituting worldviews, which we come across in myths, religions, political utopias, ideologies as well

---

[42]   As Scheler puts it, "it is thus ultimately the *same spirit* – as the one attribute of absolute being – that determines the structure of the 'possible world,' of the essential world in its *ideas* and *original phenomena*" (Scheler 2021, 165). According to Scheler's reinterpretation of this theistic thesis, since mere spirit does not have the power needed to phantasmically constitute reality, it must be the unity of spirit and impulses, that is, the metaphysical unity of the human and the divine, that constitutes reality" (See Scheler 2021, 165).

as arts and sciences. These worldviews are no less phantasy-laden than they are world-constituting. We can view individual phantasy content as world-constituting if it participates in these transsubjective formations of world-constituting phantasy. If such an interpretation of Scheler's concept of *Alleben* is legitimate, then Scheler's metaphysical considerations do seem to provide the resources needed to schematize social phantasy not just historically, but also culturally.

Phantasy and Desire

Scheler's emphasis on the role that productive phantasy plays in the constitution of the surrounding world largely rests on the insight that productive phantasy is inseparably tied not only to drives and impulses, but also to instincts and desires. In this way, Scheler binds productive phantasy to embodiment. This does not mean, however, that Scheler is an early proponent of the Sartrean perspective, which suggests that precisely because phantasy is rooted in desire, it is fundamentally cut off from reality. In contrast to Sartre, Scheler maintains that "phantasy does not necessarily lead into deception and error but can also serve both cognition of the real and truth" (Scheler 2012, 117). In Scheler's view, productive phantasy is *indifferent* to values and this is the reason why it can be of service to both falsehoods and truth. This indifference is to be explained by the fact that productive phantasy derives from the vital stratum of our emotional lives. Productive phantasy relates to drives, impulses and wishes, which are just as closely aligned with positive values as with negative values.[43]

For Scheler, the actual world we inhabit is largely constituted instinctually and affectively, which, among other things, means that desire plays an important role in its constitution. We see this already in the world of animals: the bird does not build its nest after reflecting on the nests it has seen or heard about, or by comparing

---

43   Scheler further suggests that here we discover the reason why Kant would no less famously than mysteriously proclaim that imagination (*Einbildungskraft*) is a blind power of the soul. According to Scheler, the blindness in question concerns a blindness to values, be they positive and negative.

what it builds and what others have built. Rather, the nest it builds (much like the structures that ants build in the absence of any blue-print) is a direct expression of the drives and instincts that underlie this activity. We have here an example of a reality-constituting ac-tivity rooted in the vital stratum of animal life.

This dependence on instincts and drives is characteristic not only of animal, but also of human existence. Humans accentuate, more than animals do, desires, instincts, urges and wishes, which are expressed not only in direct practical activities, but also phan-tasmatically. With attention to distinctly human life, Scheler main-tains that productive phantasy plays an irreducible role in the life of a businessman, statesman, artist and scholar. Productive phan-tasy largely shapes the highly diverse aesthetic, practical as well as theoretical formations. In all these cases, we are confronted with productive phantasy as it expresses the vital stratum of our emo-tional lives, as it expresses that part of our lifeworld which is fun-damentally rooted in our bodies. In all these cases, phantasy is not only pictorial, but also emotive and impulsive: precisely because phantasy is embodied, it is fundamentally productive.

Scheler has provided us with two significantly different con-ceptions of productive phantasy. My earlier remarks on the distinc-tion between conscious and unconscious phantasy provides the means needed to clarify this distinction. To maintain that produc-tive phantasy is an irreducible dimension of perceptual experience is to conceive of phantasy as a reality-constituting power, which lacks self-consciousness in the sense that it does not recognize itself as mere phantasy. By contrast, to speak of productive phantasy as it functions in the life of a businessman or a statesman is to conceive of productive phantasy as an already self-conscious mental activity, which recognizes that it intends an irreality and which it subse-quently aims to realize. Phenomenologically, we are faced here with two different types of experience, while conceptually we are confronted with two different structures of seemingly one and the same activity.

To further clarify these differences, alongside the distinction drawn between conscious and unconscious phantasy, one should also distinguish between immediate and mediate phantasy. While immediate phantasy is an activity that directly shapes the look of our surroundings, mediate phantasy performs the same constitutive function by means of, firstly, intending a fictive realm, which it then, secondly, transfigures into the field of reality. Scheler himself does not thematize these phenomenological and conceptual differences. Suffice it to note that his broad employment of the term, *productive phantasy*, suggests that it can be determined in diverse ways, at different levels of experience and in different frameworks of analysis. From the terms of these levels and frameworks, productive phantasy manifests itself as a reality-constituting power, no matter whether it functions in an immediate or mediate way or if it is unconscious or self-conscious.

The Development of Productive Phantasy

As we saw, Scheler's reflections on productive phantasy suggest that productive phantasy is at work in the midst of our most basic perceptual activities. As we further saw, productive phantasy is in full force at the level of original perception (*Urperzeption*). For this very reason, the world of a child is incomparably richer when compared with the world of an adult, just as the ancient world of a primitive society is incomparably richer when compared with the positivistic world of an overripe civilization. Should we, then, confirm Nietzsche's insight that "everything essential in human development occurred in primeval times, long before those four thousand years with which we are more or less familiar" (Nietzsche 1984, 14)? Should we take Nietzsche's insight to mean that productive phantasy is fundamentally pre-conscious? In other words, does phantasy transform at the moment it gains self-consciousness into reproductive phantasy? Furthermore, does this mean that there are two and only two fundamental types of phantasy: immediate unconscious phantasy, on the one hand, and mediated self-conscious phantasy, on the other?

Yet for Scheler, productive phantasy is at work not only at the early stages of psychic and historical development, and not only before conscious life establishes the distinction between different types of intentional presentations. The birth of self-conscious phantasy does not bring about the collapse of productive phantasy. Even as it loses its unrestrained, wild, magical flavor, productive phantasy continues to function in more advanced stages of psychic and historical development, both individual and social. Yet now it functions not only in the service of the constitution of largely diverse personal worlds. Once restrained and "civilized," it also enters into the service of purely aesthetic goals and purposes. If art is to be conceived as a field, where productive phantasy constitutes its formations, it must be further understood as a *late* formation in the course of psychic and historical development, which relies upon and transfigures productive phantasy's more basic unrestrained manifestations.

Although productive phantasy is controlled and diminished, it is not extinguished in the course of experience. At the more advanced stages of psychic and historical development, it is reducible neither to its merely aesthetic manifestation nor to its service in various practical and theoretical fields. Psychic life, in all its individual and social forms, continues to depend upon drives, instincts, needs, urges and wishes, and productive phantasy is the vehicle of their expression. While tracking the continuous role that these vital urges play in human life, Freud argues that, in the course of psychic development, the child learns how to transform his activities of play into pure phantasies, namely, into dreams and daydreaming. Supposedly here, in these purely phantasmic activities, one can safely play out one's desires and wishes (see Freud 1959). Although Scheler admits (at least on one occasion) that no one other than Freud and his early students has given such a detailed account of the function of drives (Scheler 2021, 194), Scheler's view at the same time significantly departs from the Freudian perspective. For Scheler, "our natural perception is not only initially, but always a complex structure, which entails sensations, memory, and phantasy.... The drive structure, and also the dynamic modification of the drive structure in the aging process, are for the phantasy world *and* the perceptual world a *dynamic constant*" (Scheler 2021, 159). For

Scheler, no fundamental break separates what Freud identifies as the stage of play and the stage of pure phantasies.

Scheler's opposition to the view that all our phantasies are re-productive activities thereby becomes understandable. According to Scheler, the contention that phantasy formation is either a repro-duction or a creative assembly of previously given perceptual for-mations is misguided, among other reasons, because it does not consider the possibility that perception itself is always already soaked in phantasy. In direct contrast to sensualism in general and to British empiricism in particular, Scheler maintains that what comes first in the flow of experience is not a pure sensation, but a wild fusion of phantasy, memory, anticipation and perception, which Scheler names *original perception* (*Urprezeption*). For Scheler, phantasy has always already been, and will always continue to be, an irreducible perceptual component.

The Limits of Productive Phantasy

So far, I have focused on the vertical depth and horizontal breadth of Scheler's reflections on productive phantasy. The vertical depth concerns the historical and psychological genealogy that underlies the relation between the subject of experience and the world at large. The horizontal breadth concerns the irreducible presence of productive phantasy in our most basic perceptual, affective and cognitive activities. Scheler's reflections might lead us to wonder whether there is any activity immune from the effects of productive phantasy. Are there any limits that constrain productive phantasy? Can any power resist its force?

These questions can only be answered if we pay close atten-tion to the general framework of Scheler's analysis. As we already know, Scheler's reflections on productive phantasy unfold in the context of his critique of pragmatism, which Scheler conceives of as a position with limited legitimacy. Due to its emphasis on the pri-macy of the practical, Scheler commends pragmatism for having brought to light that our perceptual relation to the world at large is nested in impulsion, drives, affects and needs. Nonetheless, accord-ing to Scheler, pragmatism has overstated the significance of the primacy of the practical. To recognize the limits that constrain the pragmatist's thesis is at the same time to recognize the limits that constrain productive phantasy.

Scheler's critique can be characterized as the contention that pragmatism suffers from what one of its greatest spokespersons, William James, has identified as the psychologist's fallacy. "The great snare of the psychologist is the confusion of his own standpoint with that of the mental fact about which he is making his report. I shall hereafter call this the 'psychologist's fallacy' par excellence" (James 1950, 196). According to Scheler, this is very much the confusion that characterizes pragmatism itself. Pragmatism confuses its own description of reality with the reality, which it describes. It absolutizes its own descriptions and takes them for reality itself.[44] Like King Midas, who cannot help but transform everything he touches into gold, pragmatism cannot help but reduce everything non-practical to the practical. It is the specifically philosophical attitude that enables us to recognize the fundamental limits of pragmatism.

According to Scheler, the philosophical attitude can only be established on the basis of the phenomenological reduction.[45] Scheler conceptualizes the reduction as the imaginative process *sui generis*, which consists of dismantling the intuitive content that covers the presumed reality of things. Let every color fade; let every tone die away; let all of the embodied forms of reality disappear; let space, time and all the categories of being be leveled. Such a process of dismantling (*Abbau*) the presumed reality of things leads to the realization that resistance (*Widerstand*) constitutes the essential and irreducible nature of reality. Emphasizing each and every word,

---

[44]   "Pragmatic philosophy is for us an attempt to consciously and one-sidedly *reduce* all knowledge to *practical knowledge*; it is an attempt to regard the possible transformation of the world for the purposes of our willed goals as the sole meaning and value of knowledge" (Scheler 2021, 21).

[45]   "Philosophy *begins originally* with the conscious bracketing of all possible desiring and practical spiritual dispositions and with the conscious bracketing of the 'technical principles' by which the object of knowledge is chosen according to the order possible mastery" (Scheler 2021, 19). Moreover, according to Scheler, "to cognize something about the being of the thing is not the concern of positive science, but rather of metaphysics" (Scheler 2021, 29).

Scheler writes: *"Realsein ist nicht Gegenstandsein ... es ist vielmehr Widerstandsein"* (Scheler 1977, 237).[46]

Such a conception of reality is sharply opposed to the insight that the reality of our surrounding world is constituted through the powers of productive phantasy. The reduction, conceived as the process of dismantling the presumed reality of things, is nothing other than the process of bracketing the achievements of productive phantasy. We face here a tension between two fundamentally different conceptions of reality. This tension makes it comprehensible why Scheler would qualify the objects we come across in our surrounding world not as things, but as phantasmic images (*Bilder*).[47] It thereby becomes also comprehensible why, in the concluding pages of *Cognition and Work*, Scheler would qualify the world of these images (that is, our actual surround world) not only as objective, but also as essentially contingent (*zufällige objektive Bilderwelt*). This qualification suggests that there is no necessity that underlies the emergence of those configurations of sense, which make this phantasmatic world into what it is; the content of this contingent world of phantasmatic images might just as well have been different.

Yet, no matter how great the tension between the practical and the philosophical conceptions of reality might be, Scheler holds the view that for philosophical purposes alone, it is not only possible, but also necessary to overcome this tension. He writes: "It is only in the greatest *tension* between both these dispositions [the practical and the philosophical—SG] and primarily through the *overcoming* of this tension in the unity of the person, that genuine philosophical cognition is born" (Scheler 2021, 168).

Although Scheler does not clarify the meaning of this highly intriguing claim, it is hard to overestimate its significance as far as the scope and limits of productive phantasy are concerned. Thus, in what follows, I will offer a concise interpretation of this claim

---

[46]   *"Being real is not objective being,* that is, it is not the identical being-thus correlate of any intellectual act; rather, it is being resistant to the original arising spontaneity that is one and the same in willing, in attending of any kind" (Scheler 2021, 168).

[47]   For an informative analysis of this concept, see Frings 2001, 236-241.

with the aim of demonstrating how it affects our understanding of productive imagination.

We do not face here irreconcilable claims: it is possible to conceive of reality as resistance while at the same time hold the view that reality is largely a constitutive accomplishment of productive phantasy. What is more, to make good sense of the concepts of resistance and productive phantasy, one needs to think of them alongside each other. After all, if reality were nothing more than resistance, it would be an entirely empty concept that lacks positive determinations; so also, if reality were nothing more than a product of phantasy, it would be anything the subject of experience would want it to be. It is highly fruitful to think of productive phantasy alongside the concept of resistance, since one thereby obtains the philosophical means to claim that, even though phantasy is one of the essential powers that constitute our surrounding world, it nonetheless does not have the power to give this world any shape or form. If phantasy fails to absorb the reality of things with its own projected sense-formations, this is because something resists it, and yet what resists it is nothing other than reality itself. The insight that the being of reality is the being of resistance mitigates the claims of productive phantasy, while the recognition that reality is a constitutive accomplishment of phantasy liberates the concept of reality from empty indeterminacy.

In his brief critique of Dilthey, which he offers at the end of *Cognition and Work*, Scheler maintains that we misunderstand the concept of resistance if we think that it is originally experienced when drives and impulses lead to disappointment. Scheler inverts such a view and contends that it is precisely the experience of resistance that sparks the activities of drives and impulses (Scheler 2021, 176). He thus maintains that the phantasy-driven constitution of reality is established on the basis of, in spite of, and within the limits of, resistance. We can take this as Scheler's direct admission that his philosophical conception of reality limits the powers of productive phantasy, although it does not rob phantasy of all constitutive force. To return to the earlier question, which concerns the limits of productive phantasy, we can now state that it is nothing less than the original experience of reality that resists the force of productive phantasy.

Yet the reverse also holds: just as the determination of reality as resistance limits the claims of productive phantasy, so also the recognition of the constitutive function of phantasy refashions the concept of resistance. Thinking of these terms alongside each other invites one to concede that resistance is adaptable, flexible and plastic. Thinking of the concept of resistance alongside that of productive phantasy invites one to maintain that the being of reality is not just the being of resistance, but rather, the being of *compliant resistance* – a form of resistance, which sometimes opposes and sometimes cooperates with the constitutive force of productive phantasy. From such a perspective, our cultural worlds turn out to be constitutive accomplishments derived from the play of resistance and productive phantasy.

One might wonder if such an interpretation of the conception of resistance can be justified based on Scheler's writings. Yet only if one accepts such a paradoxical notion of *compliant resistance* – that is, only if one admits that the concept of reality as resistance is commensurable with the concept of reality as the constitutive effect of productive phantasy – can one understand why Scheler would conceptualize resistance as a malleable term, which enables him to typologize different levels of reality. Here, I have in mind the fourfold stratification of reality that Scheler discusses the end of his *Cognition and Work*. Scheler distinguishes between (1) the reality of the absolutely real, which he further qualifies as "all-powerful reality," (2) the reality of the community, conceived as the *you-sphere* and the *we-sphere*, (3) the reality of the "outer world," which he claims has priority over the "inner-world," and, finally, (4) the reality of the bodily being (*Leibsein*) – a sphere within which animate beings are granted priority over inanimate beings (See Scheler 1977, 252-253). According to Scheler, the greater the resistance inscribed in a particular sphere of being (*Sphäre des Seins*), the greater is its reality. Scheler takes this to mean that the absolute reality of things, which he locates at the highest sphere of reality, is most resistant to modifications that stem from drives and impulses. This standpoint has the most reality, while the sphere of one's own bodily being (*die Sphäre Leibsein*) contributes the least resistance and has, therefore, the least reality.[48] Such a typology of the four spheres of being presupposes that the concept of resistance is a malleable term, while this malleability rests, in turn, upon the tacit admission that reality is just as resistant as it is compliant.

Scheler takes his fourfold typology of the spheres of being to mean that human domination over nature is in truth domination over the lowest spheres of being, which have least reality. Should we take this to mean that the sphere he identifies as absolute reality is immune not only to human domination, but also to productive phantasy? Moreover, should we take this to mean that Scheler refuses to grant productive phantasy far-reaching ontological significance in that he circumscribes the effects of phantasy to the lower spheres of being, which remain extraneous to the highest sphere, which Scheler identifies as absolute reality? I will bring my analysis of Scheler's concept of productive phantasy to its end with reflections on this very issue.

Life, Spirit, and Productive Phantasy

With these questions about human domination and productive phantasy in mind, we uncover a far-reaching ambiguity in Scheler's thought. Concerning Scheler's final work, *Man's Place in Nature*, I would maintain that in his writings, Scheler never managed to dispel this ambiguity. What is at stake here is the dualism of life and spirit, which lies at the heart of Scheler's metaphysics and philosophical anthropology.

Let us recall that for Scheler, "phantasy is a capacity of the vital soul" (Scheler 2012, 116). Moreover, let us recall that for Scheler, philosophical cognition originates with the phenomenological reduction, which is understood as the liberation of cognition from its dependence on the vital soul. This already tells us quite a lot about philosophy's relation to phantasy. Consistency demands that

---

[48]   Scheler further takes this to mean that human domination over nature is in truth domination over the sphere of being which has least reality.

reduction marks the distance that separates philosophical cognition not only from drives and impulses, but also from productive phantasy. Yet such a view is highly counter-intuitive and Scheler himself explicitly denies its validity. For Scheler, metaphysics begins at the point where sensory experience ends and therefore, all the metaphysical positions "are works of phantasy" (Scheler 2012, 117). It would seem, however, that Scheler wants to have it both ways—he wants to situate phantasy within the boundaries of the vital stratum and, at the same time, conceive of phantasy as the vehicle of philosophical thought. Yet his conception of the phenomenological reduction, which introduces a sharp divide between the vital and the metaphysical strata, does not justify such a perspective. Scheler ends up holding the same view that he himself considers to be illegitimate.

If phantasy is indeed "a capacity of the vital soul," then phantasy does not have any metaphysical significance. Alternatively, if "in metaphysics phantasy leads to evident knowledge" (Scheler 2012, 118), then phantasy cannot be qualified as a capacity of the vital soul. How is one to resolve this dilemma? There seem to be three ways. First, one could bite the bullet and proclaim that phantasy has no role to play in metaphysics. Such a view, however, would hardly be convincing, since it would deprive metaphysics of all content and meaning. As far as other possibilities are concerned, one could either give up the claim that phantasy is the capacity of the vital soul, or give up the view that the phenomenological reduction liberates one from the effects of the vital soul. Scheler, however, dismisses both options. The reason for this dismissal is grounded in the fundamental distinction that underlies his metaphysics, namely, the dualism of life and spirit. Such being the case, it becomes understandable why, in his final work, *Man's Place in Nature,* this ambiguity is intensified instead of resolved.

One could of course argue that in Scheler's final work, we come across an attempt to resolve this ambiguity. Consider Scheler's account of the interaction of spirit and life:

> It is precisely the spirit that initiates the repression of instincts. It does so in the following manner: Subject to its own ideas and values, the spiritual

> "will" withdraws from the opposing vital impulses the images necessary for action. At the same time, *it lures the drives with a bait of appropriate images* in order to coordinate the vital impulses so that they will execute the project set by the spirit. (Scheler 1961, 62) [emphasis added—SG]

Yet how can spirit "lure the drives with a bait of appropriate images" if, being cut off from phantasy, it does not have the capacity to generate any images? We face here a question-begging strategy: Scheler's explanation of how spirit establishes contact with the vital soul already presupposes an established bond between spirit, on the one hand, and drives, impulses and phantasy, on the other hand. What Scheler calls sublimation, conceived as the vitalization of spirit and the spiritualization of drives, already presupposes a deeper tie between spirit and life.

Where is this deeper tie to be found? One could argue that it is to be found not in the framework of philosophical anthropology, but in the specifically metaphysical domain. If so, the answer to the outlined dilemma must lie in Scheler's reflections on the highest form of Being, which he calls "the world-ground."

According to the fundamental principles of Scheler's metaphysics, spirit is originally impotent, while demonic drives and impulses are powerful yet blind. This insistence on the powerlessness of spirit forces him to give up the idea of the creation *ex nihilo* as an untenable position. Scheler rethinks this idea in the following way:

> In order to realize its *deitas*, or its inherent plenitude of ideas and values, *the Ground of Being was compelled to release the world-creative drive*. It was compelled, as it were, to pay the price of this world process in order to realize its own essence in and through this temporal process. And this Being would deserve to be called divine being only to the degree to which it realizes its eternal *deitas* in the processes of world history and in or through man. (Scheler 1961, 70-71) (emphasis added—SG)

Yet, if it is impotent, how can "the ground of being release the world-creative drive"? Moreover, how else is one to think of such a form of release if not in terms of creation *ex nihilo*? Last but not least, how can such a form of release take place without the objectification of what is not yet there, that is, without the objectification which appears to be only conceivable as *productive phantasy*? We face here the same unresolved ambiguity that we have already encountered in *Cognition and Work*. If the reduction marks the suspension of the vital sphere, then it must also mark the suspension of productive phantasy; but, if this is its effect, how can the reduction enable metaphysical reflections? This ambiguity becomes all the more pronounced when Scheler passes from phenomenological to anthropological and metaphysical reflections.

Conclusion

Scheler's phenomenology of productive phantasy, despite the above-mentioned ambiguities, provides a sufficient basis to respond to some of the more recent critiques that have been directed against phenomenology of imagination in general. Arguably the sharpest critique is to be found in Ricœur's works on imagination. Ricœur repeatedly maintains that the classical phenomenological tradition has addressed imagination only alongside perception and, for this reason, is unable to say anything substantial about productive imagination. This is why Ricœur provocatively asks: "But if an image is not derived from perception, how can it be derived from language?" (Ricœur 1991, 121). Scheler's reflections on productive imagination clearly demonstrate that there is a lot to be said about productive imagination when it is conceptualized along with perception. In fact, precisely because Scheler addresses imagination in such a framework, he discloses what in Ricœur's writings remains unexplored, namely, the possibility that our perception is largely soaked in phantasy.

    While inquiring into the limits of productive phantasy, I was led to the conclusion that Scheler's arguments are weakest at the moment of thematizing these limits. This brings up a further problem: to the extent that his philosophy fails to demonstrate the limits of productive phantasy, does it not thereby also fail to define productive phantasy? This philosophy rejects the option of defining phantasy by distinguishing it from perception, anticipation and memory. It even dismisses the possibility of distinguishing it from conceptual consciousness. Yet if any form of intentional consciousness can be qualified as a form of phantasy, then we lose the possibility of understanding what phantasy is. By becoming everything, phantasy becomes nothing. It becomes a superfluous term, which can no longer designate a circumscribed field of phenomena. Such being the case, it seems that we are better off if we drop this term and replace it with other concepts, which are better suited to describe a limited phenomenal domain.

Let me close this chapter by suggesting that one of the great merits of Scheler's phenomenology of productive phantasy lies in its capacity to provide us with an answer to this objection. According to this answer, just because phantasy forms a significant dimension of our multifaceted intentional relation to the world, it does not lose all determinacy. The reason for this lies in the distinction between productive phantasy and "mere phantasy," that is, between productive phantasy and that type of phantasy that does not contribute to the constitution of reality.

CHAPTER IV
Between Phenomenology, Ontology and Philosophy of Culture: Productive Imagination and the Cassirer-Heidegger Disputation

Introduction

In this chapter I wish to revisit the Davos disputation between Cassirer and Heidegger and interpret it as a debate over the meaning, nature and significance of productive imagination. As I showed in Chapter I, at least since Kant, the concept of productive imagination (*Einbildungskraft*) has been defined in terms of a transcendental function: it has been identified as a transcendental power that shapes human experience by forming the contours of intuition, experience, knowledge and understanding. Yet how is one to understand the transcendental status of productive imagination? Should one identify productive imagination as an original (that is, non-derivative) ground of human experience, a power more primitive and fundamental than reason itself? Or should one, on the contrary, identify productive imagination not as a transcendental ground, but as a mediating power between understanding and sensibility? Is productive imagination formative of reason, or is it rooted in reason? As far as productive imagination is concerned, these are the fundamental questions that we come across in the Cassirer-Heidegger debate.

After sketching the historical setting of the Davos disputation, I will proceed by addressing the common ground that underlies Cassirer's and Heidegger's analysis: both conceive of productive imagination as a transcendental power that determines the essence of subjectivity. This common ground, however, conceals far-reaching differences: since Cassirer and Heidegger understand productive imagination in significantly different ways, their respective conceptions of the "subjectivity of the subject" are also significantly different. So as to clarify the differences in question, I will focus on

Cassirer's and Heidegger's interpretations of Kant's Copernican revolution, on the methodological orientations of their respective analyses, and on their conceptions of human freedom. Following such a path, I will argue that Cassirer's and Heidegger's conceptions of productive imagination are not just different, but are, in fact, irreconcilable. So as to highlight the philosophical relevance of such an irresoluble difference, I will lastly turn to the relation between productive imagination and temporality.

The Historical Setting

Cassirer and Heidegger met in person on only three occasions (in Hamburg in 1923, in Davos in 1929, and in Freiburg in 1930),[49] yet they knew each other's published works quite well and the philosophical discussion between them spanned more than twenty years. Their meeting at the Davos *Hochschule*, which ran annual three-week meetings from 1928 to 1931, was the most important one of the three. The meeting was designed as a platform for presenting the audience with the central philosophical standpoints of the day. Cassirer was seen as the most important representative of neo-Kantianism, whose contributions to philosophy of culture were unprecedented, while Heidegger's name was associated with existential phenomenology, whose popularity after the publication of *Being and Time* (1927) was on the rise. Otto Friedrich Bollnow, Rudolf

---

[49]   Cassirer initiated the philosophical exchange with Heidegger when he invited his younger colleague from Freiburg to deliver a lecture at the Hamburg section of the Kant Society in December of 1923. Heidegger's lecture was titled "Tasks and Ways of Phenomenological Research." The Davos disputation followed from this meeting in 1929. A year later, Heidegger invited Cassirer to Freiburg. In the form of conversations, reviews and critical observations, their discussion continued until Cassirer's death in 1945. Both had enormous respect for each other's work, so much so that, as Hans-Georg Gadamer once remarked, Heidegger considered Cassirer to be "the only one worth publicly responding to" (Quoted from Kaeigi 2002, 72). Cassirer's appreciation of Heidegger was equally unmatched. As he put it in a letter to Maximilian Beck on August 15, 1928, "however much I disagree with Heidegger in terms of 'standpoint,' I nonetheless prize his work as an achievement of the highest significance, which everywhere bores back into the philosophical depth of philosophical problems" (Quoted from Meyer 2006, 157).

Carnap, Emmanuel Levinas, Herbert Marcuse, Erich Maria Remarque, Joachim Ritter and Leo Strauss were among the audience.

The disputation was preceded by a week of independent lectures. Cassirer presented morning lectures on philosophical anthropology (on problems relating to space, language and death), while Heidegger delivered afternoon lectures on Kant (on laying the foundations of metaphysics).[50] In its planning stage, this open discussion was conceived as an intellectual exchange between two outstanding German philosophers. The newspapers publicized the event as a "representative encounter" between "the new and the old ways of thinking" (see Gordon 2004, 221).

In the second half of the twentieth century, the debate was reinterpreted in a new light. Triggered by the controversies that surrounded Heidegger's political engagement and by Cassirer's political critique of Heidegger in *The Myth of the State*,[51] a tendency was

---

50   In itself, this can already be seen as an attempt on the part of both Cassirer and Heidegger to demonstrate how the themes that are central to their opponent can be treated from within their own philosophical standpoint. Thus, Cassirer's discussion of issues relating to temporality, finitude and death was meant to show what his revised version of neo-Kantianism had to say about issues germane to Heidegger's existential phenomenology. So also, Heidegger's analysis of Kant was designed to demonstrate why existential phenomenology provides a more compelling understanding of Kant's legacy than the neo-Kantian framework. Both Cassirer and Heidegger were well equipped for such an undertaking. On the one hand, Cassirer's transformation of the Neo-Kantian framework into a philosophy of symbolic forms (the first two parts of which were published in 1923 and 1925, while the third part was published in 1929, soon after the Davos disputation) provided him with a strong foundation to address issues relating to finitude. On the other hand, Heidegger's *Marburger Vorlesungen* from the WS 1925/26 (see Heidegger 2010a) and WS 1927/28 (see Heidegger 1997b) provided him with a solid foundation not only to lecture on Kant in Davos, but also for his *Kant and the Problem of Metaphysics*, which he began writing immediately after returning from Davos and which he published in the same year, in 1929 (see Heidegger 1997a). As one commentator has recently noted, between 1927 and 1936, Heidegger had written close to a thousand pages of textual commentary on Kant (see Golob 2013, 345).

51   In his last published work, *The Myth of the State* (1946), Cassirer interpreted Heidegger's philosophy as one that "did enfeeble and slowly undermine the forces that could have resisted the modern political myths." As he went on to argue, "such philosophy renounces its own fundamental theoretical and ethical ideals. It can be used, then, as a pliable instrument in the hands of the political leaders" (Cassirer 1974, 293). Moreover, in this work, Cassirer went on to argue

born to interpret Heidegger's alleged victory symptomatically. As Michael Friedman has forcefully emphasized (see Friedman 2000), from that point on it seemed that the Cassirer-Heidegger disputation marked a moment of rupture between the old humanism and a new anti-humanism, the old Enlightenment and a new anti-Enlightenment, the old rationalism and a new irrationalism. The Davos debate was interpreted as "a parting of the ways": it signaled that the ideals of modernity had receded into the background and had left the space open for the birth of a new era, which replaced faith in reason with attention to the precarious condition of human existence and the old commitment to the moral and rational essence of humanity with the new pledge to the "hardness of fate."[52]

I will stay clear of the political interpretations of this debate.[53] Although numerous circumstances invite political interpretations, they have the tendency to direct us away from the philosophical issues that were discussed in the debate.[54] There are, however, also good reasons to avoid the contrary tendency, namely, that of reducing the debate to a dispute over the correct interpretation of Kant's

---

    that Heidegger's emphasis on thrownness marks the self-surrender of autonomy and thus is a return to political "fatalism," conceived as a form of "myth." See in this regard also Barash 2012, 448-450.

[52]   In recent years, we have come across alternative interpretations of the debate that bring into question a sharp opposition between Cassirer's and Heidegger's respective philosophical standpoints. As Steve G. Lofts argues in his recent study, Cassirer's and Heidegger's projects are *different*, yet they are not *antithetical* in that they "both share in the development of a new ontology as a response to a fundamental crisis in Western ontology" (Lofts 2015, 234).

[53]   For political readings of the debate, see Bourdieu 1991, esp. 48 and Habermas 2001, esp. 26. For interpretations that bring into question the validity and significance of the political readings, see Skidelsky 2008, esp. 218.

[54]   Peter E. Gordon presents a similar claim when he argues, addressing mainly intellectual historians, that "neither Ernst Cassirer nor Martin Heidegger was primarily concerned with matters political, and if one places undue emphasis upon their political disagreement one may miss what most mattered to them; and, just as seriously, one may fail to appreciate why their debate remains of such moment for European intellectual history even today" (Gordon 2004, 224-25). Consider also Rudolf Bernet's telling observation: "in order to better understand what is at issue in the debate, we should distrust the overly simple and covertly ideological images employed by the protagonists and their communities of the faithful" (Bernet 2010, 51). To this, one can further add that the political matters were salient neither for the discussion partners nor for the audience (see Kaegi 2002).

critical writings. While political interpretations tend to place the Davos disputation in too broad a framework, the textual accounts, concerned with Cassirer's and Heidegger's allegiance to Kant, tend to diminish its scope and significance. We cannot deny the obvious fact that Cassirer had significantly expanded both the Kantian and the neo-Kantian versions of transcendental idealism into a comprehensive philosophy of symbolic forms. So also, we cannot overlook Heidegger's unwillingness to offer a philologically correct reading of Kant's *Critique of Pure Reason*, neither in *Kant and the Problem of Metaphysics* (hereafter *Kantbuch*) nor in the lectures from the WS 1925-26 (see Heidegger 2010a) and 1927-28 (see Heidegger 1997b) on which the *Kantbuch* was based.[55] To be sure, almost all of the central themes in the dispute can be found already in Kant; so also, both thinkers explicitly focus in the debate on those issues, which we come across in Kant's philosophy. Nonetheless, this debate concerns not only, and not primarily, the meaning that various themes, such as the Copernican revolution, productive imagination, or freedom, have in Kant's writings. Rather, for both Cassirer and Heidegger, Kant's texts provide a springboard to defend issues germane to their own standpoints. What is at stake in this debate concerns a creative and in some important ways anti-Kantian development of those themes that we come across in the works of both thinkers. As Rudolf Bernet remarks in his analysis of the Davos disputation, "beyond the quarrel over the right way to read and extend the thought of Kant, it is the question of the status of philosophy itself which is at stake" (Bernet 2010, 54).

---

[55]   Heidegger's interest in productive imagination can be traced back to his *Marburger Vorlesung* on logic from the WS 1925/26 (see Heidegger 2010a). While preparing these lectures, Heidegger realized that Kantian schematism provided him with a new angle from which to formulate the question of Being. Heidegger's unexpected recognition, while preparing these lectures, of the temporal formation of the categories through schematism forced him to abruptly change the outline of these lectures (see Schalow 1994, 104).

Productive Imagination and the Subjectivity of the Subject

Although the concept of *productive imagination* plays a central role in the Davos disputation, I am not familiar with a single study that has interpreted this debate as a controversy over the nature of productive imagination. This is highly surprising, since both Cassirer and Heidegger identify productive imagination as the central theme of their own respective philosophical projects. The central importance of productive imagination in Heidegger's reading of Kant is well known and well recognized. According to his central thesis, productive imagination is the hidden root from which the two stems of knowledge, pure sensibility and pure understanding, grow. Neither Husserl nor Scheler granted such as central role to productive imagination as Heidegger did in his *Kantbuch* and in his early lectures from the WS 1925-27 and WS 1927-28, on which this book was based. Heidegger does not address productive imagination in *Being and Time*, for in this work, Heidegger strives to outline fundamental ontology by relying on new concepts. Within such a framework, the concept of productive imagination is rethought as the "constitution of the being of Dasein" (*Seinsverfassung*) conceived on the basis of the transcendental-ontological determination of time. Regarding Cassirer, consider his remarks during the Davos disputation: "for me as well the productive power of imagination appears in fact to have a central meaning..." (Heidegger 1997a, 194); "the extraordinary significance of schematism cannot be overestimated" (Heidegger 1997a, 195). In his review of Heidegger's *Kantbuch* that was to appear in *Kantstudien* in 1931, Cassirer emphasizes just as strongly that there is an overall agreement between him and Heidegger as far as the recognition of the importance of productive imagination is concerned.[56] This should not surprise us, for

---

[56] "Ich selbst kann an diesem Punkte nur die volle Zustimmung zu Heideggers Auffassung und meine prinzipielle Übereinstimmung mit ihm betonen; denn die Lehre von der 'produktiven Einbildungskraft' erscheint nur – wenngleich unter völlig anderen systematischen Gesichtspunkten – als ein schlechthin unentbehrliches und als ein unendlich-fruchtbares Motiv der Lehre Kants wie der gesamten 'kritischen Philosophie'" (Cassirer 1931, 8-9).

according to Cassirer, a human being is an *animal symbolicum*, while the making of symbols itself rides on the back of productive imagination. The lack of attention given to productive imagination in this debate is not only surprising, but also unfortunate, since one could rightfully consider the Davos disputation to be the most important philosophical debate over the nature of productive imagination to have ever taken place. The publication of this debate, arguably, resulted in one of the most important texts on productive imagination in the 20th century.

For both Heidegger and Cassirer, productive imagination is of fundamental significance because it largely determines the *subjectivity of the subject*. This expression, "*Subjektivität des Subjektes*," is used by Heidegger repeatedly, and especially in the *Kantbuch*, which Heidegger wrote shortly after the Davos debate and which appeared in print in 1929. This expression refers to the peculiar characteristic — however one is to define it — to capture the nature of the subject, conceived specifically as a *human* subject. Indeed, this is what Heidegger identifies as the decisive question for the Kantian project of laying the ground of metaphysics: "Is the transcendental power of imagination, as previously laid ground, solid enough to determine originally, that is, cohesively and as a whole, precisely the finite essence of the subjectivity of the human subject?" (Heidegger 1997a, 120) Heidegger's qualification of human essence as *finite* is of fundamental importance, for it indicates that, for Heidegger, productive imagination is itself rooted in finitude. The reason for this lies in the fact that, according to Heidegger, productive imagination is a power that is not just spontaneous, but also receptive: it shapes *human* knowledge, rather than divine knowledge; as *human*, it is characterized by "original presenting" (*exhibitio originaria*) instead of by divine "creative intuition" (*intuitus originarius*); it is *intellectus ectypus*, not *intellectus archetypus* (as Cassirer puts it in his critical evaluation of Heidegger's *Kantbuch* [See Cassirer 1931, 6]). "Divine knowing is representing which, in intuiting, first creates the intuitable being as such" (Heidegger 1997a, 17). In contrast to such purely spontaneous intuition, human knowledge is marked by spontaneity *and* receptivity. Human

knowing cannot help but "take things in stride," as Heidegger repeatedly claims in the *Kantbuch*; it is a "hinnehmendes Anschauen,
das sich das Seiende geben lassen muß" (Heidegger 2010b, 117). In
Being and Time, this insoluble unity of receptivity and spontaneity
(which one could also call "spontaneous receptivity," or "the
grounding of spontaneity upon receptivity") is conceptualized under the heading of "thrownness" (*Geworfenheit*). Yet such a receptive taking of things in stride, which is rooted in Dasein's finitude,
is at the same time subject to highly diverse syntheses, and especially to the spontaneous formations of the given in accordance
with the categories of understanding. In the present context, let me
stress that, for Heidegger, productive imagination is no more and
no less spontaneous than receptive.

Cassirer and Heidegger are thus in agreement that the essence
of human subjectivity is largely shaped by productive imagination.
Yet this agreement only sets in sharper relief the far-reaching differences between them, which are derived from significantly different conceptions of productive imagination. For Heidegger, productive imagination is a transcendental power, qualified as both spontaneous and receptive, and itself grounded in finitude: it prefigures
the form in which things appear; it shapes the look of things, irre-
spective of how, psychologically, one might have wished to shape
them.[57] By contrast, for Cassirer, productive imagination is not a receptive, but a spontaneous power, a power guided by, although not

---

[57]   Cassirer felt that Heidegger's talk of receptive spontaneity was inappropriate
as far as Kant scholarship is concerned. In his review of Heidegger's *Kantbuch*,
Cassirer stressed that "a purely receptive spontaneity" and "sensuous reason"
could not have been thought by Kant in the sense that was ascribed to him by
Heidegger. He further emphasized that although Heidegger had the right to
offer an alternative philosophical approach to the Kantian system, he did not
have the right to conceal and deny that his "monism of the productive imagination" is incompatible with Kant's "radical dualism" (see Cassirer 1931, 16-
17). Cassirer therefore maintained that Heidegger was not a commentator, but
a "usurper, who, so to speak, penetrated the Kantian system with the force of
arms.... A restitution is required to oppose this usurpation: a *restitutio in in-
tegrum* of the Kantian doctrine" (Cassirer 1931, 17). Such a restitution required
that one reintegrates the doctrine of productive imagination within the Kantian
system, for the chief shortcoming of Heidegger's interpretation of Kant was that
it focused on one moment (namely, on the doctrine of schematism), while for-
getting about its place within the general architectonic of Kant's thought.

subservient to, intuition, and which has its own limits, beyond which lies the domain of reason, which enables human beings to break out of the confines of finitude and enter the domain of infinity. For Cassirer and Heidegger, productive imagination grounds the subjectivity of the subject, although in fundamentally different ways, and thereby leads to significantly different answers to the Kantian question, which lies at the heart of the Davos dispute: *what is the human being*? While for Heidegger, the answer to this question lies within fundamental ontology, for Cassirer, the answer is rooted in philosophy of culture. Heidegger conceives of the subjectivity of the subject as Dasein, determined existentially by "care" (*Sorge*) and illuminated through thrownness (*Geworfenheit*), fallenness (*Verfallenheit*) and existence (*Existenz*). By contrast, Cassirer conceptualizes the subjectivity of the subject in terms of the human capacity to constitute symbolic forms, such as language, myth, religion, art, technology and science, which predetermine the meaning of all objectivities. For Cassirer, a human being is not just an *animal rationale*, but also an *animal symbolicum*, an animal whose world experience is shaped by symbolic relations and forms.

To clarify what is at stake in these significantly different conceptions of productive imagination, I will focus on three themes: (1) different conceptions of Kant's Copernican revolution; (2) different orientations of Cassirer's and Heidegger's analyses; and (3) different conceptions of human freedom.

The Copernican Turn

Although it would be too restrictive to interpret the Davos disputation as a polemic over the correct understanding of Kant's *Critique of Pure Reason*, it is nonetheless undeniable that Kant's Copernican revolution plays a central role in this disputation. As Cassirer puts it, "but here an essential difference appears to me to exist, namely, with respect to what Kant called the Copernican Turn" (Heidegger 1997a, 205). For Cassirer, the insight that our knowledge does not conform to objects, but, rather, that objects themselves conform to our knowledge, stems from the realization that for us humans the world of pure immediacy is always already lost, that we always already live in a world that is mediated symbolically. Cassirer's broadening of neo-Kantianism from the theory of knowledge to a philosophy of culture relies upon a specific reading of the Copernican turn, derived from the insight that *human intuition is never "pure," but is always symbolic*; and insofar as it is symbolic, it is always already shaped by productive imagination. The *"symbolische Prägnanz"* (see Cassirer 1963, 191-204) that envelopes each and every phenomenon is the stamp of the spontaneous and creative power of imagination, which, in turn, is tractable to both practical and theoretical *reason*.

According to Cassirer, the Copernican turn brings to light that the question concerning the constitution of the Being of objectivity in general precedes the question concerning the determinacy of the object. Moreover, and this is crucial, Cassirer interprets the Copernican turn as a further apprehension that "there is no longer one single such structure of Being, but that instead we have completely different ones. Every new structure of Being has its new a priori presuppositions" (Heidegger 1997a, 206). The structure of Being thereby proves to be historical and socio-cultural through and through, which means that, paradoxically, for Cassirer, the ontological has ontic origins. As Cassirer sees it, the Copernican turn ultimately finds its fulfillment in a philosophy of symbolic forms, where different forms are conceived as different structures of Being, which, in turn, predelineate the horizon of sense within which each object gains its determinacy. Thus, for Cassirer, the Copernican turn leads to the insight that Being ultimately relies upon functional determinations and meanings: "the essential point which distinguishes my position from Heidegger's appears to me to lie here" (Heidegger 1997a, 206).

How does Heidegger interpret Kant's Copernican turn? In the Davos disputation, we do not come across Heidegger's explicit reflections on this issue. However, in his lectures from 1927-28 as well as in the *Kantbuch*, Heidegger speaks of the Copernican turn and its constant misinterpretations (see Heidegger 1997a, 8, and Heidegger 1997b, 38). The fundamental misinterpretation concerns the assumption that the Copernican turn replaces the primacy of receptivity with the primacy of spontaneity and the primacy of sensibility with the primacy of understanding. Resisting such an interpretation, which was prevalent among neo-Kantians (in his lectures from 1925-26 and 1927-28, Heidegger was an outspoken opponent of Hermann Cohen and Paul Natorp especially, whom he considered were the main neo-Kantian advocates of this interpretation), Heidegger maintains that the Copernican turn lies in the realization that not all knowledge is ontic and that all ontic knowledge is only possible through ontological knowledge. "The Copernican revolution states simply that *ontic knowledge of beings must be guided in advance by ontological* knowledge" (Heidegger 1997b, 38) For Heidegger, this means, among other things, that the correspondence theory of truth is not the fundamental determination of truth and that it relies upon a more primordial conception of truth, conceived in terms of ontological self-manifestation, which Heidegger qualifies as the "unveiledness of the constitution of the Being of beings (ontological truth)" (Heidegger 1997a, 8-9). In contrast to Cassirer, this truth lends itself neither to functional determinations and meaning, nor to diverse ontic origins, nor to the constitution of the multiplicity of symbolic forms, nor to a quasi-Platonic qualification, such as "truth beyond being," which presumably escapes the boundaries of both human receptivity and spontaneity. As Hans Blumenberg aptly remarks with reference to the Davos disputation, "he who is able to raise the question of the 'meaning of being' will not think highly of symbols" (Blumenberg 2000, 78).[58] Heidegger goes so far as to suggest that philosophy's focus on the constitution of diverse symbolic forms bespeaks the forgetfulness of Being, for with regard to ontological truth, our attitude is first and foremost *receptive*, and even though for Heidegger human receptivity is shot through with spontaneity, it is nonetheless not arbitrarily spontaneous and constitutive. Thus, while Cassirer conceives of productive imagination as *pure spontaneity*, Heidegger describes it as "spontaneous receptivity." Only by being "spontaneously receptive" can we recognize productive imagination not only as the

---

[58]   "Wer nach dem 'Sinn von Sein' fragen kann, wird von Symbolen nicht viel halten" (Blumenberg 2000, 78).

intermediary "midpoint," but also as the "central grounding" and as a "hidden stem" of both understanding and sensibility (see Wang 2018, 84-86). For Heidegger, productive imagination is not a spontaneous absorption of sensations within the fields of meaning that consciousness itself projects upon phenomena; on the contrary, it is the unity of understanding and sensibility, which marks a finite deliverance of Dasein to that which gives itself. But if this is so, by paying attention to different readings of Kant's *Critique of Pure Reason*, we can state that Heidegger's critical interpretation of Kant's transcendental power of imagination, as it is presented in his lectures from 1925-26 and 1927-28 as well as in his *Kantbuch*, does not belong either to the so-called "triad thesis" camp, which suggests that besides understanding and sensibility, imagination constitutes the third origin of cognition, nor does it belong to the "duality thesis," which, as was common among the neo-Kantians, aimed to reduce transcendental imagination to understanding. Rather, in Heidegger's reading, transcendental imagination turns out to be the "common root" out of which the other two "stems" grow. As Qingjie James Wang has recently put it, "it is an 'existential' and 'ontological' root that does not only make our cognition of the cognitive phenomenon possible, but it also enables our existence, our life, as well as 'the objects of phenomenon'" (Wang 2018, 87).

With this difference between the two thinkers in mind, one can say: for Cassirer, the subjectivity of the subject has the productive capacity to constitute diverse symbolic forms, conceived as diverse functional determinations of Being, which, in turn, form the transcendental dimensions of sense that prefigure the meaning of particular objectivities (for example, mythical, religious and scientific). Whereas for the Heidegger of *Being and Time*, the feeling of *Unheimlichkeit* disrupts the comfort of the "they"-dominated everydayness and leads to the discovery of authenticity and finitude, for Cassirer, human life is intrinsically homeless. Because of this, it can transgress the boundaries of its merely natural existence and enter into the domain of culture, thereby securing for itself the only available "seal of its infinitude" (Heidegger 1997a, 201).[59] For Cassirer,

---

[59]   See in this regard Skidelsky 2008, 211-212.

the fundamental *Unheimlichkeit* of human life is the reason that motivates humanity to perpetually create and re-create symbolic forms, which one can interpret as the human capacity to transform the natural environment into a home. Such a "metabasis which leads him [a human being] from the immediacy of his existence into the region of pure form" (Heidegger 1997a, 201) is very much what makes up the subjectivity of the subject. [60] By contrast, for Heidegger, because such a perpetual re-creation of cultural homes expresses Dasein's perpetual fleeing into the domain of inauthenticity, it only leads to the (re)-creation of the "they"-world and to a deeper forgetfulness of one's ontological roots. For Heidegger, the subjectivity of the subject can be discovered only insofar as one recognizes the arbitrariness of such a world, only insofar as one transgresses its boundaries and opens oneself up to the ontological, which both resists functional determinations and, fundamentally, precedes them, as it forms the ultimate horizon of sense, which might be covered up, yet cannot be extinguished.

Terminus a Quo and Terminus ad Quem

Let us supplement the first difference with a second difference, with a difference which concerns the distinctive orientation of Heidegger's and Cassirer's respective analyses. With reference to the lecture that Cassirer delivered at Davos before the disputation, Heidegger writes: "In the first lecture, Cassirer used the expressions *terminus a quo* and *terminus ad quem*. One could say that for Cassirer the *terminus ad quem* is the whole of a philosophy of culture... For Cassirer, the *terminus a quo* is utterly problematic. My position is the reverse" (Heidegger 1997a, 202). After indicating that his analysis is oriented towards the *terminus a quo*, Heidegger asks: "Is the *terminus ad quem* as clear for me?"

---

[60]   In the words of Fritz Kaufmann, "in the neo-Kantian interpretation subjectivity is 'nothing but' the system of objectifying functions read from the cultural documents in which they have manifested themselves and in which alone they are said to have their true life and being" (Kaufmann, 807). Or as Peter E. Gordon puts it, "Thus, for Cassirer, the human being was understood as a *spontaneous and creative agency* whose own activity as *animal symbolicum* cleared its path to an 'immanent infinity'" (Gordon 2010, 186).

What does Heidegger mean when he claims that, for Cassirer, *terminus ad quo* is utterly problematical? What is at stake here is the very way Cassirer appropriates Kant's concept of productive imagination. Cassirer transforms productive imagination into the power that constitutes diverse symbolic forms. This power manifests itself through the constitution of language, myth, religion and science, conceived as diverse symbolic forms that prefigure the meaning human beings assign to concrete objectivities. Yet what is the transcendental basis that underlies the human capacity to accomplish such remarkable feats, whose significance is not ontic, but ontological, just as it is not empirical, but transcendental? This is the question, Heidegger suggests, that Cassirer cannot answer. His analysis is fully absorbed in the *terminus ad quem* without being sufficiently absorbed in the *terminus a quo*. What is of concern in Cassirer's analysis relates to the *accomplishments* of productive imagination; what is missing are reflections on the transcendental *grounding* of these accomplishments. For Cassirer, the question concerning the subjectivity of the subject is to be determined not in terms of its concealed ontological origins, but rather in terms of the concrete historical unfolding of subjective life. As seen from the Heideggerian standpoint, Cassirer's analysis is marked by a constant confusion of the empirical and the transcendental, the ontic and the ontological, reminiscent of Kant's own analysis of productive imagination in his *Anthropology*, which does not subscribe to the immaculate bifurcation between the transcendental and the empirical that underlies his analysis in the first *Critique*.

All of this means that, for Heidegger, Cassirer's interpretation of productive imagination remains *ontologically groundless*. Heidegger stresses this point especially forcefully in his lecture course, *The Fundamental Concepts of Metaphysics* (1929-1930), where his critique of Cassirer is even more piercing than it is in the Davos debate:

> It is a widespread opinion today that both culture and man in culture can only be properly comprehended through the idea of expression or symbol. *We have today a philosophy of culture concerned with expression, with symbol, with symbolic forms.* Man as soul and spirit, coming to expression in forms that bear an intrinsic meaning and which, on the basis of this meaning, give a

sense to existence as it expresses itself: this, roughly speaking, is the scheme of contemporary philosophy of culture. Here too almost everything is correct, right down to the essential. Yet we must ask anew: Is this view of man an essential one? (Heidegger 2001, 75)

For Heidegger, philosophy of culture "unties us from ourselves;" it "does not grasp us in our contemporary situation;" it "does not concern or grip our Da-sein" but rather "necessarily misses it" (Heidegger 2001, 75-76). This means that, for Heidegger, philosophy of culture, which is concerned with expression, symbol and symbolic forms, fails to give an account of the subjectivity of the subject: "not only does it factically fail to attain it, it is of necessity unable to attain it, because in itself it blocks the path to doing so" (Heidegger 2001, 76).

What kind of an alternative understanding of productive imagination does Heidegger offer? For him, productive imagination is not an empirico-transcendental power, but is, instead, a solely transcendental power. In his lectures on Kant from the WS 1927/28 (see Heidegger 1997b, esp. 48) and in the *Kantbuch* (see Heidegger 1997a, esp. 148-150), Heidegger downplays the significance of Kant's account of imagination in the *Anthropology from a Pragmatic Point of View*, arguing that it provides an empirical but not a transcendental determination of productive imagination. More generally, Heidegger argues throughout his studies of Kant and elsewhere that philosophical anthropology does not address the fundamental question of its subject matter (what is a human being?), which, according to Heidegger, can only be addressed transcendentally, that is, ontologically. The genuine significance of Kant's reflections on productive imagination lies, Heidegger argues, in the *Critique of Pure Reason*, where Kant's analysis of productive imagination is thoroughly transcendental.[61] Heidegger's own goal is to

---

[61]   In a recent contribution, Alfredo Ferrarin emphasizes the differences between Kant's accounts of the imagination in the *Anthropology* and in the first *Critique*, arguing that while the first *Critique* presents an account of the imagination in a genuinely new sense, the *Anthropology* provides us with an account that is largely borrowed from the philosophical tradition stemming from Aristotle up to Hume and Baumgarten (see Ferrarin 2018, 30-33). "[W]hen he summarizes productive imagination in the *Anthropology* he conflates the senses (phantasy

show that this transcendental analysis is in truth ontological, irre-spective of what Kant himself might have thought of it.[62] Moreo-ver — and this is crucial — for Heidegger, the transcendental analysis of productive imagination is fundamentally *regressive*, in the sense that it must be concerned with the *origins* of subjectivity, conceived as the starting point in the laying of the ground for metaphysics. Thus, in contrast to Cassirer, whose analysis one could qualify as *progressive*, Heidegger presents us with a strategy that questions the subjectivity of the subject. His strategy focuses on the fundamental elements that form the core of the subject in a transcendentally and ontologically anterior way, as they predelineate the horizon of pos-sibilities in order to shape the multiplicity of forms, which, in turn, as Cassirer shows in great detail, constitute the variety of worldviews and forms of understanding. For Heidegger, to answer the question concerning the subjectivity of the subject one needs to turn to fundamental ontology, within which productive imagina-tion occupies an exceptional place.[63] According to Heidegger's

and schematism) in the same paragraph. In §28, he writes that productive im-agination is an *exhibition originaria* prior to experience as opposed to reproduc-tive imagination, whereas a few lines below reproductive imagination is op-posed to phantasy rather than to schematism" (Ferrarin 2018, 31). In contrast to this, in the first *Critique*, Kant offers a new meaning of productive imagination, where he conceptualizes it as a determination of time and schematization of pure concepts.

62   As Kearney remarks, "by thus bringing the humanist philosophy of imagina-tion to the point of its own self-overcoming as *Dasein*, Heidegger anticipates the end of imagination — and by implication the end of man" (Kearney 1998, 224).

63   What sense are we then to make of the puzzling fact that in *Being and Time*, Heidegger does not employ the concept of imagination? There are a few reasons for this. First, we should not forget that Heidegger was planning to develop an interpretation of the *Critique of Pure Reason*, and especially of schematism, in Part II of *Being and Time*, but this was never written. According to Heidegger's plan, the First Division of Part II should have focused on "Kant's doctrine of schematism and time, as a preliminary stage in a problematic of temporality." Yet the publication of the *Kantbuch* made Part II obsolete, since it served, in Heidegger's own words, as a fitting supplement" and a historical introduction to Part I of *Being and Time*. Secondly, and no less importantly, the reason con-cerns Heidegger's conviction that the ontological perspective he articulated in this work called for new terminology. Thus, even though Heidegger credited Kant with having elaborated a fundamentally novel theory of time, nonetheless, as Jeffrey Andrew Barash remarks, "the model of consciousness in terms of

controversial reading of Kant, productive imagination is the hidden root of sensibility and understanding: it forms the fundamental horizon that embraces all that subjectivity can experience, intuit, know and understand. With this unprecedented move (which is deeply contentious, as far as Kantian scholarship is concerned), Heidegger collapses the distinction between pure sensibility (time) and pure understanding (the categories) by reinterpreting productive imagination, which he also identifies as primordial temporality, as the hidden root of the two stems of cognition.[64] Heidegger does not claim that this was the conclusion reached by Kant in the *Critique of Pure Reason*. He rather maintains that Kant recognized the destructive implications that followed from the recognition of the primacy of productive imagination over understanding and sensibility. This is why Kant rewrote crucial passages and removed others, thereby retreating from the realization that productive imagination is the origin of our knowledge, selfhood and being. "He saw the unknown. He had to shrink back" (see Heidegger 1997a, 118).[65]

which this theory was elaborated only obscured the fundamental question of being; it therefore remained dependent upon a philosophical tradition that Heidegger aimed to overcome" (Barash 2012, 444). More precisely, as Richard Kearney insightfully remarks, "This is why he [Heidegger] replaced the term 'imagination' — which he deemed excessively charged with metaphysical connotations — with the more neutral term *Dasein*. This latter concept embodies the temporalizing activity of imagination..." (Kearney 1998, 223). Cassirer appears to be one of the first to have realized this, for as he notes in his review of Heidegger's *Kantbuch*, in the framework of his fundamental ontology, Heidegger was forced from the very start to displace Kant's concepts and enwrap them within "a modified spiritual *atmosphere*" (Cassirer 1931, 23).

64 Heidegger realizes that his interpretation of Kant departs from the letter of Kant's text. Yet let us not overlook the conclusion that a distinction between philological and phenomenological interpretation is operative in Heidegger's reading of Kant's texts (see, for instance, Heidegger 2010a, 145). While a philological reading sticks to the letter of the text, the phenomenological interpretation focuses on the issues (*die Sache selbst*) addressed in the text. Heidegger explicitly and repeatedly points out that his concern is not with what Kant said, but with what Kant wanted to say: "our intention and task, in properly understanding Kant's *Critique of Pure Reason*, necessarily includes the claim to understand Kant better than he understood himself" (Heidegger 1997b, 2-3).

65 Hartmut Boehme and Gernot Boehme suggest that Kant's refusal to grant productive imagination autonomous status is derived from a psychological

This difference between Cassirer and Heidegger tells us quite a bit about their respective conceptions of productive imagination. For Cassirer, productive imagination has its roots in *reason* and *understanding*, so much so that one could qualify imagination as a tool of reason and understanding. From this conception, productive imagination proves to be a fundamentally spontaneous force, capable of shaping the forms of the world autonomously and in a large variety of ways. For the same reason, Cassirer's conception of productive imagination does not result in a form of indiscriminate pluralism, which would place equal value on each symbolic form. Rather, for Cassirer, language and myth are of inferior value when compared to science. Sooner or later these inferior types of symbolic forms reach their limits and must transform themselves into science.[66] Cassirer defended this view until the end of his life: science marks the culmination of symbolic accomplishments. By contrast, for Heidegger, productive imagination is the hidden root of reason and understanding, and therefore, it cannot be exclusively spontaneous. Insofar as it brings understanding and sensibility into an indissoluble unity, it limits both, and thus is the ground of human

---

misapprehension that establishes a close association of the imagination with emotions and the body (see Boehme and Boehme 1996, 106). It is important to stress that, for better or worse, Heidegger's account does not oppose the Kantian reduction of productive imagination to reason with an opposite reduction of productive imagination to the body. Rather, as Qingjie James Wang highlights, if we bind imagination either to the mind or to the body, then in effect we "drive the transcendental power of imagination into an awkward situation of homelessness" (Wang 2018, 84) and consequently block the possibility that is so important for Heidegger, namely, that productive imagination "could be the essential ground for ontological knowledge" (Heidegger 1997a, 113). In Heidegger's reading of Kant, productive imagination proves to be just as autonomous of the body as it is of consciousness. Heidegger's account of the phenomenological framework distinguishes his approach to productive imagination both from Husserl's and from Scheler's accounts. In contrast, they each strove to show the rootedness of productive imagination either in consciousness (Husserl) or in the body (Scheler).

66   Or, as Peter E. Gordon puts it, Cassirer's theory of form "cannot be credited with a non-hierarchical pluralism. Indeed, the internal 'logic of philosophy' required that humanity awaken from mythic devotion to acknowledge its own responsibility in creating its symbolic order. Cassirer was therefore unabashedly a modernist, and self-reflexively so, in that his theory of symbolic development seemed to underwrite his own theoretical labor" (Gordon 2004, 236).

finitude. Productive imagination is spontaneous insofar as it *forms* human finitude; yet, it is just as much receptive since what it forms is precisely *finitude*, which is fundamentally marked by *transcendence*, that is, openness and receptivity to that which gives itself. Heidegger recognizes this as the Being of beings. It is crucial to notice that Heidegger's project of laying the hidden ground for metaphysics turns out to be a project of overcoming metaphysics. In the *Kantbuch* and the *Marburger Vorlesungen* on Kant, Heidegger aims to show how laying the ground is also an overcoming of metaphysics by dislocating reason from the place it had occupied in metaphysical thinking. In this regard, Cassirer's and Heidegger's projects could hardly be more distant from each other.

Freedom

Yet another fundamental difference between Cassirer and Heidegger concerns their respective conceptions of *freedom*. Cassirer maintains that freedom, understood as the cornerstone of practical reason, cannot be schematized, and for this very reason, "we conceive only of the inconceivability of freedom" (Heidegger 1997a, 194). Following Kant, Cassirer maintains that, as a cornerstone of practical reason, freedom escapes the jurisdiction of productive imagination: it cannot be schematized. The fact that freedom is not rooted in imagination but that imagination itself springs from freedom invites us to raise further questions about the sources of freedom. Along with Kant, Cassirer maintains that these sources lie in practical reason. Thus, for Cassirer, productive imagination rides on the back of freedom, which, on its own, is rooted in reason. For Cassirer, freedom ultimately is freedom for the creation of symbolic forms, and productive imagination is, at its core, the manifestation of freedom. It thereby becomes understandable why Cassirer would conceive of productive imagination as a fundamentally spontaneous force with irreducibly subjective origins.

It is precisely this subjectivism that comes under attack in Heidegger's reflections on the subjectivity of the subject. Heidegger maintains that "the difference [between Cassirer and Heidegger — SG] is clearest in the concept of freedom" (Heidegger 1997a, 208).

According to Heidegger, we misunderstand freedom when we conceive of it as a form-creating power. For Heidegger, productive imagination is not only the common root of understanding and sensibility; it is just as much the source of freedom, and precisely because productive imagination shapes freedom, freedom is inseparable from finitude, so much so that Heidegger qualifies it as "freedom for the finitude of Dasein" (Heidegger 1997a, 203). It would be a misunderstanding to reduce this enigmatic claim to a suggestion that freedom is freedom for the inner transcendence of Dasein, which, insofar as it is always already shaped by productive imagination, is fundamentally finite. Such an interpretation cannot account for the difference between freedom and its absence. In one way or another, human beings are *destined* for inner transcendence, no matter whether they use their freedom or not. Of central importance is the recognition of a conflict that lies at the heart of freedom, which Heidegger qualifies in terms of thrownness: "I did not give freedom to myself, although it is through Being-free that I can first be I myself" (Heidegger 1997a, 203). For Heidegger, freedom for finitude is to be conceived as the human being's potentiality to disclose the Being of beings in their truth, including both the Being of transcendent entities as well as the Being of Dasein itself. One could say that freedom, conceived as freedom for finitude, is nothing other than the human being's reflective openness to the shaping powers of productive imagination when it is conceived as an unyielding refusal to distort its ontological significance. As such, freedom proves to be fundamentally *receptive*, so much so that one can qualify it as freedom *from* the spontaneous production of symbolic forms, which, besides shaping the look of the surrounding world, also cover up its ontological presuppositions (such as thrownness and finitude).

Thus, for Cassirer, because it is rooted in reason, freedom is the fundamental presupposition of productive imagination and the vehicle of the production of symbolic forms; however, for Heidegger, freedom is shaped by productive imagination and is the capacity of authentic self-understanding, conceived as the disclosure of the forming powers of productive imagination. As far as the subjectivity of the subject is concerned, this means that, for Cassirer, the essence of subjectivity reaches its fulfillment in freedom when the life of subjectivity becomes the manifestation of freedom. On the other hand, for Heidegger, the freedom of human subjectivity is at most a possibility to receive what gives itself without transforming into something other than it is.

The Possibility of Reconciliation

If Heidegger's analysis is primarily concerned with the *terminus a quo* while Cassirer's reflections are absorbed in the *terminus ad quem*, then could one conclude that Heidegger's analysis complements Cassirer's investigations by providing them with the transcendental grounding they otherwise lack, while Cassirer's philosophy of symbolic forms supplements Heidegger's fundamental ontology with a detailed description of the effects of productive imagination, which is missing from Heidegger's reflections? Could such a dialectic result in a comprehensive and systematic account of productive imagination, which would cover not only its origins (in fundamental ontology), but also its meaning and significance (in the constitution of symbolic forms)?

Such a form of synthesis is compatible with the reconciliatory reading of Steve G. Lofts: "The philosophical projects of Cassirer and Heidegger are not antithetical, they are *different* and, through the opposition of their difference, they not only belong-together but require each other" (see Lofts 2015, 234). Lofts' arguments to the contrary notwithstanding, it seems to me that such an attempt at reconciliation would result in a muddled syncretism, a reconciliation which would distort both Heidegger's and Cassirer's analyses of productive imagination as well as blind us to their fundamentally different conceptions of the subjectivity of the subject. As seen from a Heideggerian standpoint, the philosophy of symbolic forms conceals the ontological significance of productive imagination, for it distorts the relation between imagination and reason and therefore covers up the receptive nature of productive imagination. Heidegger is therefore right to deny the possibility of such a synthesis (see Heidegger 1997a, 199-200 and 202-203) and to claim that, for him, the *terminus ad quem* does not concern philosophy of culture, but it does, instead, concern the question, *what is being?* By contrast, for Cassirer, because Heidegger was unwilling to recognize the fundamentally spontaneous nature of productive imagination and its rootedness in freedom and reason, Heidegger fails to provide productive imagination with a sufficient ontological grounding, which would initiate the transition from finitude to infinity (see Heidegger 1997a, 195-196) and disclose the manner in which productive imagination shapes the human world. Moreover, for Cassirer, Heidegger's unwillingness to thematize productive imagination at the level of its cultural manifestations results in an illegitimate restriction of its analysis to the level of fundamental ontology (which Cassirer, like Husserl, conceived as a form of anthropology). Heidegger's unwillingness marks his abandonment of phenomenology, since it expresses his refusal to address productive imagination in terms of how it shows itself.

Here we touch on a possible reason why, as the critics often remark, Cassirer's tone in the debate was so conciliatory, that is, why he was persistently willing to identify the common features characteristic of both Heidegger's and his own thought. By the time the disputation took place, Cassirer had already finished working on the third volume of his *Philosophy of the Symbolic Forms*; however, since it remained unpublished, Heidegger could not have been familiar with it. Cassirer believed that in this third volume (the subtitle reads, *The Phenomenology of Knowledge*), he unified the two greatest living German traditions of philosophy — neo-Kantianism and phenomenology. [67] For this very reason he so adamantly

---

[67]   Admittedly, in the Preface to the Third Volume of his *Philosophy of Symbolic Forms*, in which he offers a detailed study of the "phenomenology of knowledge," Cassirer remarks: "In speaking of a phenomenology of knowledge I am using the word 'phenomenology' not in its modern sense but with its fundamental signification as established and systematically grounded in Hegel" (Cassirer 1965, xiv). The Hegelian spirit behind Cassirer's analysis cannot be either denied or underestimated. Yet it also cannot be denied that Cassirer's central themes in this work are the very themes that have been at the center of attention in the phenomenological literature. Moreover, the way that Cassirer addresses these themes also brings his analysis into proximity with

proclaimed at the beginning of the disputation that "absolutely no essential difference arises" (Heidegger 1997a, 193) between these traditions of thought. For the very same reason, Cassirer further argues that he has "found a neo-Kantian here in Heidegger" (ibid).

By contrast, Heidegger considered the disputation to have been a failure because "Cassirer was almost too obliging. Thus I found too little opposition, which prevented me from giving the problems the requisite sharpness of formulation" (Storck 1989, 30). Heidegger did not accept Cassirer's solution to the dispute between neo-Kantianism and phenomenology (nor would he ever accept it afterwards), which originated not with Cassirer's and Heidegger's debate, but with the exchange between Natorp and Husserl. For Heidegger, phenomenology, conceived as fundamental ontology, and Cassirer's neo-Kantianism, conceived as a philosophy of culture, represented two mutually exclusive paths, and it was by no means merely a question of taste which path one preferred over the other. As Heidegger saw it, if his proposed path was worth taking, then Cassirer's alternative had outlived its day.

It is certainly not easy to see how the differences between Cassirer's and Heidegger's conceptions of productive imagination can be reconciled. Any attempt to resolve these differences would call for such far-reaching modifications that their implementation would cancel out each position and subsume one under the other. To see this, we need to turn to the relation between productive imagination and temporality.

Temporality

In the *Kantbuch*, Heidegger argues that Kant was "the first and only" thinker in the Western philosophical tradition to have stumbled across the fundamental significance of temporality for the

---

phenomenology. In this regard, Rudolf Bernet's observations are well-worth quoting: "Cassirer's hermeneutics thus seems to be compatible with conceptions of intentionality and constitution that scarcely differ from those developed by Husserl's transcendental phenomenology" (Bernet 2010, 53). This suggests that Cassirer's use of the term "phenomenology" is in fact not so different from its modern usage. See, in this regard, also Möckel 1992 and Luft 2004.

constitution of phenomena. According to Heidegger, Kant is the first modern thinker to interpret being in terms of time. Heidegger takes to mean that Kant's *Critique of Pure Reason* prefigures the ontological account of being offered in *Being and Time*. Nonetheless, Heidegger contends that Kant did not elaborate on the problematic of time in an original manner, and that he only understood it derivatively as sequence of nows. Still, according to Heidegger, in the first edition of the *Critique of Pure Reason*, Kant inadvertently uncovers a "decisive connection" between time and the "I think," which must accompany all representations. For Heidegger, the "I think," or, in other words, transcendental apperception, is itself rooted in primordial temporality.[68] That is, if the "I think," must be understood as the transcendental unity of apperception, then this unity, insofar as it is a unity at all, must rely upon a synthesis. This deeper synthesis is itself rooted in productive imagination (see Kant 2007, A118/123). We can thus say that imagination provides the original synthesis that apperception (the "I think") needs so as to bring appearances into a single experience.

Although Heidegger admits that Kant did not explicitly address the relation between primordial temporality and productive imagination, he nonetheless maintains that in Kant's reflections, productive imagination constitutes the ripening of time. More precisely, while Heidegger equates productive imagination with primordial temporality (understood in terms of the threefold synthesis of apprehension, reproduction and recognition), he further maintains that it generates "secondary time" (scientific or metaphysical time, understood as sequence of nows), which, in turn, means that, as Duane Armitage puts it in a recent contribution, the "categories of the understanding are formal abstractions from a more primordial temporal horizon" (Armitage 2016, 477).

For Kant, the synthesizing power of productive imagination is of an essentially temporal character. This is because it produces three syntheses — pure apprehension, pure reproduction and pure recognition (Kant 2007, A98-A110) — which Heidegger interprets as

---

[68]   For Heidegger's critique of Kant's account of the "I think," see *Being and Time*, §64 (Heidegger 1996, 292-297).

the syntheses of the three modalities of time. As a *facultas formandi*, productive imagination forms the present through apprehension; as a *facultas imaginandi*, it constitutes the past through reproduction; as a *facultas praevidendi*, it shapes the future through recognition. In *Being and Time*, as well as in Part Four of his *Kantbuch*, Heidegger reconceptualizes such a threefold synthesis of productive imagination under his own conception of Dasein, understood as ecstatic temporality. In *Being and Time*, Heidegger rethinks the threefold temporal syntheses through the primordial unity of the three *existentialia*. Each privileges a specific temporal orientation: "thrownness" — the past, "fallenness" — the present and "existence" — the future. Through such a tripartite temporal structure, Dasein makes sense of Being.

Heidegger's identification of productive imagination with primordial temporality is not without problems. It involves what John Sallis calls "the effacement of imagination" (Sallis 1990, 109) for the sake of Dasein's temporality and understanding of Being. As Heidegger himself states in the *Kantbuch*, "in the end, what has hitherto been known as the transcendental power of imagination is broken up into more original 'possibilities' so that by itself the designation 'power of imagination' becomes inadequate" (Heidegger 1997a, 98). We can take this to mean that, as Roxana Baiasu writes, "for Heidegger, imagination becomes an inappropriate name to designate the condition of possibility of the understanding of Being" (Baiasu 2020, 64). Thus, not only in Husserl's, but also in Heidegger's writings, Kant's concept of productive imagination becomes reconceptualized under the heading of many other phenomenological notions and themes, although these notions and themes are significantly different in Husserl's and Heidegger's respective phenomenologies.

Productive imagination, understood as primordial temporality, forms the horizon of time, thereby predelineating the temporal mode in which phenomena manifest themselves. Precisely because it is time-constituting, productive imagination is the root of all transcendence: whatever appears, must appear in time. As such, productive imagination proves to be primordial temporality itself, which Heidegger, in his *Marburger Vorlesung* from the WS 1925/26 and in his *Kantbuch* explicitly, equates with "pure apperception." As such, productive imagination, understood as primordial temporality, proves to be a pure self-affection. By constituting various schemata, productive imagination forms the horizon of transcendence; it pre-delineates the look of things and the manners of their givenness. Productive imagination thereby proves to be not just the intermediate faculty between sensibility and understanding, but the original "root of both stems" — that very basis, upon which all ontological knowledge (and, by implication, all knowledge whatsoever) rests and from which it takes its departure.[69]

For Heidegger, productive imagination, understood as primordial temporality, must be further conceptualized as self-affection (see Heidegger 1997a, §34, Heidegger 1997b, §25e and Heidegger 2010a, §28). As it forms the horizons of the present, past and future, primordial temporality must affect itself if experience is to have temporal unity and reference to the self. In such a basic way, productive imagination constitutes the ultimate temporal horizon, which delimits the boundaries of intuition, understanding and reason. Heidegger further suggests that productive imagination, understood in such terms, is the very subjectivity of the subject, the "ich selbst." So as to avoid unnecessary misunderstandings, Heidegger adds that such a self is rooted in primordial temporality and therefore must be understood as a finite self. That is, for the ego to secure its enduring character, productive imagination must first shape the horizon of identity and permanence. This allows Heidegger further to maintain that even though for Kant, *The Critique of Pure Reason* is sharply separated from the *Critique of Practical Reason*, nonetheless, the moral notion of the self outlined in the second *Critique* relies upon the formative powers of productive

---

[69]   Precisely due to the temporalizing nature of productive imagination, the transcendental subject is itself temporal. Needless to say, the transcendental subject does not change the way the empirical subject changes. While the empirical subject is temporalized externally, the transcendental subject is temporalized internally: the transcendental is thus an "abiding and unchanging I," and yet, in its abiding nature, it is the ecstatic unity of the future, present and past.

imagination just as much as the transcendental ego relies on this in the first *Critique*.

One might wonder whether such a view does not overemphasize the significance of productive imagination. At least for Kant, and in contrast to Heidegger, practical reason retains its freedom from the schematizing effects of productive imagination. Cassirer considers this point to be crucial: "the greatest misunderstandings in the interpretation of Kant creep in at this point. In the ethical (*Ethischen*), however, he forbids Schematism" (Heidegger 1997a, 195). Insofar as the ethical is conceived in terms of absoluteness and infinity, in Cassirer's judgment, Heidegger has failed to conceptualize the transition from relativity to absoluteness and from finitude to infinity. Heidegger's answer to this objection relies upon the insight that not only pure theoretical reason, but practical reason, too, is rooted in temporality, and more precisely, finitude. As soon as we pose the question of the meaning of the moral law, as soon as we inquire into the manner of how lawfulness is constitutive of the person, we come to realize that the concept of the imperative has an inner reference to finitude. Only Dasein, conceived as a fundamentally finite being, can submit itself to the moral law. Does this not mean that the question of the inner constitution of Dasein lies at the root not only of theoretical, but also of practical reason? To emphasize this point, Heidegger remarks: "Kant describes the power of imagination of the Schematism as *exhibitio originaria*" (Heidegger 1997a, 197). Here the term "originarius" must be understood in the etymological sense: to let something spring forth. Does this mean that productive imagination is not just spontaneous, but also receptive? Does this mean that only a being whose relation to the world is shaped by the schematizing power of productive imagination can impose the moral law upon oneself? Such, at least, is Heidegger's view: only a finite being, marked by thrownness and receptivity, is capable of submitting itself to the law.

This intimate and irreducible connection between temporality and reason jeopardizes the fundamental role that Western philosophy assigns to reason. According to Heidegger's controversial reading of Kant, the first edition of the *Critique of Pure Reason* culminates in the realization that reason itself takes root in productive imagination, conceived as the original mode of temporality. The disparaging implications of such a reading are far-reaching: Heidegger's recognition of the centrality of productive imagination culminates in the destruction of the history of that metaphysics, which ascribed central significance to reason and which ultimately saw world history as the self-manifestation of reason. For Heidegger, the "I think" is rooted not in reason, but in the schematizing power of productive imagination, that is, in original temporality. It thereby becomes clear how such a reading culminates in the ontological destruction of that very style of thinking, which in the Germany of the late 1920s, Cassirer's philosophy of symbolic forms forcefully represented. In Heidegger's own words, "the point of departure in reason has thus been broken asunder," which implies the "destruction of the former foundation of Western metaphysics in reason (spirit, logos, reason)" (Heidegger 1997a, 192).

In Heidegger, the primacy of productive imagination replaces the primacy of reason; in the framework of fundamental ontology, we can only understand the centrality of productive imagination as a hermeneutical alternative to the metaphysical centrality of reason The opposition to neo-Kantianism implied in this standpoint constitutes one of the reasons why, in *Being and Time*, Heidegger still identifies the conditions of experience as "existential," rather than "transcendental," for they are rooted not in reason, but in productive imagination and primordial temporality.[70]

---

[70] Heidegger's opposition to the neo-Kantian reading of Kant is especially strongly expressed in his *Marburger Vorlesungen* from 1925/26 and 1926/27 (see Heidegger 2010a and 1997b), on which the *Kantbuch* was heavily based. Paul Natorp and Hermann Cohen are Heidegger's constant "partners in dialogue" in these lectures, in the sense that Heidegger develops his own reading of Kant in opposition to their attempt to reduce transcendental aesthetics to transcendental logic under the category of modality. "Cohen and Natorp noticed as clearly as no one else before that the *Critique* lacks an ultimate encompassing unity, in the sense namely that this unity and *the ground of this unity of the transcendental aesthetic and logic was not explicitly brought to light by Kant*, and also *could not* be brought to light. Thus what disturbed those thinkers was genuinely motivated, but they looked for the solution in the wrong direction" (Heidegger 1997b, 54). That is, the neo-Kantians looked for the solution in understanding,

Here we arrive at a fundamental point of contention between Cassirer and Heidegger. In Cassirer's view, these far-reaching implications are built upon a misconception of the power of productive imagination. According to Cassirer, Heidegger's fundamental mistake lies in the refusal to acknowledge the independent character of both reason and understanding. In this regard, it is crucial to limit imagination and to acknowledge reason's independence from both imagination and intuition. Understanding might serve intuition, yet it is not subsumed by, and therefore, not receptive to understanding, but is, instead, fundamentally and irreducibly spontaneous. Moreover, once we move from the transcendental analytic to the transcendental dialectic, we are forced to say the same about reason. Reason is not constrained by phenomena, but is fundamentally unconditioned, or in Cassirer's words, infinite, in the sense that it places us in front of the noumenon.

In contrast to Heidegger, for whom productive imagination limits the power of reason, for Cassirer, productive imagination is itself limited by the power of reason. Cassirer thus ascribes to productive imagination those very functions that classical empiricism had ascribed to sensibility. In the framework of a philosophy of culture, the centrality of productive imagination marks the predominance of spontaneity over receptivity and of understanding over sensibility. This means that, for Cassirer, productive imagination is the power that shapes the phenomenal world according to reason's own forms of intelligibility. Therefore, while in Heidegger productive imagination ultimately marks the collapse of Western metaphysics and its rootedness in reason, in Cassirer productive imagination proves to be the force that preserves the foundations of Western metaphysics in reason (precisely because it stands at the

---

while according the Heidegger, the solution lies in productive imagination, understood as the hidden root of the two stems of knowledge. In his lectures from 1927/28, Heidegger formulates his approach to the neo-Kantian reading of Kant unambiguously: "with the phenomenological interpretation we oppose in principle the conception of Kant of the Marburg School" (Heidegger 1997b, 54); "a phenomenological interpretation of the *Critique* is the only interpretation that fits Kant's own intentions, even if these intentions are not clearly spelled out by him" (Heidegger 1997b, 49). "We are for Kant, against Kantianism" (Heidegger 1997b, 90).

service of understanding and reason). It thereby becomes understandable why John M. Krois would note that "there was really not a Davos debate; instead, two ships were floating away from each other in the darkness" (Krois 2002, 234). Indeed, both Cassirer and Heidegger recognized the central importance of productive imagination, yet they both interpreted it in accordance with fundamentally different paradigms (see Lengyel 2015, 313).

Conclusion

When Cassirer and Heidegger discuss productive imagination and both recognize its centrality in Kant as well as in their own respective philosophical frameworks, are they addressing one and the same phenomenon, or are they focusing on different themes, which they give one and the same name? Kant had argued that "the schema of a pure concept of understanding can never be brought into any image whatsoever" (Kant 2007, A142/B181). *Mutatis mutandis*, both Cassirer and Heidegger agree with this estimation and recognize that this agreement constitutes how one can speak of productive imagination as a common phenomenon in their reflections. Cassirer and Heidegger are in full agreement that productive imagination does not produce empirically-intuitable images.[71] This corresponds to Kant's explicit claim that schemata are not pictures, but "rules" by which imagination schematizes time (Kant 2007,

---

[71]   One should note in passing that Heidegger's interpretation of the Kantian warning is not as straightforward as one might wish. By introducing a distinction between *Bild* and *Abbild* as early as in his Lectures from WS 1925/26, Heidegger maintains that although a schema is not an image, conceived as an empirical copy (*Abbild*), which characterizes the relation between photographic images and the things they represent, it is nonetheless a picture of sorts (*Bild*), which Heidegger calls a schema-image (*Schema-Bild*). More precisely, in Heidegger's reading, while a schema is a general rule for the sensibility of concepts, a schema-image is the look that structurally belongs to the schema. Schema-images are not copies of empirically intuitable things, but *pictures as rules*, which are presupposed by experience. To stick to Heidegger's own example, without a schema-image of a house, an intuition of a particular house *as* house would not be possible. Without schema-images, concepts would have no meaning, which in Heidegger's interpretation further suggests that concepts are abstracted from schema-images, and not the other way round, as classical readings of Kant propose.

A142/B181). So also, for Cassirer and Heidegger, although schemata provide the basis on which empirical imagination can construct images, by themselves, schemata are not images. For both,
productive imagination constitutes horizons of sense, which one
could call *operational fields* (see Schrag 1967, 94) that prefigure intuition and understanding. Productive imagination establishes the
conceptual and phenomenal frameworks that pre-determine the
look and sense of phenomena. For both Cassirer and Heidegger,
productive imagination gives rise to the mode of vision (*Sicht*) that
makes seeing possible (see Bernet 2010, 44). The thesis that anything
and everything that appears is always already shaped by productive imagination constitutes the central point of agreement in Cassirer's and Heidegger's respective conceptions of productive imagination.

Thus, if one were to ask – "what does productive imagination
produce?" – both Cassirer and Heidegger would offer very similar
answers: productive imagination produces the transcendental horizons of sense, the operational fields, or the modes of vision, which
pre-determine human experience. Metaphorically, one could say
that for Cassirer and Heidegger, productive imagination produces
the light without which seeing is not possible. However, Cassirer
and Heidegger determine this light in significantly different ways.
While Cassirer interprets it in terms of objective forms, Heidegger
interprets it ontologically, as an essential characteristic of fundamental ontology, hence as something characteristic of Dasein, as
something irreducibly subjective. Because they have such fundamentally different re-interpretations of the transcendental schema,
Cassirer and Heidegger offer us two diverging conceptions of the
limits of productive imagination. For Heidegger, precisely because
it is understood ontologically, productive imagination is boundless:
it is nothing other than original temporality itself, which the
Heidegger of *Being and Time* interprets as Dasein. By contrast, for
Cassirer, precisely because it is interpreted through objective forms,
productive imagination is limited by understanding and reason. It
thereby becomes understandable why Heidegger's account of productive imagination leads him to speak of the destruction of the

foundation of Western metaphysics in reason. So also, it becomes understandable why, in Cassirer, productive imagination performs the contrary role, namely, that of preserving faith in reason.

Yet, paradoxically, precisely because in Heidegger productive imagination is boundless, it is also the mark of finitude. While, presumably, an infinite being could itself produce the object of intuition, a finite being can only *receive* what gives itself, and therefore, finite intuition is fundamentally contingent, reliant and receptive. Moreover, what a finite being receives comes in the form of a question mark: it is something that calls for interpretation and understanding. Thus, for a finite being, intuition always synergizes with understanding, and this unity of intuition and understanding is the accomplishment of productive imagination.

By contrast, for Cassirer productive imagination is that very power which lifts the subject above the confines of finitude and opens up the field of infinity. By this we are to understand that a finite being is always capable of determining objects in a way that transcends the bounds of finite experience. This act of transcendence is accomplished through the medium of forms by objectively shaping lived experience. For Cassirer, language, myth, religion and science are all figures of the infinite, conceived as the fulfillment of finitude.

In his noteworthy study, Rudolf Bernet argues that Heidegger's great insight in the Davos disputation was the realization that just as Dasein "cannot shrink from the question of its own being," so philosophy "cannot escape from the fate of human finitude" (Bernet 2010, 55). By contrast, according to Bernet, Cassirer's *Philosophy of Symbolic Forms* relies upon the viewpoint of absolute knowledge, a "view from nowhere." In Bernet's terms, Cassirer's philosophy is a *philosophical hermeneutics* yet not a *hermeneutic philosophy*. With this distinction, we are to understand that while hermeneutic philosophy thinks its own finitude, philosophical hermeneutics withdraws from the recognition of finitude.

Yet, arguably, Cassirer's and Heidegger's conceptions of productive imagination differ from each other, not because the former recoils from while the latter faces up to finitude, but rather because they express two fundamentally different ways of conceptualizing finitude. Heidegger understands Cassirer's preoccupation with objective forms symptomatically, as a matter of absconding finitude. Yet, as seen from Cassirer's point of view, insofar as Heidegger's fundamental ontology is a *philosophical* doctrine, it must find a way to transcend the bounds of finitude: as a philosophy, it must find a path to infinity, in a similar way to how Goethe conceives of it when he writes that "if you want to step into infinitude, just go in all directions into the finite" (Heidegger 1997a, 201). Leaving Dasein's existence aside, let us ask: to what degree is philosophy as such bound to finitude? In what sense, if any, can philosophy rise above finitude? And most importantly, should philosophy strive to rise above finitude, or should it, on the contrary, commit itself, not just thematically, but also methodologically, to finitude? These appear to be the central philosophical questions the Davos dispute has left us with. It should not be overlooked that Cassirer and Heidegger rely on their respective conceptions of productive imagination to justify their fundamentally different answers to these questions.

On the one hand, Cassirer provides a more nuanced conception of productive imagination, which admits of a variety of structures of Being, conceived as symbolic forms (such as language, myth, religion or science). On the other hand, Heidegger's alternative builds productive imagination up as having greater fundamental significance, since it conceives of imagination as the fundamental origin of intuition, understanding and reason. What one loses in breadth, one gains in depth, and vice versa.

CHAPTER V
From Phenomenology to the Kyoto School: Miki Kiyoshi and the Logic of Imagination

Introduction

Miki Kiyoshi (三木清) was a multifaceted thinker: a prominent member of the Kyoto School, an advocate and a critic of Japanese Marxism, a model for comparative philosophy, an early representative of philosophy of technology and of philosophy of culture. In this chapter, I will be mainly concerned with his contribution to the phenomenological tradition, which I will address while focusing on his *magnum opus*, *The Logic of the Imagination*, and especially on the chapters "Myth" and "Institution/s," which were originally published as journal articles and subsequently incorporated into Part I of *The Logic of the Imagination*. Although Miki's writings on imagination are still little known to the broader philosophical community, it will not be difficult to see that *The Logic of the Imagination* is of great significance for phenomenology — the phenomenology of imagination in general, and the phenomenology of productive imagination in particular.

Miki spent three years in Europe (1922-25), the first two of which he spent in Germany, in Heidelberg and then in Marburg. He traveled to Germany so as to study under Heinrich Rickert, who was the leading neo-Kantian thinker in Heidelberg and who was even more appreciated at that time in Japan than in Germany. After spending a little over a year in Heidelberg, Miki moved to Marburg to study under Heidegger, who himself had studied under Rickert at the University of Freiburg more than a decade earlier, still before Rickert had moved from the University of Freiburg to the University of Heidelberg in 1915. After spending ten months in Marburg, Miki left for Paris, where he stayed for a year before returning to Japan. It is not my goal in the present study to delve into the biographical details, no matter how interesting they might be (see in Yusa 1998). I mention these details so as to stress that neo-

Kantianism and phenomenology (especially the Heideggerian version) were the Western philosophical traditions that Miki was well acquainted with.

It is philosophically fruitful to interpret Miki's philosophy of the imagination alongside the Heidegger-Cassirer controversy that was presented in the last chapter. On the one hand, the Heideggerian background of Miki's analysis is hard to overlook. As we will see, for Miki, imagination is fundamentally the mediating link between λόγος and πάθος. At the same time, Miki maintains that the logic of the imagination is original logic, and in this sense, imagination underlies both λόγος and πάθος. Thus, much like Heidegger before him, Miki also fuses together the mediating and grounding functions of imagination. At the same time, Miki appropriates those insights that we have come across in Cassirer's analysis. He maintains that the logic of the imagination is largely a logic of symbols and a logic of forms. He explicitly contends that "what Cassirer refers to as 'the philosophy of symbolic forms' needs to be rewritten in accordance with the logic of the imagination" (Miki 2016, 8). Moreover, much like Cassirer, Miki does not subscribe to an immaculate distinction between the transcendental and the empirical, but maintains that "creative society is indeed the true transcendental subject" (Miki, unpublished, 29).[72] Thus, even though it was not the primary goal of Miki's analysis, his philosophy of the imagination offers a highly creative reconciliation of Heidegger's and Cassirer's accounts of productive imagination.[73]

Miki began writing *The Logic of the Imagination* in 1937 and continued working on it until his untimely death. He died in the detention center of the Toyotama prison in Tokyo in late September of 1945, six weeks after the end of World War II. Part I of *The Logic of*

---

[72]   The English translation of Miki's *Logic of Imagination* still remains unavailable. I would like to express my sincere gratitude to John W.M. Krummel for sharing his translation of Chapter 2, "Institution/s." In the present context, I will quote this text as follows: Miki, unpublished, page numbers.

[73]   One must further stress that this reconciliation is successful only to the degree that it is presented within the framework of a philosophy of action. It is therefore unlikely that either an orthodox Heideggerian or an orthodox Cassirerian would find this reconciliation convincing, for it demands that one give up some of the central commitments that we come across in their respective works.

the Imagination was published in 1939 and Part II was published posthumously in 1946. *The Logic of the Imagination* is an experimental and programmatic study, not a comprehensive and conclusive investigation.[74] Still, despite its fragmentary nature, it deserves to be referred to as Miki's *magnum opus* (see Fujita 2011).

In the framework of this study, Miki understands productive imagination as a transcendental power that shapes the human experience of the actual world by forming the contours of action, intuition, knowledge and understanding. Some identify this power as a modality of intentional consciousness (Husserl); others link it to bodily instincts and drives (Scheler); others, still, maintain that imagination should be understood as primordial temporality that is fundamentally prior both to consciousness and the body (Heidegger). These controversies notwithstanding, phenomenologically-oriented thinkers agree that imagination is a capacity of experience that augments and transfigures our cultural lifeworlds. Miki conceives of imagination along these phenomenological lines. His philosophy of the imagination is not the philosophy of fancy (*sōzō* 想像), but of productive imagination (*kōsōryoku* 構想力). By *kōsōryoku*, Miki understands a power more original than reason, which is constitutive of the sociocultural world, conceived as a horizon of shared meanings (see Krummel 2017, 256). My goal in this chapter is to show that Miki conceptualizes productive imagination in three fundamental ways: as a power that shapes our world-understanding, that configures our world-organization, and that generates world-transformation.[75] Miki thus articulates his philosophy

---

[74]   As Susan Townsend puts it, this study consists of "a rather haphazard collection of notes, not unlike Pascal's *Pensees*" (Townsend 2009, 214). Or, as Fujita Masakatsu remarks, the papers contained in Miki's *magnum opus* were originally written in the form of research notes, which made their further articulation excessively complicated (Fujita 2011, 306).

[75]   Miki's analysis of myth—conceived not as a phenomenon of antiquity, but as a perpetual cultural force—demonstrates how the human world-understanding is shaped by the imagination. His analysis of institutions shows how our social and historical worlds are organized by the imagination. Finally, Miki's account of technology brings to light that the transformations of the historical world are also largely driven by the imagination.

of the imagination in terms of three domains: myth, institutions and technics (see Curley 2019 and Krummel 2017).

In this chapter, I will focus on how productive imagination shapes our world-understanding and world-organization, and I will argue that it does so by generating collective representations, symbols, forms, conventions and customs. My goal is to show that, in all of these frameworks, we can identify one and the same logic of the imagination, which one can conceptualize by binding three terms: *formation, reformation and transformation.*

Miki as a Phenomenologist

At the end of the first section of "Myth," Miki writes: "what then is the imagination and what sort of thing is the logic of the imagination itself? Leaving a generalizing answer for later, we shall instead proceed with a phenomenological investigation" (Miki 2016, 28). As Miki further explains: "following the path Hegel took from phenomenology to logic, we shall pursue logic amidst the analysis of phenomena" (ibid). Thus, much like Cassirer before him, Miki identifies his approach as phenomenological *in the Hegelian sense of the term.*

Hegel conceives of phenomenology as a science of appearances. For Hegel, a phenomenological analysis modifies the Kantian conception of the transcendental, since it addresses phenomena as they manifest themselves in social and historical contexts. As Tom Rockmore puts it, "Hegel relativizes the distinctions between falsity, appearance, and truth in calling attention to false appearance as a stage on the way to truth. Mere falsity, which is not truth, is replaced by appearance (*Schein*) that, under the right circumstances, becomes true appearance (*Erscheinung*), or truth" (Rockmore 2018, 12). Within such a phenomenological framework, Hegel demonstrates that cognition does not need to be grounded, but that it can justify itself in the process of its unfolding. For Hegel, it is precisely in the process of its cognitive extension that phenomenology reaches its justification.

In a Hegelian way, Miki proceeds in *The Logic of the Imagination* by offering a chain of progressive approximations. Taken in their totality (which, in light of the fragmentary nature of this study, is an *open* totality), these approximations provide us with Miki's conception of the logic of the imagination. Miki's analysis is phenomenological in the Hegelian sense of the term, insofar as his analysis is a matter of a progressive series of approximations, which justify themselves in their unfolding. It thereby becomes clear that Miki employs the term "logic" in his studies not just with reference to laws of thought, but also, and more importantly, with reference to what Fujita calls "a logic or a philosophy that brings to light the essence of human being as an embodied existence that acts through the medium of its body, and also the reality that is encountered within the field of this activity" (Fujita 2011, 308). In this broad sense, the logic of the imagination is not a logic of thought, but a logic of action. Thus in "Myth," the logic of the imagination is said to be a logic of emotions, a logic of creation, a logic of history and historical creation, a logic that takes the standpoint of the subject, a logic of symbols, a logic of forms, a logic of individuals, a logic of formed images (dynamic and developmental) and a logic of love. Insofar these approximations form an open totality, they provide us with an understanding of the logic of the imagination.

There is, however, another way to identify Miki's approach as phenomenological. This second, implicit, way comes from the classical phenomenological tradition. This tradition brings together the background that Miki's own analysis both relies upon and also aims to transgress. Using Husserl's terminology, one could say that Miki's philosophy of the imagination is an implicit phenomenology of the lifeworld; using Scheler's terminology, one could speak of imagination as a phenomenology of reality; using Heidegger's terminology, one could also say that it offers an implicit phenomenology of the practical everyday world.[76]

---

[76]   According to Miki, the everyday world of our experience needs to be clarified phenomenologically, yet it cannot be clarified either in accordance with Husserlian or Heideggerian principles. In a short text from 1930 entitled "Is Phenomenology the Science of Tomorrow?" Miki argues that neither Husserlian phenomenology, conceived as phenomenology of reason and the science of pure consciousness, nor Heideggerian phenomenology, conceived as the

To read Miki's *Logic of the Imagination* as a phenomenological study in this second way is to contend that it offers an implicit phenomenology of the world of experience. Miki conceives of the world of experience not as an object of contemplation, but as a sphere of action—a distinctly human world, which human actions continuously transform and enrich.[77] Put in phenomenological terms, Miki conceives of the human world as a constitutive accomplishment and of the logic of the imagination as a logic of world-constitution.

Miki's unique contribution to the phenomenology of logic lies in his explicit identification of the logic of experience as a logic of the imagination. Indeed, while some phenomenologists have recognized imagination as a fundamental and irreducible component of everyday experience, no one has gone so far as to suggest that the logic of everyday experience is a logic of the imagination. In this regard, the novelty of Miki's philosophy of the imagination can be best evaluated against the background of Heidegger's philosophy. Following Heidegger's destructive reading of Kant, which ultimately strives to replace the "primacy of logic" (Heidegger 1997a, 117) with the primacy of imagination, Miki further contends that imagination has a distinctive logic and that this logic is more primordial than the logic of reason. Herein lies Miki's unique and

---

analysis of the conditions of human existence and the phenomenology of being, can be identified as a "phenomenology for tomorrow." According to Miki, both need to be supplanted with a phenomenology that studies "the conditions of even more realistic and historical human existence" (MKZ, 13: 105; John Krummel's translation). This short text does not clarify in detail how, exactly, Miki conceives of the phenomenology of the future. However, it does help to clarify Miki's conception of phenomenology by explaining it as a synthesis of Marxism and phenomenology. Miki thus writes that phenomenology "requires the analysis of human conditions that would complete the self-alienation particularly in its contemporary sense or more precisely in the sense of a commercial "product" (*shōhin* 商品). This type of phenomenology would probably not comprise the science of tomorrow. It is the science of today. But it is also the science *for* tomorrow." Presumably, Miki identifies his own writings with this kind of "third wave of phenomenology."

77   As John Krummel has it, "Miki in developing his philosophy of the imagination aims to take the standpoint of the actor acting *within* history as opposed to the philosopher who merely theorizes about facts from outside of their historical happenings. The point is that the practical and historical dimension is essential in Miki's understanding of the imagination" (Krummel 2017, 261).

highly significant contribution to the phenomenology of logic and the phenomenology of productive imagination. Consider the following claims: "the reality of this world must be founded by means of the logic of the imagination" (Miki 2016, 39); "we seek to conceive the imagination at the root of the historical world" (Miki 2016, 48); "What is really creative is actuality itself, and it is within the actual itself that we recognize the imagination" (Miki 2016, 63); "We must conceive the imagination at the root of the world's creation" (Miki 2016, 64). No earlier phenomenologist has ever spoken of the logic of imagination explicitly, and no other phenomenologist has qualified the logic of everyday experience as a logic of the imagination. Only by acknowledging the phenomenological orientation of Miki's *Logic of the Imagination* can we recognize his unique contribution to this philosophical tradition.

In *The Logic of the Imagination*, Miki's methodological approach is based on a creative fusion of these two phenomenological strategies. On the one hand, Miki consistently speaks in the voice of others and presents his arguments by means of detours and approximations. On the other hand, all these detours and approximations have one and the same goal—that of deepening our understanding of the world of experience.

The Standpoint of Contemplation and the Standpoint of Action

It would seem only natural to begin a philosophical analysis of the imagination with the question, "what is imagination?" For Miki, however, this is exactly the question with which philosophy of the imagination should *not* begin. One should recognize two other questions as more fundamental, the first of which concerns the context of analysis, while the second of which concerns the critical standpoint. For Miki, the question concerning the critical standpoint is the most fundamental.

We face here methodological considerations, which concern the significance of *Einstellung* (let us not overlook the fundamental role this concept plays in classical phenomenology). At the outset of his analysis, Miki draws a distinction between the *standpoint of contemplation* and the *standpoint of action*. Besides drawing a distinction between these standpoints, Miki also contends that the standpoint of contemplation is ill-suited to address imagination. For Miki, even though the essence of imagination cannot be disclosed from within the standpoint of contemplation, it can nonetheless be studied from within such a standpoint. Miki claims that the logic of the imagination is the logic of action. This means, in effect, that the essence of imagination can be understood only from within the standpoint of action.

These are provocative claims. On the one hand, Miki holds the view that a philosopher who addresses imagination in his day-and-age is prone to undertake his analysis from within the contemplative attitude. This tendency is derived from the weight of the philosophical tradition, which has almost exclusively focused on imagination from within the standpoint of contemplation. However — and this is what makes Miki's analysis polemical — he also holds the view that this standpoint is inadequate to address imagination. The contemplative attitude follows the guideline of formal logic and its two fundamental principles: the law of non-contradiction and the law of identity. According to Miki, these laws do not apply to imagination.

Here we encounter one of the central reasons why, in the title of this work, Miki speaks not just of imagination, but of the *logic* of imagination. This turn of phrase suggests that the laws of logic do not apply to imagination. To grasp what imagination is, one must rely on other principles. According to Miki, imagination generates its own principles and it must be judged according to these principles.

From within the standpoint of contemplation, imagination manifests itself as a reproductive mode of consciousness. When I am reading Miki's writings on imagination, from time to time my thoughts are interrupted by various sounds that reach me through the open windows. Even though I no longer hear these sounds once I have closed the windows, I can, nonetheless, still imagine hearing them. I then reproduce the more original experiences and intend these sounds as a series of modifications. How exactly are phenomena given to me in imagination? Following Sartre,[78] one can single out four possibilities: phenomena are given in imagination either as absent, as existent elsewhere, as non-existent, or as neutralized. In all of these cases, imaginary objects are given as non-actual, as fundamentally cut off from the field of actuality. Things appear from within the contemplative attitude. But what about the standpoint of action? At first glance, it would seem that such an *"Einstellungsänderung"* does not bring about any significant changes. Whether one thinks of images from the standpoint of contemplation or from the standpoint of action, images are still intended as non-actual possibilities. Yet action has no patience for mere possibilities; it is interested in possibilities only insofar as they can be actualized. While from the standpoint of contemplation, imaginary objects are given as pure possibilities, from the standpoint of action, possibilities are intended as real possibilities, or possible actualities. While in the contemplative framework, imagination performs an irrealizing function, in the framework of action, its central function is transformative. From within the standpoint of action, imagination does not cut us off from actuality; instead, it enables the modification of actuality. While from the standpoint of contemplation, imaginary consciousness is fundamentally reproductive, from the standpoint of action, it proves to be fundamentally productive, in the sense that it strives to transform the world of everyday experience.

Let us stress that Miki does not conceptualize these two attitudes alongside each other. Rather, he contends that the standpoint of action is more basic and that the standpoint of contemplation is its modification. This means that, for Miki, the logic of imagination does not exist on the same plane as formal logic, nor does it exist on the same plane as any other logic. The logic of imagination is the most original logic: every type of logic that is grounded on theoretical reason arises as a modification of the logic of imagination.

---

[78]   For Miki's remarks on Sartre's writings on the imagination, see Miki 2016, 49.

The Field of Imagination as the Field of Action

How is one to map out the field of productive imagination and where is one to place Miki's contribution within this field? One option would be to follow Ricœur's lead and to speak of four fundamental forms of productive imagination: poetic, epistemological, socio-political and religious. Keeping in mind Miki's observation that "action … is essentially social" (Miki 2016, 27), one would be tempted to place Miki's analysis within the framework of socio-political imagination. To do this would lead to a significant broadening of what we usually understand by socio-political imagination.

Although such a way of conceiving the field of productive imagination has its own merits, it nonetheless suppresses the full-fledged significance of Miki's analysis. While Ricœur's goal is to typologize the field of productive imagination in terms of its four fundamental fields, Miki's goal is to ground productive imagination in the basic experience from which productive imagination as such arises. In this regard, Miki is closer to Heidegger than to Ricœur, whose phenomenology of imagination we will address in later chapters. Yet Miki does not simply repeat the claims that we have addressed in Chapter IV. Rather, according to Miki's intriguing thesis, all modes of productive imagination have the same experiential roots; namely, they are all rooted in action. *The logic of imagination is the logic of action*, which, for Miki, further means that the real transcendental subject is the acting society.

According to Miki, action has four fundamental characteristics: it is embodied, expressive, social and historical. First, to claim that action is *embodied* is to suggest that it takes root in our embodied relation to things and the world at large: "it is through our bodies that we collide with things themselves in their materiality" (Miki 2016, 26). Second, the qualification of action as *expressive* can be understood in two complementary ways: in terms of self-expression and world-expression. Acts are forms of self-expression and simultaneously expressions of the world's own possibilities: they realize the world's potentiality by rendering it as an expressive world. Third, to claim that action is *social* is to suggest that it is neither individual, nor universal, but collective (see Muramoto 2010, 15-16).

In Miki's words, the logic of action refers to group psychology. "Everything that can be seen as a product of group psychology, such as language, myth, manners, custom, institutions, etc., cannot be grasped by formal logic" (Miki 2016, 27). Finally, precisely because it is social in the collective sense of the term, action is fundamentally *historical*: the logic of action is the logic of history, conceived not from the perspective of comprehension, but from the perspective of historical action.

Thus, for Miki, productive imagination is grounded in action and, as such, it is fundamentally embodied, expressive, social and historical. To a certain degree, it thereby becomes understandable why Miki would claim that the logic of imagination is the logic of action; yet only to a degree, for it still remains unclear how one is to understand Miki's general contention that besides the logic of the intellect there is another kind of *logic*, which must be identified as the logic of imagination. One could list three fundamental reservations; (1) Clearly, it is one thing to qualify certain experiences (say, those of dreams or daydreaming) as pre-logical or a-logical; it is an altogether different matter to contend that at least some of the experiences that do not subscribe to the principles of formal logic are nonetheless logical, although in an unusual sense of the term. (2) So also, it still remains unclear why one should identify this pre-conceptual logic as the logic of imagination, and not as some other kind of logic. And (3), it is unclear why one should qualify the logic of imagination as a proto-logic (*Urlogik*).[79]

In "Myth," Miki argues that productive imagination shapes the human experience of the world by generating collective representations, symbols and forms. With this in mind, he qualifies the logic of imagination as a logic of collective representations, a logic of symbols and a logic of forms. In "Institution/s," he further maintains that the logic of imagination is the logic of conventions and customs. In what follows, I want to turn to Miki's analysis of these themes and show that, insofar as we see them as accomplishments

---

[79]   While commenting on Aristotle's and Hegel's logic, Miki writes: "as a kind of *Urlogik*, the logic of the imagination educes these two from within itself as configurations of self-reflection" (Miki 2011, 706-707).

of productive imagination, we can derive from them a certain common structure. It is this common structure—I will contend—that makes up the logic of imagination. With regard to the three questions listed above, we understand the following: (1) insofar as experiences that do not subscribe to the principles of formal logic are governed by the structure of formation, transformation and reformation, they are not just a-logical or pre-logical, but are, nonetheless, logical, even though not in the sense of formal logic. (2) The logic of which we here speak is none other than the logic of the imagination. And (3) this logic is "a kind of *Urlogik*" in the sense that all forms of the logic of the intellect are abstracted from it.

The Logic of the Imagination as the Logic of Collective Representations

Miki is committed to the view that myth is not a phenomenon of the past, but that each epoch has its own myths, that the cultural worlds we inhabit always have, and always will have, mythical dimensions. In direct contrast to the positivists and the spokesmen of the enlightenment, Miki asserts that "freedom and equality were myths of the eighteenth century. In the present age, there are myths for the present age" (Miki 2016, 33). So also, democracy and communism, the rise of ethno-nationalism in Europe and the European Union, Xi Jinping's China and Shinzo Abe's Japan, the fight against terrorism and the COVID crisis – are the myths of the twenty-first century. For Miki, myths are fictions, although they are not illusions; because they are fictions, they are constitutive ingredients of any social life. With this stipulation in mind, Miki opens a dialogue with anthropological and sociological literature on mythical consciousness, "in order to obtain some suggestions" (Miki 2016, 29). Miki is interested in that type of suggestion that helps us to understand myths as constitutive formations of our historical, socio-cultural worlds.

Following Durkheimian sociologists, and especially Lévy-Bruhl, Miki contends that collective representations govern the domain of mythical consciousness. These representations are both social and historical. They are social in the sense that they are common to members of a certain social group. They are historical in the sense that they are common to different generations of the same social group (see Miki 2006, 29). Collective representations are multidimensional: they are not merely cognitive phenomena, but entail emotive, kinetic and intellectual strata.

Following Lévy-Bruhl, Miki draws a sharp distinction between *the law of contradiction*, conceived as the fundamental principle of formal logic, and *the law of participation*, conceived as the fundamental principle that guides the generation of collective representations.[80] Insofar as consciousness is governed by the law of participation, it is indifferent to the principle of contradiction: the one and the many, the same and the other, the here and the there, do not constitute sets of oppositions and do not compel us to give up one alternative even if we choose another. In some cases, the primitive mind can plainly go against the principle of non-contradiction, as happens when it conceives of things as both within and simultaneously outside of its surroundings. To use Miki's example, the members of the Bololo clan believe that they are red parrots. They do not believe that their ancestors were red parrots before they were born, or that they will become red parrots once they die. But they do believe that they *are* red parrots here and now. Such a somatic and mystical symbiosis can only be understood in a twofold sense: as the identification of the individual person with the social group and as the identification of the person with things in the surrounding world. Such a twofold symbiosis is an accomplishment of productive imagination.

However, the effects of productive imagination are not reducible to the generation of such identifications. Following Lévy-Bruhl, Miki contends that myth is born precisely when the above-mentioned symbioses are not accepted at face value. Precisely when their validity comes into question, the need is born for the

---

[80]   In Lévy-Bruhl's words: "In the collective representations of primitive mentality, objects, beings, phenomena can be, though in a way incomprehensible to us, both themselves and something other than themselves. In a fashion no less incomprehensible, they give forth and they receive mystic powers, virtues, qualities, influences, which make themselves felt outside, without ceasing to remain where they are" (Lévy-Bruhl 1985, 76-77).

reinforcement of the social ties that bind the members of the social group to each other. Myth is born from the need of such reinforcement.[81] Not surprisingly, therefore, myths represent solidarity not only with things we come across in the surrounding world, but also with the past of the social group. We are confronted here with myth's *ideological* function: while the loss of commitment to the established collective representations gives rise to a crisis of established meaning, myth strives to overcome such a crisis by re-establishing the bond that ties the present to the past, by demonstrating that the present is the child of the past and thereby by reinvigorating the power of collective representations.

Miki's appropriation of Lévy-Bruhl's standpoint, disregarding the question of its legitimacy,[82] lies beneath his identification of myth as a form of productive imagination. For Miki, productive imagination is the power that shapes our world-understanding through collective representations, whose functioning is governed

---

[81]   As Miki has it, "the continuity of time is suspended by a period of crisis. We can probably say that all myths are products of the consciousness of crisis" (Miki 2016, 60).

[82]   Starting with his early studies on the subject, Lévy-Bruhl has consistently defined "primitive collective representations" as non-cognitive and non-conceptual (see Mousalimas 1990, 37). By contrast, Miki interprets Lévy-Bruhl's collective representations as synthetic unities that comprise cognitive, emotive and kinetic elements. This is Miki's conception of collective representations, not Lévy-Bruhl's. Even more importantly, Many anthropologists have criticized Lévy-Bruhl for drawing too sharp a distinction between primitive and civilized minds. As Evans-Pritchard has it, Lévy-Bruhl made "civilized thought far more rational" and "savage thought far more mystical" than they both were and thus offered a "caricature" of the "primitive mentality" (Evans-Pritchard 1934, 7, 9). In light of this widespread criticism, which was also shared by Malinowski, Lowie and Radin, Lévy-Bruhl modified his position in his later works by abandoning the controversial concept of the pre-logical, which stirred up the controversy in the first place. The question of whether the abandonment of this concept signalled a substantive or merely a terminological revision appears to be a contentious issue (see Mousalimas 1990, 41). The controversy concerning the sharp opposition between the primitive and the civilized mind plays no role whatsoever in Miki's interpretation of Lévy-Bruhl's writings. Moreover, according to Miki, no such distinction between the primitive and the civilized mind exists. "Will pre-logical modes of thinking vanish as a consequence? Lévy-Bruhl claims that this is impossible. Even in advanced societies, traces of the pre-logical ways of thinking, instead of vanishing, remain in the majority of concepts" (Miki 2016, 31). Here, again, we face Miki's, and not Lévy-Bruhl's position.

by the law of participation. Moreover, in light of the fact that this law does not subscribe to the principle of non-contradiction, Miki claims that imagination is "a priori" to reason and that historical, socio-cultural worlds are constituted not by reason, but by imagination.[83]

Miki's analysis of myth in light of Lévy-Bruhl's studies brings to light ideological function of mythology: it reinvigorates the established collective representations. However, myth can also perform a "utopian" function, as Miki's engagement with Georges Sorel's revolutionary syndicalism demonstrates (see Sorel 2004).[84] While in Lévy-Bruhl's studies, myth primarily has to do with the historical past, "what Sorel calls myth primarily has to do with the creation of the future" (Miki 2016, 46). Miki appreciates Sorel's recognition of the role of imagination in the constitution of cultural worlds. "What he [Sorel] refers to as myth is nothing other than a product of the imagination" (Miki 2016, 45). Miki also appreciates Sorel's emphasis on the dynamic, developmental and, more broadly, historical nature of productive imagination, and on the voluntary and affective dimensions of productive imagination ("Sorel states that myth is an expression of the will" [Miki 2016, 43]). Nonetheless, Miki is critical of Sorel's persistent attempts to remove all intellectual elements from myth and, more generally, from imagination. In this regard, Miki distances himself from Sorelianism, which he understands as a branch of irrationalism.

According to Sorel, while myth is an expression of the irrational will, utopia is a product of intellectual labor.[85] Miki accepts

---

[83]   According to Miki, "imagination is more primordial than reason" (Miki 2016, 44). Miki returns to this assertion on a number of occasions: "the originariness of the imagination vis-à-vis the intellect must be acknowledged" (Miki 2016, 45); "we can recognize the existence of the imagination at the root of the intellect" (Miki 2016, 46).

[84]   We will soon see why the concept of utopia can be used here only metaphorically, and thus, in quotation marks.

[85]   As Sorel puts it in his "Letter to Daniel Halévy," "men who are participating in great social movements always picture their coming action in the form of images of battle in which their cause is certain to triumph. I proposed to give the name of 'myth' to these constructions…: the general strike of the syndicalists and Marx's catastrophic revolution are such myths" (Sorel 2004, 20). "A utopia

the validity of this distinction, although with important reservations. Even though both myth and utopia entail cognitive, emotive and kinetic dimensions, in the case of myth, the emotive and kinetic elements are fundamental, while in the case of utopia, the cognitive element is primary. The primacy of the cognitive dimension in the case of utopia suggests that utopia is a product of individual consciousness. By contrast, in the case of myth, the primacy of emotive and kinetic dimensions suggests that myth is a form of social imagination. It would seem that, for Miki, individual consciousness is capable only of reproductive imagination and that, by contrast, creative society is "the true transcendental subject" (Miki, unpublished, 29) precisely because productive imagination is social through and through. With this in mind, Miki contends that "we can probably view myth as belonging to productive imagination (*produktive Einbildungskraft*) and utopia as belonging to the reproductive imagination (*reproduktive Einbildungskraft*)" (Miki 2016, 43). This point is as true for Miki as it is for Sorel: it is myth, not utopia, that anticipates and builds the future world.

We can now understand Miki's central and highly intriguing claim: "we must conceive imagination at the root of the world's creation" (Miki 2016, 64). For Miki, the world as we know it is always already given as a horizon of shared meanings (see Krummel 2017, 255-256) and this horizon is largely shaped by collective representations and is largely understood as accomplishments of productive imagination. Herein we encounter *the primary function of productive imagination*. Its function is to shape collective representations and thereby to transform a formless universe into a cultural world, conceived as a horizon of shared meanings, that is, as a synthetic totality of historical forms. It is important to see that it is not individual consciousness, but a certain social group that shapes collective representations. The very fact that the human world is fractured into a

---

is, on the contrary, an intellectual product; it is the work of a theorists who, after observing and discussing the facts, seek to establish a model to which they can compare existing societies in order to estimate the amount of good and evil they contain.... It is a construction which can be broken into parts and of which certain pieces have been shaped in such a way that they can (with a few alterations) be fitted into future legislation" (Sorel 2004, 28).

variety of cultural worlds provides the evidence needed to maintain the thesis that the human world is shaped neither by sensations nor by reason (both of which are, presumably, common to all of humanity), but, instead, by productive imagination. Yet the very fact that these forms are irreducibly historical also indicates their fragility and signals that, sooner or later, all of the established collective representations will lose their validity. At such moments when collective representations no longer speak to us, we witness the transformation from the historically-formed world into a universe of pure indeterminacy — a transformation which one could further characterize as the world's dehumanization, or as a crisis of the overarching meaning that gives human life its sense and unity. It is precisely at such moments of crises that we come across the *secondary function of productive imagination*. Besides shaping collective representations, productive imagination also counterbalances their nullification. It does this in two fundamental ways: either, as in Lévy-Bruhl, by reinvigorating the validity of those collective representations that are no longer accepted at face value, or, as in Sorel, by replacing them with the creation of novel collective representations. In short, to conceive of imagination at the root of the world's creation is to recognize that not only the formation, but also the reformation and transformation of collective representations is the work of productive imagination. *Formation, reformation, transformation*: these are the key terms in the logic of imagination.

The Logic of Imagination as the Logic of Symbols

Although our everyday worlds are largely shaped by collective representations, they are nonetheless not reducible to collective representations. Miki's identification of the logic of imagination as the logic of symbols significantly broadens the field of productive imagination by incorporating within it not only what is collective, but also what is individual. For Miki, all forms of logic perform one and the same function: they enable a human being to transcend the boundaries of immediate experience. Miki appears to think of the world, given through immediate experience, as analogous to how Hegel thinks of sense-certainty, namely, as a field of pure indeterminacy. Nonetheless, from Miki's analysis one can derive some general features characteristic of immediate experience. Immediate experience consists of an embodied encounter with things themselves in the surrounding world. Miki takes this to mean that our embodied "collision with things themselves" (see Miki 2016, 26-27) is largely motivated impulsively and instinctually. The view that drives, impulses, instincts, bodily passions and needs in various ways shape our embodied encounter with things themselves is of great significance for our understanding of the logic of imagination. It allows Miki to identify πάθος as the basis that underlies the logic of imagination.

Miki employs the concept of πάθος with reference to the lived-body (which in his earlier works, Miki called "the inner body"[86]), conceived as the pre-conscious locus of instincts, drives and impulses that shape consciousness not outwardly, but inwardly. Precisely because these instincts, drives and impulses are pre-conscious, πάθος is more original than λόγος, just as the inner body is more original than consciousness. Shigenori Nagatomo argues that "of the πάθος, Miki recognizes two major tendencies: he assigns the state of being to the passive phase and impulse to the active phase of πάθος. It is the active impulse which animates a creation of image" (Nagatomo 1995, 55). Since desires, drives, impulses and

---

[86]   Miki employs the concept of the "inner body" in earlier works, such as "On Πάθος" and "Ideology and the Logic of Πάθος" (1933). This concept suggests that, in a good sense, materiality is more fundamental than form. Thus in "Ideology and the Logic of Πάθος," Miki writes: "Contrary to the Greek way of thinking, that which is material or physically substantial is more primary than that which has form or is ideal" (Quoted from Fujita 2011, 312). With regard to these studies, one could qualify Miki's philosophy as materialistic phenomenology. However, such a qualification would be inappropriate with regard to *The Logic of the Imagination*. According to Fujita, already in *Philosophical Anthropology*, Miki carefully avoids using the concept of the "inner body" and replaces it with the concept of nothingness (see Fujita 2011, 313). Presumably, in *The Logic of the Imagination*, Miki holds the view that insofar as human life is determined by πάθος, it is determined by genuine nothingness, conceived as the ground of existence. This nothingness is not to be conceived as matter, but as "formless form": "The one that ties together the many forms is formless rather than being a form, it is a so-called 'formless form'" (Miki 2016, 40). Thus, in *The Logic of the Imagination*, the body is not conceptualized as the original locus of πάθος, but as a *medium* that binds being and nothingness.

needs lie at the bottom of immediate experience, human life cannot content itself with the indeterminacy characteristic of immediate experience. No matter how insatiable they might be, impulses would not be impulses if they did not strive for fulfillment. Precisely because immediate experience is not merely passive, but is largely shaped by active πάθος, human life is always already on the other side of immediate experience.

How should this transcending of immediate experience be understood? Along with Théodule Ribot, the author of *The Essay on Creative Imagination* (see Ribot 1906), Miki sees only two possibilities: one can "venture to the yonder side of that which can be raised by immediate experience" (Miki 2016, 33) either by means of (1) *inference* or (2) *imagination*. Following Ribot, Miki contends that originally, these two procedures were intermingled and that they were only subsequently distinguished from each other. Miki qualifies the original inseparability of these two forms of logic as the logic of imagination. Here, we encounter one of the reasons why Miki identifies the logic of imagination as the logic of emotions and then further qualifies it as the logic of love. Miki maintains that it is precisely through *eros* that the daemonic impulse that lies at the root of immediate experience develops into an idea, thereby accomplishing the transition from πάθος to λόγος: "Idea… is born from the daemonic πάθος, and this πάθος contains an *eros* as its impulse in its longing from nothingness to being, from the unrestrictedness to restricted, from darkness to light."[87]

How does imagination accomplish this transition from the pure indeterminacy of immediate experience to the determinate ideality of the λόγος? The things we collide with through our bodies in the field of immediate experience obtain their meaning through the symbolizing power of productive imagination. Through the imagination, human life symbolizes what it lives through by means of externally formed images. So also, through imagination, human life animates the things it has collided with by offering them symbolic

---

[87]   Miki, Bungeiteki ningengaku [「文芸的人間学」 ; Anthropology via the Arts and Literature], Vol. 11, 1967, 473 (quoted from Nagatomo 1995, 56).

meaning. Besides being the logic of emotions and the logic of love, the logic of imagination is also the logic of symbols.[88]

Miki emphasizes that one should not confuse symbolization with allegorization or pictorialization, both of which employ images as illustrations. Illustrations are by definition secondary: they rely upon the anterior givenness of the thing being illustrated. By contrast, symbolization is fundamentally primary: it marks the original way things obtain their meaning. So as to emphasize this priority, Miki speaks of "symbolization without the symbolized" (Miki 2016, 38). By this, we are to understand that symbolization is the means whereby productive imagination performs the transition from the indeterminate chaos of original experience to the field of determination. We can think of it as a specific reinterpretation of Kantian schematism.

Thus, the world reaches determinacy through acts of symbolization, understood as accomplishments of productive imagination. Presumably, insofar as an active πάθος lies at the root of immediate experience, such a symbolic world serves the function of their fulfillment. Nonetheless, desires and impulses that lie at the heart of immediate experience are in principle insatiable. We face here a peculiar dialectic between fulfillment and insatiability, which relies upon the same logic we have already encountered in Miki's analysis of collective representations. Here also we need to draw a distinction between the primary and secondary function of productive imagination. The *primary* function concerns the transformation of the field of immediate experience into a determinate, symbolic world. However, the validity of such a symbolic world comes into question as soon as this world no longer provides the life-forming impulses with their self-realization. At such moments of disillusionment, we come across the *secondary* function of productive imagination, namely, the function of either reforming the validity of established symbols or replacing them with other symbols.

---

[88]   As Fujita has it, "Miki's unique philosophy was made possible on the basis of the fact that he discovered, in the imagination, a power capable of giving logical (that is, λόγος-informed) expression to the impulses of πάθος, which we inevitably harbor insofar as we exist as embodied human beings" (Fujita 2011, 317).

Formation, reformation, transformation: once again we discover that these three concepts make up the logic of imagination. Just as productive imagination is the power that forms collective representations, so also it is the power that envelops immediate experience within symbolic meanings. Moreover, just as productive imagination is the power that either reforms the validity of collective representation or generates new collective representation, so also it proves to be the power that either reconstitutes the legitimacy of established symbols or replaces symbols with other symbols. The logic of collective representations and the logic of symbols are guided by the same logic, which Miki invites us to conceive of as the logic of imagination. The logic of imagination is not only the logic of collective representations, but also the logic of symbols.

The Logic of Imagination as the Logic of Forms

Just as the logic of imagination is not reducible to the logic of collective representations, so also, it is not reducible to the logic of symbols, and it is especially not reducible to symbols that are understood as impulsively driven expressions of imagination. The foregoing account of the logic of symbols is psychological, and even though Miki invites us to draw such psychological implications, nonetheless, we cannot overlook Miki's explicit observation that "we ought not to understand the imagination, from the outset, in a psychological sense" (Miki 2016, 41).

Eros, conceived as the active impulse that underlies immediate experience, is not reducible to desire, which means that it cannot be accounted for in terms of merely subjective satisfaction. For Miki, the logic of love is not the logic of gratification, but the logic of transgressing the merely subjective boundaries of immediate existence. The striving that characterizes the original impulse is the striving for being, for light, for determination, that is, for *form*. Following Dilthey, Miki maintains that imagination produces "something ideal," namely, it produces *forms*, or *types* (*kata*) (see Miki

2006, 36).[89] By this we are to understand that the particulars we come across in the everyday world already typify commonalities, and these commonalities are to be understood as accomplishments of productive imagination. The concept of form, or type (*kata*) signifies the subsumption of the particular within the intersubjective context of mutual understanding. Forms, or types, are of subjective origin, yet their validity is not psychological: the cultural worlds we find ourselves in are shaped by the accomplishments of typifying consciousness, which constitute communal meanings and values.

For Miki, forms are conceivable only insofar as they overcome two sets of binary oppositions. First, forms are both subjective and objective.[90] Second, forms are both individual and universal.[91] Yet, we have to admit that the field that stretches between the merely subjective and the merely objective as well as between the merely individual and the merely universal – is remarkably broad, which means that Miki's concept of form admits of highly diverse degrees of generality. At its lowest level, the determination of any empirical

---

[89]   Since Miki's concept of form is heavily indebted to Dilthey, it is worthwhile noting how Dilthey himself conceives of forms, or types: "the particular manifestations of life that confront the understanding subject can be considered as belonging to a sphere of commonality, to a type. The commonality sets up a relation between manifestation of life and spirit such that as soon as we locate the manifestation in a common context, a spiritual meaning attaches to it (Dilthey 2002, 230). More generally, in his own writings, Dilthey thematizes productive imagination as poetic, historical, and scientific. To a large degree, he conceives of it as productive phantasy. As Eric Nelson has argued in a recent contribution, besides playing a constitutive role in aesthetics, Dilthey's imagination also codetermines the processes of understanding and interpretation in everyday life by enabling humans for shape the meaning of the whole. For Dilthey, the central function of productive imagination is to expound how we inhabit the human, sociohistorical world. Thus, Dilthey reinterprets productive imagination as the formative-generative imagination and thereby demonstrates that imagination is productive in that it shapes the implicitly historically embodied orientational contexts that are presupposed and utilized by the human efforts to reach knowledge and truth. See Nelson 2018.

[90]   Insofar as forms arise out of the insatiable impulse, they are subjective. However, they are not merely subjective, for they have objectified themselves in the sensuous world.

[91]   Insofar as we can recognize many individuals as having the same form, they are universal. However, they are not universal in the strict sense of the term, because forms are by definition manifold: "forms are not one. Forms in relation to forms are forms by being many" (Miki 2016, 40).

object as an object of a certain type is already an accomplishment of typifying consciousness. When we name the things we come across in our surroundings, we rely upon the accomplishments of productive imagination.[92] At its highest level, language, myth, science and technology are also forms, although much more general forms. On this basis, Miki asserts that Cassirer's philosophy of symbolic forms needs to be rewritten as a logic of imagination (see Miki 2016, 36).

At the core of Miki's analysis of imagination, we discover a conception of human life that is ruled by the impulse to overcome the indeterminacy characteristic of immediate experience. This impulse is the driving force behind the generation of forms that subsume all the experiential particulars. All these forms, without exception, are creations of the human will and imagination, even though no particular individual is ever in a position to generate these forms in their entirety. This means that the forms we are here speaking of are not only the results of human creation, but also the goals of human appropriation.[93] Only insofar as they are appropriated by a particular community can they suitably perform their function as the world's humanization. However, there are at least two fundamental conditions that need to be met for the world to be humanized. A community must not only establish the fundamental forms that will subsume experiential particulars, but the members of the community must also accept the validity of the forms in question. Yet, the very fact that these forms are historical means that sooner or later their validity will no longer accepted at face value.

---

[92]   To use Dilthey's telling example, "every square planted with trees, every room in which chairs are arranged, is understandable to us from childhood because human tendencies to set goals, produce order, and define values in common have assigned a place to every square and every object in the room" (Dilthey 2002, 209). While we are "always already immersed in the medium of commonalities" (ibid.), this medium itself is a subjective accomplishment, which Miki interprets as an accomplishment of productive imagination.

[93]   To return to Dilthey, "the child grows up within the order and ethos of the family that it shares with the other members and in this context it accepts the way the mother regulates things. Before the child learns to speak, it is already wholly immersed in the medium commonalities. The child only learns to understand the gestures and facial expressions, movements and exclamations, words and sentences, because it constantly encounters them as the same and in the same relation to what they mean and express. Thus, the individual becomes oriented in the world of objective spirit" (Dilthey 2002, 229-230).

At such moments of disenchantment, forms lose their objective validity and are recognized as arbitrary projections of subjective will — mere fictions, which have no hold on reality.

Formation, reformation, transformation: we once again discover the same logic of imagination, yet this time in the context of form constitution. The logic of imagination is not reducible to the original configuration of forms, and if one should qualify their configuration as the *primary* function of productive imagination, then to this one should further add that the reconfiguration of forms, conceived either as the reformation of existent forms or as their replacement with alternative forms, makes up the *secondary* function of productive imagination.

The Logic of Imagination as the Logic of Institutions

In every πάθος, there is something of the λόγος, just as in every λόγος, there is something of the πάθος, and such is the case because both πάθος and λόγος are rooted in imagination. This means that besides binding πάθος and λόγος, the logic of imagination is also the source from which both πάθος and λόγος spring, which further implies that "pure" πάθος and "pure" λόγος are abstractions derived from their original unity in imagination and from their actual manifestation in history. There are, thus, good reasons to suggest that in *The Logic of the Imagination*, Miki rethinks the dual role that Heidegger ascribes to imagination. Just as for Heidegger, productive imagination both mediates and grounds understanding and sensibility, so also for Miki, productive imagination both binds and shapes πάθος and λόγος.

Now the very fact that both πάθος and λόγος manifest themselves in history suggests that the logic of imagination cannot be restricted to the logic of images. However, insofar as the logic of imagination is understood as the logic of representations, symbols and forms, it is precisely a logic of socially-formed images. Only insofar as it is institutionalized can the logic of imagination be said to be truly embodied in the historical world. Not surprisingly, therefore, Chapter II of *The Logic of the Imagination* focuses on institutions. Here we find out that imagination is bound to the body not only because, as a symbolizing power, it is rooted in our embodiment, but also because it strives for its own unique social embodiment, which it reaches through institutionalization. Thus, the logic of myth finds its further articulation in institutions: religious, moral, political and social.

Miki presents his account of institutions against the background of Paul Valéry's analyses of conventions [*kanshū* 慣習]. Valéry conceptualizes conventions in a broad way, including under this concept morality, law, politics, language, art and even society itself. Moreover, and this is especially important for Miki, Valéry qualifies conventions as *fictions* that are necessary for social existence.[94] Social life relies on trusting these fictions, so much so that the collapse of this trust would signify the collapse of the fabric of society. In his further elaboration, Miki takes this to mean that social life itself is rooted in productive imagination, which continues to shape and reshape social life throughout its historical existence. With Valéry's broad conception of conventions in mind, Miki suggests that we "adopt, in place of Valéry's term *convention*, the term *institution* [*seido* 制度] that is still closer to cases of ordinary terminology" (Miki, unpublished, 1).

The transition from the analysis of myth to the analysis of institutions significantly broadens the scope of Miki's investigation and also marks the transition to the analysis of distinctly normative social phenomena. While both myth and institutions are figures of social imagination that mediate between the πάθος and the λόγος, they bring the two into unity in different ways. Thus, with reference to institutions, Miki remarks that "it may be fitting to use the Greek word νόμος in opposition to the word μῦθος (myth) that we have been using" (Miki, unpublished, 1). So as to stress the difference further, he writes that "while myths are something mystical, by contrast institutions are more intellectual" (Miki, unpublished, 2). This means that the synthesis of λόγος and πάθος can take different shapes, some of which are closer to the πάθος (myth), while others are closer to the λόγος (institutions).

---

94   "*Fiction* does not mean *illusion*. In the world of history, what is *real* is *fictional* and what is *fictional* is *real*" (Miki, unpublished, 28).

So as to provide the concept of institutions with greater precision, Miki draws a distinction between three meanings of the term. First, institutions refer to *conventions* in Valéry's sense of the term. They are fictions generated by social imagination. Relying on the etymological sense of the term, Miki emphasizes that conventions refer to what is assembled, or brought together, and therefore signifies a consensus among members of a social group. Second, institutions refer to *customs*, understood as social habits: customs are social and traditional. While conventions, as social agreements, rely upon the λόγος, customs, as social habits, relate to the πάθος: insofar as we are born into the institutionalized world, we do not generate institutions, but inherit them. Third, institutions have the quality of being lawful and have their own authority: they regulate and coerce. In short, understood as creations of productive imagination, institutions at the same time relate to λόγος, πάθος and νόμος.

This tripartite distinction allows us to understand with greater precision the logic of imagination as the logic of formation, reformation and transformation. The establishment of the institution relies upon the formative power of productive imagination. In this regard, "creative society is indeed the true transcendental subject" (Miki, unpublished, 29). In Heidegger's reading of Kant, transcendental imagination generates transcendental schemas which predelineate the look of things, or the mode of vision that makes seeing possible; similarly, Miki's transcendental imagination schematizes different modes of belief, thinking and action. "By becoming one with that creative society, the inventive individual can thus be inventive" (Miki, unpublished, 29), which we can take to mean that only at the social level can the individual participate in the shaping of institutionalized life.[95] Yet, we do not just shape our own institutionalized existence. To use Heidegger's terminology, we are thrown into an institutionalized world and the established institutional framework marks our own facticity. Or as Miki has it, institutions are not just conventions, but also customs that have their

---

[95]   This is, admittedly, a problematic claim, which brings into question the relation between society and the individual. For a good analysis of this issue, see Curley 2019.

own normative force: they have a "*nomos*-logical quality" (Miki, unpublished, 2). Yet like any authority, institutions retain this *nomos*-logical quality only insofar as the members of society believe in them. Just as the formation of institutions rests on the power of productive imagination, so the belief in the normative power of institutions also rests on this same power, and it can be sustained only in virtue of diverse reformations and transformations. As Miki has it, "institutions that have thus become fixed can no longer be adapted to societies that continue developing. But because institutions are not something like a hat that one can put on or take off at will, when that happens people make an effort to adapt that institution by some method to the altered society" (Miki, unpublished, 28). This adaptation can take the form of either reformation or transformation. In other words, the validity of the established institutionalized forms can either be reaffirmed, or, alternatively, can undergo transformation. In short, *formation, reformation, transformation*: the same logic of imagination that we already encountered in Miki's account of representations, forms and symbols, is also at work in his account of institutions.

As we saw in the earlier sections of this chapter, the logic of myth is the logic of participation. By contrast, the logic of institutions is the logic of imitation. It is important to stress, however, that for Miki, just as for Gabriel de Tarde (on whose analysis of the institution of morality Miki's analysis heavily relies), imitation is creative, and not just repetitive. If it were just repetitive, the logic of imitation would not be said to be a logic of history, where nothing repeats itself but everything is always transmuted and modified. History entails not only the steady constancy of what productive imagination has generated, but also its transformations and reformations. The logic of imagination, understood as the logic of history, proves again to be a logic of formation, reformation, transformation.

Formation, reformation, transformation: this is the logic of imagination that appears in Miki's analysis in "Myth." We can now recognize that this is also the same logic that appears in Miki's account of institutions. Productive imagination is what shapes them; it is also what reforms them when their validity becomes questionable; it is also what transforms them when they can no longer be accepted in their present form.

Conclusion

To what degree is Miki's philosophy of imagination a product of its time? It provides a powerful explanation of the world of the 1930s and 1940s, characterized by all its disturbing myths, alarming collective representations, symbols and forms. One can only smile ironically as one tries to think of such a world either as the manifestation of reason, or as a spiritual formation that relies upon the resources of sensuous experience. A philosophy that grants primacy to imagination over reason and sensibility provides a viable alternative to rationalism and empiricism and a much more compelling account of the Japanese (of course, not just Japanese) world of his time than any rationalist or empiricist position could ever provide. Still, if this philosophy is nothing more than a product of its time, then one can quality it as a *Weltanschauung* that has outlived its day — a page in relatively recent intellectual history, which carries little genuinely *philosophical* significance. While it might explain the mindset of the 1930s and 1940s, it appears incapable of saying anything of importance about the structure of the sociocultural world itself.

As a response to such an objection, it is important to stress that here, in Miki's reflections on imagination, we come across the very same insights that other phenomenologically-oriented Western thinkers will present a few decades later. In his recent study, John W. M. Krummel also emphasizes this point, bringing Miki's philosophy of imagination into dialogue with Cornelius Castoriadis, Paul Ricœur, and Charles Taylor. According to Krummel, "in comparison to Ricœur or Castoriadis, Miki still seems to be caught in a residual transcendentalism inherited from Kant when he emphasizes the transcendentality of the imagination and uses the terminology of German transcendentalism" (Krummel 2017, 264). I would suggest that in this "residual transcendentalism" lies Miki's important contribution to the phenomenology of productive imagination and that it constitutes one of the significant strength of his philosophical standpoint.

In another contribution, Iwasaki Minoru also problematizes Miki's transcendentalism and especially his allegation to which I have already referred in the beginning of this chapter: "by becoming one with that creative society, the inventive individual can thus be inventive" (Miki, unpublished, 29).[96] Such an apparently anti-individualistic stance and (as Iwasaki maintains) the militaristic mobilization that it further implies is both philosophically doubtful and politically alarming. Melissa Curley remarks on this with passages such as the following: "the individual person is here made a puppet of history in a way more brutal than anything Hegel proposes" (Curley 2019, 7).[97] Yet, when Miki is read against the phenomenological background, this objection starts losing its sting. As we saw, among all its other qualifications, the logic of the imagination is a logic of symbols, which means that it is grounded in the individual's embodied relation to the world. The logic of imagination is a logic that both binds πάθος and λόγος as well as grounds λόγος in πάθος, which, among other things, means that it is not anti-individualistic, but designed to integrate the social and the individual. As Fujita Masakatsu puts it in his analysis of λόγος in πάθος in Miki's thought, "πάθος has an 'impulsive' character; it urges us to action through our bodies" (Fujita 2011, 311). For Miki, it is productive imagination that binds such an active body with the λόγος. Not only does the body "seep up into" consciousness, but also, the body largely determines it. This means that Miki's logic of imagination does not unfold on the other side of everything individual, but is a logic that succeeds only insofar as it binds the individual and the social. If not for this integration, the logic of imagination could not entail either reformative or transformative dimensions, which rely upon the relation between the individual and the social.

The logic of imagination, interpreted as the logic of formation, reformation and transformation of collective representations,

---

96   See, in this regard, Iwasaki 1998.
97   According to Curley, a dialogue opened up between Miki and post-Marxist thought, and especially Henri Lefevbre, provides the resources needed to answer this objection.

symbols, forms and institutions, is indicative of the fact that there is a constant need for cultural renewal and rejuvenation. On the one hand, each culture produces its own identity by means of self-objectification. On the other hand, since it reaches its own self-objectification in the irreducibly historical collective representations, symbols and forms, it is only a question of time until each culture finds itself locked within its own self-objectifications. In Miki's own words,

> Humans form a world and by producing culture discover within it a dwelling place and gain life.... That which was the developing form of life will in due time become a negation of life and will become a shackle for life. Culture become the so-called humans' "self-alienation" rather than an objectification of life. Life that has thus achieved a formative synthesis of self, by producing the culture, now falls again into a separation and an opposition.[98]

The perpetual transformation of the objectification of life into its self-alienation is indicative of the perpetual crisis of humanity.[99] Yet in a world ruled by imagination, only imagination itself can provide the resources needed to counteract the perpetual crises that it itself breeds. If the crisis is not momentary, but perpetual, and if the task of rebirth is not relative, but absolute, then this crisis can only be countered, and this task can only be met, by affirming the idea of *absolute creativity*.[100] For Miki, life itself is necessarily situated not

---

[98]   Miki, *Huymanizumu no testugakuteki kiso* [「ヒューマニズムの哲学的基礎」; *The Philosophical Foundation of Humanism*], Vol. 5, 1967, 176-177 (quoted from Nagatomo 1995, 14).

[99]   Shigenori Nagatomo argues that Miki's philosophy of productive imagination should be understood as a philosophical response to the looming crisis of the day. "The 'mixed' connotes a degree of chaos as a counter concept to form (*eidos*), and the chaos is formless, presenting itself as a state of the world in which Miki believed he and his contemporaries lived. Therefore, as a way of correcting this situation, Miki attempts to give 'form' though his philosophical endeavors to the otherwise formless world. Basically, Miki sees in contemporary anxiety, springing from the formless world, a lack of artfully creative, productive spirit which he tried to exhort us to embody through the act of 'creative imagination' by assuming the standpoint of acting self-awareness" (Nagatomo 1995, 6-7).

[100]   As Miki has it, "the one that ties together the many forms is formless rather than being a form, it is a so-called 'formless form'" (Miki 2016, 40). Not only do all forms arise out of nothingness; they also all return to nothingness. Absolute creativity appears to be Miki's response to the perpetual crises that such a play of nothingness and being generates.

only between πάθος and λόγος, but also between hope and despair, elation and disenchantment, cultural crisis and its overcoming. Miki's philosophy of productive imagination is a philosophy of absolute creativity.[101]

---

[101] A word of gratitude is due to John W. M. Krummel for his kind help with the preparation of this chapter.

CHAPTER VI
From the Phenomenology of the Body to the Ontology of the Flesh: Maurice Merleau-Ponty and Embodied Imagination

Introduction

Merleau-Ponty is first and foremost a philosopher of perception. To understand his contribution to phenomenology requires that one clarify why perception occupies a central place in his thinking. Because scholars focused, for many decades, on the primacy of perception in Merleau-Ponty's work, there was little interest in his phenomenology of the imagination, which is latent in many of his writings, from his earliest to his final work. In the last few decades, however, the situation has started to change. Richard Kearney (see Kearney 1998), James Morley (see Morley 2002), James Steeves (see Steeves 2004), Annabelle Dufourcq (see Dufourcq 2011 and 2018), Kathleen Lennon (see Lennon 2015 and 2018) and Glen Mazis (see Mazis 2016) are among those scholars who have argued that it would be a serious misunderstanding to think that imagination is only of secondary importance for Merleau-Ponty. These scholars have shown that Merleau-Ponty's ever deepening reflections on perception led him to discover that perception is inseparable from imagination. But what kind of imagination is this? Merleau-Ponty's reflections often appear incoherent because different conceptions of imagination are implicit in his analysis. Within such a framework, the distinction between productive and reproductive imagination proves to be highly significant, for it allows us to resolve many apparent contradictions and allows us, in effect, to recognize the transcendental and ontological importance of Merleau-Ponty's implicit phenomenology of productive imagination. I do not mean thereby to suggest that, in his diverse analyses, Merleau-Ponty returns to classical conceptions of productive imagination. Rather, in what follows I wish to show that Merleau-Ponty's multifaceted reflections on imagination provide us with the basis to reconceptu-alize productive imagination in a new fashion. As we will see, once reconceptualized in such a framework, productive imagination manifests itself as a *sui generis* mode of embodied intentionality through which embodied subjectivity relates to the invisible dimen-sion of the visible world and enables us to recognize the imaginary texture of actuality.

To show this, I will proceed by taking three major steps in my analysis. First, I will begin by focusing on Merleau-Ponty's early phenomenological studies, in which we will come to recognize Sar-tre's influence. I will maintain that due to this influence, Merleau-Ponty's reflections on productive imagination are only implicit in these studies, and I will substantiate this claim with a number of references from Merleau-Ponty's analyses. Second, I will turn to the analysis of imagination that we come across in various lectures that Merleau-Ponty had delivered in the late 1940s and 1950s. In this framework, we will come to recognize an opening gap in Merleau-Ponty's explicit reflections, which are directed at both productive and reproductive functions of imagination. The merely implicit dis-tinction between reproductive and productive imagination in Mer-leau-Ponty's early writings will become much more explicit in these lectures. In the third and last part, I will turn to Merleau-Ponty's final writings, especially to "Eye and Mind," and in such a frame-work, will address the "ontological turn" in Merleau-Ponty's phe-nomenology of imagination. As we will see, in "Eye and Mind" and *The Visible and the Invisible*, Merleau-Ponty's phenomenology of per-ception proves to be inseparable from the phenomenological ontol-ogy of productive imagination.

Merleau-Ponty's Early Phenomenology of Imagination

In 1936, Merleau-Ponty's review of Sartre's *L'Imagination* – the first of Sartre's two books on imagination – was published in *Journal de Psychologie normale et pathologique*.[102] In this review, Merleau-Ponty

---

[102]   For the English translation, see Merleau-Ponty 2012b.

interprets Sartre's early study as a systematic elaboration of a brand of phenomenology which was "only initiated" by Husserl (Merleau-Ponty 2012b, 171). He interprets *L'Imagination* as a preparatory study that eventually led to the publication of *L'Imaginaire*, which Sartre was to publish four years later, in 1940. Merleau-Ponty's review was generally favorable, yet it also included a few critical observations. According to Merleau-Ponty, Sartre was not entirely fair to the plethora of thinkers he addressed in his historically-oriented study; he was especially unfair to Henri Bergson, whose concept of the image in *Matter and Memory* is, Merleau-Ponty claims, an anticipation of Husserl's concept of the *noema*. Moreover, according to Merleau-Ponty's assessment, Sartre placed himself too close to Husserl in the sense that he ignored the difficulties that surround the Husserlian distinction between *hyle* and *morphe*. Despite these critical observations, Merleau-Ponty concluded his review by stating that "these injustices, if there be any, are covered by the rare merits of the work: the rigour and vigour of critical thought, and the constant good fortune of expression" (Merleau-Ponty 2012b, 171).

Throughout his writings, Merleau-Ponty regularly returned to Sartre, and especially to *The Imaginary*. As we will soon see, in *Phenomenology of Perception*, Merleau-Ponty's explicit reflections on imagination are heavily influenced by Sartre; however, his implicit analysis entails insights that are out of step with Sartre's account of the imaginary. In his later reflections, Merleau-Ponty distances himself from the Sartrean view quite explicitly by developing a philosophical standpoint that is quite close to Gaston Bachelard's phenomenology of material imagination (see Kearney 1998, 120-124 and Mazis 2016, 255-271), rejecting two features of the Sartrean account. First, in his *The Imaginary*, Sartre sharply contrasts imagination with perception while arguing that perception binds consciousness to the real and that imagination links consciousness to the unreal. Second, Sartre further contrasts imagination with perception while maintaining that the perceptual world has depth but that the imaginary doesn't. In *Phenomenology of Perception*, Merleau-Ponty accepts these tendencies as largely valid, yet in his later work he explicitly rejected them while disclosing what he calls the "imaginary texture of the real," identifying this as imaginary with the depth of actuality.

Yet even in his later reflections on the imagination, Merleau-Ponty did not aim to discredit the Sartrean view. Rather, his goal was to limit the scope of its validity. As seen from Merleau-Ponty's standpoint, Sartre had never presented us with a phenomenology of the imagination *per se*, but only with a phenomenology of *one type of* imagination. Much like Ricœur would claim after him, Merleau-Ponty also appears to think that Sartre was concerned with reproductive imagination alone and that he left productive imagination thematically unexplored in his early writings on imagination.

What does Merleau-Ponty tell us about imagination explicitly in *Phenomenology of Perception*? His explicit reflections are only of a passing nature and they are heavily influenced by Sartre's *L'Imaginaire*. Contrasting imagination with perception, Merleau-Ponty, in a heavily Sartrean fashion, contends that imagination is a form of intentionality, which is characterized by spontaneity[103] and quasi-observation,[104] and which links us not to the real, but to nothingness.[105] The four fundamental features of the image, which Sartre enumerates in the opening pages of his *L'Imaginaire,* are all present in Merleau-Ponty's analysis, although with one slight modification: while Sartre understood the intentional nature of imagination to mean that "the image is a consciousness" (Sartre 2004, 5-7), Merleau-Ponty understands this to mean that imagination is rooted in the body. This becomes especially clear in the rich and intriguing analyses of hallucination, which Merleau-Ponty interprets as a result that stems from a disturbance in the body schema (Merleau-

---

[103]   "Confronted with the real thing, our behavior feels motivated by the "stimuli" that fill it out and that justify its intention. When it comes to phantasy, the initiative comes from us and nothing responds to it on the outside" (Merleau-Ponty 2012a, 355).

[104]   "The real lends itself to an infinite exploration, it is inexhaustible." By contrast, Merleau-Ponty also writes that "imagination is without depth; it does not respond to our attempts to vary our points of view; it does not lend itself to observation" (Merleau-Ponty 2012a, 338).

[105]   "The real stands out against our fictions because in the real sense surrounds matter and penetrates it deeply" (Merleau-Ponty 2012a, 338).

Ponty 2012a, 355).[106] As we will see, much of what he states here explicitly Merleau-Ponty himself will reject in his later work, starting with the lectures that he delivered first at the Sorbonne and then later at the *Collège de France*, and ending with such works as *The Visible and the Invisible* and "Eye and Mind."

Before turning to Merleau-Ponty's later reflections, it should be stressed that alongside Merleau-Ponty's explicit remarks, in *Phenomenology of Perception* we also come across an implicit analysis of imagination, which conflicts sharply with the explicit one. As Anabelle Dufourcq shows in her various studies, in *Phenomenology of Perception* Merleau-Ponty does not circumscribe the field of the imaginary, nor does he define the concept of imagination (Dufourcq 2011, 187). Still, as she further contends with the implicit account of imagination in mind, "the notion of the imaginary pervades Merleau-Ponty's early philosophy, even though it is not thematized in *Phenomenology of Perception*" (Dufourcq 2011, 187). James Steeves expresses a similar view in his analysis: "Unfortunately, Merleau-Ponty is not always clear in *Phenomenology of Perception* about which mode of imagining he is discussing" (Steeves 2004, 77). On some occasions, imagination is treated as the polar opposite of perception; at other times, imagination and perception are conceptualized as two different ways of presenting objects of consciousness. Merleau-Ponty moves from one mode of imagination to the other without drawing a conceptual distinction between them. Indeed, Merleau-Ponty's phenomenologically-grounded conception of perception recasts the imaginary-real relation, which in effect means that we can distill Merleau-Ponty's implicit phenomenology of imagination from his rich account of the diverse dimensions of perceptual experiences. Following such a path, Glen Mazis also recently shows that Merleau-Ponty's account of perceptual faith, of the gestures of the world in movement, and of what Mazis calls "physiognomic imagination" and especially the perception of space, provides "rich beginnings of a theory of the imaginal and its sources"

---

[106]   "Every hallucination is an hallucination of one's own body" (Merleau-Ponty 2012a, 355). Slightly modifying this claim, one could also say that every phantasy is a phantasy of one's own (derealized) body.

(Mazis 2016, 177). In his later work, Merleau-Ponty returns to these beginnings and developed them further in a way that ultimately leads to phenomenological ontology as conceptualized in *The Visible and the Invisible* and "Eye and Mind."

This different figure of imagination is not accidentally present in Merleau-Ponty. The reason behind its presence concerns the central role that ambiguity plays in his phenomenology.[107] According to Merleau-Ponty, both my relation to the world and my self-relation are irreducibly ambiguous: "I only know myself in my inherence in the world and in time; I only know myself in ambiguity" (Merleau-Ponty 2012a, 360). When Merleau-Ponty qualifies our basic relation to the world in such terms as "perceptual faith" or "primordial opinion" (Merleau-Ponty 2012a, 359), he wishes to stress that just as faith does not entail apodictic certainty, so opinion does not entail knowledge. This means that the mode of the world's givenness, its inherent and irreducible ambiguity, tolerate illusions and hallucinations (see Merleau-Ponty 2012a, 308). "To have hallucinations and, in general, to imagine is to exploit this tolerance of the pre-predicative world as well as our vertiginous proximity to all of being in syncretic experience" (Merleau-Ponty 2012a, 359). There are gaps and ellipses in the world's givenness, which need to be filled in, since without such filling the phenomenal world would lack the depth we ascribe to it. This is where imagination performs its inimitable role: it proves to be our gateway to the depth of phenomena. Along with James Morley, we can say that tolerance for ambiguity is a "preconceptual acceptance that the world can never be absolutely divided between the imaginary and the nonimaginary" (Morley 2002, 93). In other words, perception can only provide us with incomplete access to the perceptual world. The

---

[107]   Labelling Merleau-Ponty's phenomenology as a "philosophy of ambiguity" has been in fashion since its earliest reception. As early as 1949, Ferdinand Alquié wrote the first long review of Merleau-Ponty's philosophy, which he titled "Une Philosophie de l'Ambiguite." A few years later, in 1951, Alphonse de Waehlens wrote the first book about Merleau-Ponty's philosophy under the same title, *Une Philosophie de l'Ambiguite.* Merleau-Ponty himself embraced this label for his philosophy in the late 1940s and early 1950's, although some scholars observe that he made less use of it in his later writings. See, in this regard, Sapontzis 1978, 538-543.

perceptual world itself has its own depths – the invisible behind the visible – and the embodied imagination provides us with access to it.

In *Phenomenology of Perception*, we come across various sketches that highlight the productive function of imagination, which appears to be quite irreconcilable with Merleau-Ponty's explicit reflections on its nature. For instance, in his phenomenological account of association (Merleau-Ponty 2012a, 20-23), Merleau-Ponty emphasizes that all of our present experiences are given within a temporal field that surrounds and envelops our perceptions. He further notes that this field, which is formed by our past experiences, is given as an "atmosphere, an horizon, or even the 'setting'" (Merleau-Ponty 2012a, 23). Perceptions, he claims, are pregnant with irreducible sense, which bursts forth "in accordance with our present intentions and with our previous experiences" (ibid). The function Kant ascribes to transcendental imagination is reconceptualized by Merleau-Ponty as a component of perceptual experiences, a dimension that does not lend itself to be explained as an a priori structure of consciousness, but which should be understood, instead, as a field of sedimentations, built upon the past experiences of embodied subjectivity.

In a different framework, we come across Merleau-Ponty's discussion of different colors – blue, which solicits a certain way of looking from me, green, which brings with it a restful quality, red, which invades the eye – and the specific affective atmospheres that they create. Merleau-Ponty emphasizes that even before we see a particular color, we have already apprehended its sense, and this apprehension relies upon a specific bodily attitude that is appropriate to specific colors. Colors are "inserted into a certain behavior" (Merleau-Ponty 2012a, 216); they have "motor significance" (Merleau-Ponty 2012a, 217). Because we are embodied beings, we apprehend colors with their specific affective qualities: "I deliver over a part of my body, or even my entire body, to this manner of vibrating and of filling space named 'blue' or 'red'" (Merleau-Ponty 2012a, 219). Colors have their own symbolic value ("red signifies effort or violence," "green signifies rest and peace" [Merleau-Ponty

2012a, 219]), derived from our embodied relation to them. This original inseparability of the experience of colors and affective atmospheres cannot be explained if one conceptualizes colors as states or
qualities. As Glen Mazis observes, "it may be that Merleau-Ponty is
giving us a unique phenomenology of how the imaginal is dove-
tailed with the perceptual" (Mazis 2016, 192). "It is," Mazis continues, "Merleau-Ponty's bringing of imagining back into embodying
being by grounding it in 'affective and motor intentionality' that
will allow him to start to reconfigure the imaginal" (Mazis 2016,
207).

Kant conceptualizes productive imagination as a synthesizing
power that overcomes the gap between the concepts of understanding and intuition. It generates the schemata that prepare the way
for the apprehension of sensible givens. In *Phenomenology of Perception*, Merleau-Ponty ascribes such a schematizing role to the body.
"The experience of the body leads us to recognize an imposition of
sense that does not come from a universal constituting consciousness, a sense that adheres to certain contents" (Merleau-Ponty
2012a, 148). The body, which Merleau-Ponty conceptualizes as "our
anchorage in the world" (Merleau-Ponty 2012a, 146), schematizes
appearances, although not by mediating between appearances and
a pregiven categorical structure. What the intellectualist tradition
ascribes to the constituting consciousness, Merleau-Ponty reconceptualizes as an accomplishment of the lived-body. The body finds
itself solicited to constitute the sense of the phenomenon, which it
does by relying on its own habitualities and by opening up a field
of possibilities that enable the phenomenon to disclose its hidden
dimensions.

Within such a framework, we can understand Merleau-
Ponty's illuminating account of the organist playing an unfamiliar
keyboard (Merleau-Ponty 2012a, 146-147). The organist does not
master the instrument by forming representations during the short
practice before the concert. He does not examine the instrument
and does not form representations. His relation to the instrument is
not conceptual, but practical. As he sits on the bench, as he engages
the pedals, "he sizes up the instrument with his body, he

incorporates its directions and dimensions" (Merleau-Ponty 2012a, 147). Through his body, he tests out the horizon of possibilities, which leads to an embodied discovery of what can be achieved while playing the organ in question. In a thoroughly dialogical fashion, he discovers "affective vectors" and "emotional sources" and thereby creates "an expressive space" (Merleau-Ponty 2012a, 147), within which the musical work can be actualized. There are various modes of realization. The decision is in the organist's hands and feet. The space of possibilities that opens up through such a practice ultimately enables the organist to bring the musical essence of the piece into reality, which Merleau-Ponty takes to mean that the organist transforms his own body into a sheer medium, or "the place of passage" that brings together the score of the piece and its sounds. This bringing of the ideal essence of music down to earth is a matter of allowing music to exist for itself: a transformation of a possibility into actuality. The organist thus finds himself at the intersection of the possible and the actual, of the real and the imaginary.[108]

The organist's relation to the new organ is in many ways similar to the blind man's relation to a new cane, to a driver's relation to a new car, or, in reference to yet another example from Merleau-Ponty's account embodied habits, to a woman's relation to the feather in her new hat (see Merleau-Ponty 2012a, 144). Neither the cane, the car nor the hat are apperceived as objects whose size is to be fixed through comparison with other objects. "The cane's furthest point is transformed into a sensitive zone," and so it is with the hat ("she senses where the feather is, just as we sense where our hand is" [Merleau-Ponty 2012a, 144], and so it is with the car ("'I can pass' without comparing the width of the lane to that of the fender, just as I go through a door without comparing the width of the door to that of my body" [Merleau-Ponty 2012a, 144]). To try out a new hat, a new car or a new cane is to relate to a field of

---

[108]   While commenting on this passage, Glen Mazis remarks that this mode of imagining that sketches out implicit senses and illuminates them in their presence as they are intimately related to the audience can be called "the physiognomic imagination" (Mazis 2016, 192). In the present work, I will call this "embodied imagination."

actualizable possibilities, to imagine what it must be like to incorporate them into one's body schema. By disclosing practical possibilities in an embodied fashion, we relate to the objects in question in terms of what they are supposed to be. Put paradoxically, it is through the embodied imagination that we transform the hat, the car and the cane into what they are.

Like Kant's productive imagination, Merleau-Ponty's embodied imagination also does not function by forming images of any kind. Rather, it schematizes phenomena by disclosing in advance a range of its possible manifestations. Both produce not images, but schemas. Embodied imagination envelops phenomena within a horizon of determinate indeterminacy – a horizon of sense that concerns possible action, perception and understanding. Just as for Kant, my apprehension of any empirical object relies upon pregiven transcendental and empirical schemata, so also for Merleau-Ponty, my embodied relation to things around me relies upon possible relations between things and my body schema. The imposition of sense upon phenomena, of which Merleau-Ponty speaks at the very end of the chapter, "The Spatiality of the Body and Motricity," concerns the discovery of the horizon of congruence between the body schema and the phenomenal field.

Many more clues are scattered throughout *Phenomenology of Perception*, which provide the basis to conceptualize imagination in significantly different terms than the Sartrean conception that Merleau-Ponty had adopted explicitly in his early writings. For our purposes, the foregoing analysis will have to suffice, for it has shown with sufficient clarity that alongside Merleau-Ponty's explicit remarks about the imagination, we also come across an implicit analysis, which recasts its function within the overall structure of embodied experience. While in his explicit remarks, Merleau-Ponty sharply separates perception from phantasy and imagination, in his implicit analysis he shows that perception and imagination are entwined with each other. We should not be too quick to conclude that Merleau-Ponty's explicit analysis is turned on its head in his implicit reflections. Rather, in his explicit and implicit analyses, Merleau-Ponty focuses on different types of imagination, although without clearly distinguishing between them. While his explicit reflections are focused on reproductive imagination, his implicit analysis traces a novel conception of productive imagination, which has its roots not in the a priori structures of consciousness, but in the lived body. The implicit analysis suggests that the imaginary and perceptual spaces are interwoven with each other and that the perceptual is soaked in imaginal and memorial meanings. With Merleau-Ponty's explicit and implicit accounts of imagination in *Phenomenology of Perception* in mind, we can say that here imagination is thought through as a continuum, at one end of which lie those pure phantasies, or fancies, which stand in sharp contrast with reality, while at the other end are phantasies of an entirely different kind — those phantasies which give perception sense and depth.

Two Forms of the Imaginary in the Sorbonne Lectures (1949-1952)

Merleau-Ponty's Sorbonne lectures (1949-1952) provide us with an important resource to trace the further development of his philosophy of imagination. Of special importance are the lectures, *Structure and Conflict in Child Consciousness*, which Merleau-Ponty delivered in 1949-1950, and *Experience of Others*, delivered in 1951-1952. The seventh part of the first of these lectures is titled "The Child's Relation with the Imaginary." This title is misleading, for in this lecture, the child's relation with the real constitutes the focus of Merleau-Ponty's attention. Merleau-Ponty's goal here is to offer a reexamination of the child's relation with the real that would, in effect, force us to reconceptualize the sphere of the imaginary (see Merleau-Ponty 2010a, 176).

Sartre's influence on Merleau-Ponty's reflections on imagination remains strong in these lectures. Not just the concepts and critiques, but even the examples that Merleau-Ponty employs are borrowed from Sartre (see for instance Merleau-Ponty 2010a, 177). Building on such a theoretical background, Merleau-Ponty suggests that imagination is essentially an *affective* and *motor* phenomenon and he further contends that "the very problem of the imagination will depend on the degree of precision given to notions of affective and motor *intentionality*" (Merleau-Ponty 2010a, 178).

Of importance for Merleau-Ponty is not only Sartre's *The Imaginary*, but also *The Emotions: Outline of a Theory* – an early study Sartre published in 1939, one year before publishing *The Imaginary*. Establishing a close relation between the insights that Sartre had developed in these studies, Merleau-Ponty contends that the imaginary has its source in the emotions and that affectivity is a mode of thing apprehension. Anger, for instance, is a matter of seeking an immediate solution to a problem (see Merleau-Ponty 2010a, 179). Emotion is nothing less than the human mode of existence, if only because we hardly ever relate to our surroundings in an emotion-free way. This provides Merleau-Ponty with the basis to develop a novel account of dreams and hallucinations. Both are specific ways of positing an imaginary world, which arises on the basis of derealization. To imagine is to believe in images and this belief rests on the ground of losing contact with the real (Merleau-Ponty 2010a, 180-181)

This is the standard story, which relies upon a sharp distinction between the real and the imaginary. While presenting this common picture with reference to Sartre's *The Imaginary*, Merleau-Ponty further notes that "in the course of his study, Sartre revises his conceptions" (Merleau-Ponty 2010a, 181):

> Sartre's absolute distinction does not suffice to resolve the imaginary. In order for the imaginary to be capable of displacing the real, we do not need to consider them antinomies, as different as day and night. In such a conception, there would be no room for myth. Myth belongs in this third, oneiric order that the author introduces in the second half of his book and which is *between* waking perception and the "fiction" of the sane adult individual. (Merleau-Ponty 2010a, 181)

It is not quite clear how one is to understand these remarks with reference to Sartre's work. On the one hand, in Sartre's *The Imaginary*, we do not come across any analysis of myth. Even the term is missing, to say nothing of its analysis. On the other hand, in the second part of his study Sartre provides a patient phenomenological description of the "image family," and here we come across a large variety of phenomena, which bring into question the validity of the sharp distinction between the image and the real that Sartre had introduced when he presented the third characteristic of the image: "the imagining consciousness posits its object as a nothingness" (Sartre 2004, 11). The consciousness of imitations, of schematic drawings, of faces in the fire, spots on walls and rocks in human form, of hypnagogic images and persons seen in coffee grounds, or in a crystal ball—all these phenomena that Sartre thematizes in the second part of *The Imaginary* belong to what Merleau-Ponty identifies as "the third, oneiric order" situated half way between perception and fiction. Such is Merleau-Ponty's interpretation of Sartre's *The Imaginary* that we come across in the Sorbonne lectures —an interpretation which one could call a matter of reading Sartre against Sartre.

For Merleau-Ponty, the child's relation with the real brings into question the validity of the absolute distinction between the real and the imaginary. "The child does not live in the bipolar world of the waking adult, but rather he inhabits a hybrid zone of oneiric ambiguity" (Merleau-Ponty 2010a, 181-182). This hybrid zone lies between the extreme poles of the imaginary-real continuum, which in effect means that the child's perceptions are fused with phantasies, and *vice versa*.

How are we, then, to draw a distinction between the real and the imaginary? "The *true distinction* between the real and the imaginary stems from the fact that both are ambiguous forms of consciousness" (Merleau-Ponty 2010a, 182). This means that the distinction between perception and imagination should not be conceptualized as the distinction between two different types of certainty (certainty in being and certainty in nothingness), but, rather, as a distinction between ambiguous forms of consciousness and their *validation*. Both phantasy and perception are conjectural and ambiguous forms of embodied consciousness in the sense that neither is ever in full possession of its object. However, while perceptual experiences are validated by subsequent experiences, phantasies lack this kind of fulfillment. Yet, because the validation in question can never remove all ambiguity, it remains always conjectural. With this in mind, Merleau-Ponty further contends that the distinction between the real and the imaginary is dialectical: just as the striving for the real can result in the lack of it, so also, the striving for the imaginary can result in a similar lack.

There are two different ways to understand what Merleau-Ponty here identifies as the third, oneiric order. On the one hand, one could interpret the oneiric space as the third intermediary zone located between the sane adult's relation to reality and her relation to the imaginary. A hybrid form of consciousness mixes the categories borrowed from two fundamentally different orders of experience. On the other hand, one could also argue that this third, oneiric order bespeaks the sane adult's everyday relation to the world and that pure perception is just as abstract a concept as pure imagination. In this regard, the oneiric zone would appear similar to the space of experience that is opened by Kant's transcendental imagination – the only sphere of experience available to us. Which of these two approaches has Merleau-Ponty himself endorsed?

No straightforward answer is possible and one could bolster both accounts with supporting passages from Merleau-Ponty's lectures. Are we then to say that Merleau-Ponty's account of the "hybrid zone of oneiric ambiguity" is itself ambiguous in the bad sense of the term – in that it leaves us with an open question regarding how this zone relates to the perceptual and imaginary fields? This would be a disappointing outcome. Yet, with some hermeneutical generosity, one could resolve this apparent contradiction. To do so, one could maintain that the child *largely* inhabits the zone of oneiric ambiguity, while the sane adult's outlook on the world is qualified by reliance on the distinction between the perceptual and the imaginary fields. Despite the presence of this distinction, the sane adult can never fully succeed in liberating herself from ambiguity altogether. Any attempt to do so would have a neurotic outcome, such as the one that Merleau-Ponty terms the neurosis of abandonment (see Merleau-Ponty 2010a, 182-184). The neurosis in question is characterized by a refusal to accept the ambiguous and by the un-restrained wish to transform the ambiguous into the certain.[109]

Following this line of interpretation, we arrive at the insight that the perceptual field is pervaded by the oneiric order.[110] The in-separability of the two orders is especially conspicuous in our rela-tion with others: "since introjection and projection are unavoidable, my behavior toward others will always be in some respect imagin-ing" (Merleau-Ponty 2010a, 184). So also, in the nature of *games, im-itations* and *dreams* we witness the continual presence of such "onei-rism of wakefulness," the brief analysis of which completes Mer-leau-Ponty's analysis of the child's relation to the imaginary (Mer-leau-Ponty 2010a, 185-186).

Merleau-Ponty continues the analysis of these themes in the lecture, "The Experience of Others," delivered in the Sorbonne in 1951-1952. The fourth and last part of this lecture course, dedicated to the examination of the lived and gestural expression, is especially important for our purposes. Here, Merleau-Ponty briefly addresses mythical consciousness, which he describes as a consciousness characterized by the absence of a distinction between feelings and significations as well as experiences and expressions. More broadly, the opposition between the natural and the cultural does not exist for this kind of consciousness. Mythical consciousness is a con-sciousness that is steeped in the third, oneiric order, in the "Lectures on the Child's Relation to the Imaginary," Merleau-Ponty qualifies as the "oneirism of wakefulness." Yet, what exactly does it mean to characterize mythical consciousness as oneiric? By turning to an analysis of the dramatic arts after addressing mythical conscious-ness, Merleau-Ponty demonstrates that "we find this connection

---

[109] In this regard, James Morley's analysis of Merleau-Ponty's phenomenology and its significance for psychopathology is especially instructive. As Morley puts it, "paranoids are infamously incapable of interpersonal trust. Obsessives strive for an imaginary control that perpetually eludes them. Compulsives ritually re-peat to unsuccessfully satisfy unending imaginary doubts…. In each condition we are witness to an *intolerance* of such ambiguity" (Morley 2002, 103).

[110] One can find further support for such an interpretation in Merleau-Ponty's *Lec-tures on Passivity* from 1944-1955, to which I will soon turn: "It is not a question of subordinating waking life to oneiric life. It is simply necessary to understand that they communicate" (Merleau-Ponty 2010b, 155).

between lived and gesture exists in certain acts in our own social life" (Merleau-Ponty 2010a, 449). Thus, according to Merleau-Ponty, in some important respects, our own social life retains the oneiric characteristics of mythical consciousness.

The dramatic arts in general, and theater in particular, provide us with a first illustration. The actor transforms his own body into imaginary appearances. He embodies imaginary experiences by de-realizing himself into an imaginary role (see Merleau-Ponty 2010a, 450-451). Everything that he *as an actor* lives through is an imaginary experience, and this mode of experience is simultaneously a mode of presentation. The inseparability of feeling and expression is no different than the one lived through by the organist, as addressed by Merleau-Ponty in *Phenomenology of Perception*. The composer creates for the performer a sheet of notes and the performer has the task to bring these notes to acoustic existence. So also, the author gives the actor a role and the actor has to construct a character out of this role through performance.

There is something magical about the theater, Merleau-Ponty repeatedly claims. It blends the real and the imaginary by enabling the imaginary content to appear in real space and real time. The actor's words and gestures make the imaginary appear. "Dramatic magic consists in how at the time that the actor's body is present, everything else is raised to the imaginary by connections established between objects" (Merleau-Ponty 2010a, 453). Just as it is for the performer of a musical piece, so it is also for an actor who transforms the imaginary into the real: "The imaginary begins to be taken as real through a perfect lapping over of the text's meaning and the actor's behavior" (ibid).

Merleau-Ponty does not stop with the insight that the mythical structures are recreated in the theater in modern societies. Returning to Sartre's *The Imaginary* (although this time not to the First Part, but to the Conclusion), Merleau-Ponty affirms Sartre's central insight that "imagination is not an empirical power added to consciousness, but is the whole of consciousness as it realizes its freedom" (Sartre 2004, 186). As Merleau-Ponty has it, "all consciousness is consciousness that imagines, that takes consciousness of the world" (Merleau-Ponty 2010a, 454); "all consciousness is thus nec-essarily imaginary consciousness" (ibid). To illustrate this point, Merleau-Ponty remarks in passing that a modern life is a life lived through vocations and that "vocation always consists in the free de-cision to derealize oneself in a role" (ibid). This is not to be misin-terpreted as a matter of bad faith. Authenticity, Merleau-Ponty fur-ther observes, is a matter of "giving without pause to the role one had decided to play" (ibid).

Of course, Merleau-Ponty realizes that he is developing Sar-trean insights in a direction that Sartre himself had not followed and would not support.[111] It is this very realization that brings Mer-leau-Ponty to the explicit distinction between different kinds of im-agination, a distinction that was presupposed, although not drawn explicitly, in *Phenomenology of Perception*. "The imaginary is of two sorts, two phenomena of different orders, such as in the hidden as-pect of real landscape that I have before my eyes, on the one hand, and, on other, the evocation of absent friend" (Merleau-Ponty 2010, 454). Thus, according to Merleau-Ponty, there is indeed an imagi-nary sphere that stands opposed to the sphere of the real. However, there is also a dimension of the imaginary that belongs to the con-sciousness of reality. Merleau-Ponty's explicit affirmation of the consciousness of the real is inseparably bound up with how the con-sciousness of the imaginary corroborates the view that the third, oneiric order is meant to characterize our everyday relation to things around us. This explicit recognition that perception is soaked in imagination clarifies Merleau-Ponty's view that "all conscious-ness of the world is at the same time imagination of the world" (Merleau-Ponty 2010a, 454).[112]

---

[111] As Richard Kearney puts it, "Merleau-Ponty reveals a concern to rescue imagi-nation from the alienated status with which Sartre endowed it, and to have it recognized as a fundamental expression of Being" (Kearney 1998, 121).

[112] This does not mean, however, that consciousness of the world has become a consciousness of the theater. Yet, the distinction between them is not that of consciousness of the real and consciousness of the imaginary. "The entire dif-ference between theater and life is that one's role in life is subjected to certain past relations with others" (Merleau-Ponty 2010a, 456). The disconnection of the theater from everyday life entails that "in the theater, we can always start again" (ibid). This is what we are deprived of in life.

In summary, we can say that the merit of Merleau-Ponty's Sorbonne lectures lies in the explicit recognition that between pure phantasy and pure perception there lies a third, oneiric order, which characterizes not only the child's consciousness, mythical consciousness or the consciousness of the theater, but also the consciousness of our everyday existence. This third, oneiric order is marked by the fusion of the real and the imaginary, which in effect means that the sphere of the imaginary is itself ambiguous: besides imagination, understood as mere fancy, or fiction, there is also a consciousness of the imaginary from which consciousness of the real is inseparable. We are thus in full right to draw a distinction between productive and reproductive imagination in the framework of Merleau-Ponty's writings.

Imagination and Perceptual Faith in The *Lectures on Passivity* (1954-1955)

The phenomenology of imagination, which is only implicit in *Phenomenology of Perception* and which Merleau-Ponty only begins to develop explicitly in the Sorbonne lectures, is further advanced in the lecture course, "The Problem of Passivity," delivered at *Collège de France* in 1954-1955. The notes from this lecture course should be read along with the notes from the "Institution in Personal and Public History," which was another lecture course that Merleau-Ponty delivered during the same academic year. As Claude Lefort remarks, "Merleau-Ponty poses the problem of passivity by means of the examination of phenomena which do not form themselves according to the model of institution" (Merleau-Ponty 2010b, xix). In direct contrast to the *Lectures on Institution*, what is at stake in the *Lectures on Passivity* is the exploration of the region of being with regard to which the subject is not sovereign. Such phenomena as sleep, dream, the unconscious and memory are at the forefront of Merleau-Ponty's attention in these lectures.

At a methodological level, Merleau-Ponty's orientation in these lectures is even more distant from Sartre's than it was in the Sorbonne lectures. Sartre's goal in *The Imaginary* is to conceptualize the image as a spontaneous form of consciousness (see Sartre 2004,

14). In his *Phenomenology of Perception*, Merleau-Ponty accepts this characterization while at the same time he aims to show that spontaneity has its resources not in consciousness, but in the lived-body. Juxtaposing his own approach to Sartre's as well as to his own earlier analysis, in these lectures Merleau-Ponty conceptualizes the imaginary at the level of passivity, which, in turn, leads him in an anti-Sartrean fashion to speak of "the imaginary in the fabric of life" (Merleau-Ponty 2010b, 125), which in principle cannot be the correlate of negativity.

The goal of the *Lectures on Passivity* is to restore to perceptual consciousness its thickness, which, in turn, leads to the realization that perception is shot through with imagination. Such a project of restoration leads Merleau-Ponty to develop a standpoint, which can, in one and the same respect, serve as an alternative to both realism and idealism: "my attempt at a solution .... [is to present] no exogenous causality and no pure, endogenous causality or *Sinngebung*" (Merleau-Ponty 2010b, 125). This "third way" relies on the insight that a "real unity of what exists" (ibid) inwardly binds embodied consciousness to the world. What we see here is a "propadeutic" to the ontology of the flesh that Merleau-Ponty will develop further in *The Visible and the Invisible* and "Eye and Mind." Indeed, as Merleau-Ponty states quite explicitly, his goal in the *Lectures on Passivity* is not psychological, but philosophical: while addressing such phenomena as sleep, the unconscious and memory, he strives to "redefine being, instead of presupposing an ontology of the In-itself and the For-itself" (Merleau-Ponty 2010b, 125). What is at stake, then, is an ontology that both escapes and provides an alternative to the Sartrean framework, as worked out in *Being and Nothingness*.[113] Merleau-Ponty thus speaks of the real existential unity that binds together the for-itself with the in-itself, without, however, extinguishing their separation from each other. We face

---

[113] This fundamental difference between Sartre and Merleau-Ponty is something that Sartre himself explicitly acknowledges in an interview he gave in 1975: "Merleau-Ponty is always referring to a kind of being for which he invokes Heidegger and which I consider to be absolutely invalid. The entire ontology which emerges from the philosophy of Merleau-Ponty is distinct from mine" (Sartre 1981, 43). See in this regard also Kearney 1998, 122-124.

here an overarching unity in difference, a unity that embraces both unity and difference. In the later writings, Merleau-Ponty will call this unity *flesh* (*chair*).

The unity in question has both a "world side" and a "subject side," and in Merleau-Ponty's account of these sides we come across deepened reflections on the specific role ascribed to imagination.[114] In his description of the "world side," Merleau-Ponty offers a brief critique of his own approach in his earlier studies, which he now characterizes as too static and too abstract. Instead of overestimating the sensing dimension ("which I have done too much" [Merleau-Ponty 2010b, 124]), one needs to develop a phenomenological account, which explicitly acknowledges that the perceptual world is not reducible to the sensory field. As he further remarks in the summary of this course, Merleau-Ponty's goal in the *Lectures on Passivity* is to extend the ontology of the perceived beyond the sensible (see Merleau-Ponty 2010b, 206). Objects, as they are given to us, already entail certain "physiognomies" and "behaviors." They are given as already humanized. As he stresses repeatedly throughout these lectures, the sensory world is full of "gaps, ellipses, allusions" (see, for instance, Merleau-Ponty 2010b, 124). The project of restoring the thickness to perceptual consciousness leads Merleau-Ponty to search for how the sensory dimension could be complemented with other dimensions, which would fill these gaps, ellipses and allusions that characterize the "world side." Merleau-Ponty's further account of the "subject side" suggests that this is to a large degree an accomplishment of the imagination. On the "subject side," besides recognizing the sensing dimension, which could be ascribed to the "natural" body, one must also account for all the sedimentations that characterize the embodied consciousness. "In particular, it is necessary to introduce imaginary fields, ideological fields, mythical fields—linguistics and not only [the] repletion of

---

114 In his Foreword to Merleau-Ponty's Lectures on Institution and Passivity (see Merleau-Ponty 2010b, xxi), Claude Lefort qualifies Merleau-Ponty's reflections on the "world side" and the "subject side" as those "reflections where he [Merleau-Ponty—SG] comes for the first time—if we are not mistaken—to separate his conception of phenomenology from equivocations to which it might be prey."

sensing" (Merleau-Ponty 2010b, 124). In such a way, we come to face the "imaginary in the fabric of life," as an irreducible dimension that allows us to understand why the sensible world does not exhaust the perceptual.

The Husserlian background is plainly visible in these lectures, although it is overshadowed by the Sartrean one. As Merleau-Ponty remarks, a thing is a thing only insofar as it has its own inner and outer horizons. The horizon enables the embodied consciousness to fill in the gaps, ellipses and allusions, thereby "transforming" the consciousness of quale into a consciousness of a thing (see Merleau-Ponty 2010b, 130). But one cannot stop with this realization, which has been masterfully accounted for in Husserl's writings. One must supplement horizons of perception with horizons of relation. One must account for the fact that the sensory field is enmeshed with the ideological, imaginary, mythical and symbolic fields. Such a broadened perspective leads us beyond what Husserl and Merleau-Ponty call the *leibhaftgegeben*: "a natural thing appears as such only in a culture" (Merleau-Ponty 2010b, 133). Such an "overcoming" of the nature versus culture distinction entails the recognition that perceptual horizons are themselves given within the horizon of historical life.

Within such a conceptual framework, Merleau-Ponty turns in his analysis to address the relation between perceptual and imagining consciousness explicitly. He poses the question initially in a Sartrean way: "is this the difference? … Consciousness of being and consciousness of nothingness? Adequation and bad faith?" (Merleau-Ponty 2010b, 146) This approach does not take us far: it is too reductive, in that it condenses imagination to one of its forms, namely, to reproductive imagination. To emphasize this, Merleau-Ponty remarks that "our real life, inasmuch as it is addressed to beings, is already imaginary" (Merleau-Ponty 2010b, 147). In further opposition to the Sartrean approach, which splits apart perceptual and imaginary consciousness, Merleau-Ponty joins them together quite explicitly by suggesting that, just as there is "oneirism of wakefulness," so also, there is "a quasi-perceptual character of dreams" (Merleau-Ponty 2010b, 147).

The Sartrean dichotomy between perception and bad faith proves inadequate when one admits that the perceived word is not adequation.[115] As mentioned above, perception cannot be reduced to sensory givens, which invite one to give up the dichotomy between perception, understood as the givenness of phenomena in flesh and blood, and imagination, qualified as a specific kind of belief. By rejecting such a dichotomy, Merleau-Ponty explicitly contends that what is properly perceptual entails its own beliefs. The presence of belief in perceptual consciousness enables us to determine the meaning of the oneirism of wakefulness with greater precision. Oneiric experience is characterized by a belief, which is, however, not a belief in the dreamed thing, but in the perceived. The oneirism of wakefulness is "the deployment of perceptual 'beliefs'" (Merleau-Ponty 2010b, 152).

Similar to the Sorbonne lectures, in this present context Merleau-Ponty contends that the perception of others entails an imaginary dimension in that it is a projection and introjection. As he notes on several occasions, projection and introjection should not be understood as operations of a 'consciousness' (see, for instance, Merleau-Ponty 2010b, 155), for they are rooted in our bodies, which entail their own sedimentations and their own imaginary.

Thus, the *Lectures on Passivity* provide us with further conceptual resources to rethink the nature of productive imagination in the framework of Merleau-Ponty's phenomenology. Here, productive imagination is primarily conceptualized as a disposition of perceptual beliefs, as a matter of utilizing them tacitly in our actions, perceptions and understanding, that is, as a matter of shaping our basic relation to the actual world. Merleau-Ponty's explicit and repeated admission that perception is not reducible to the sensory data attests to the fact that perception entails an imaginary dimension in the above-mentioned sense of the term, namely, that it relies upon perceptually-oriented beliefs through which we shape the natural world into a cultural one. The human world thereby proves

---

[115] "There is no bad faith except by contrast with adequation" (Merleau-Ponty 2010b, 147).

to be a world that is always already molded not only perceptually, but also imaginatively.

Phenomenological Ontology and the Imaginary Texture of the Real in "Eye and Mind"

The ontological investigations, which Merleau-Ponty was developing in various lectures in the 1950s, found a more mature expression in "Eye and Mind" — Merleau-Ponty's last piece of writing to be published during his lifetime. It is one of the most insightful and cryptic philosophical essays written in the second half of the twentieth century in general, which partly explains Sartre's remark that "Eye and Mind" "says everything provided one knows how to decipher it" (Sartre 1964, 282). Due to its enigmatic nature, any attempt to interpret this essay faces a genuine philosophical challenge. As Gary B. Madison has observed, "it seems that here Merleau-Ponty has pushed to the limit the possibilities of the philosophical discourse and of that way of reflecting and writing which is altogether his own" (Madison 1981, 95). In the present context, a thorough analysis of this essay would take us too far afield. I am concerned, instead, with a specific analysis of Merleau-Ponty's reflections on imagination in this essay. Nonetheless, for hermeneutical reasons, it will not be possible to cut out the relevant passages from the essay and just comment on them, while ignoring the framework in which these reflections unfold.

In "Eye and Mind," Merleau-Ponty thematizes imagination in the framework of a philosophy of art in general, and philosophy of painting in particular. Within such a context, Merleau-Ponty's reflections on imagination appear to be significantly different from those explicit remarks that we come across in *Phenomenology of Perception*. While in his early writings, Merleau-Ponty had largely conceptualizes imagination as a reproductive activity of consciousness, in "Eye and Mind" he explicitly dismisses such an approach as unsatisfactory and conceptualizes imagination as genuinely productive. "The word 'image' is in bad repute because we have thoughtlessly believed that a design was a tracing, a copy, a second thing, and that the mental image was such a design, belonging among our private bric-a-brac. But ... in fact it is nothing of the kind ..." (Merleau-Ponty 1964a, 164). What, then, is imagination, if it is not a matter of producing copies or second things? Moreover, what is a mental image if it is not a design that belongs to inner consciousness? Merleau-Ponty's answer to this question is deeply paradoxical and evocative. Insofar as the image makes itself present in a painting, it is "the inside of the outside and the outside of the inside" (ibid). Merleau-Ponty further adds that if we were to fail to take this into consideration, then we would never be able to understand "the quasi presence and imminent visibility which make up the whole problem of the imaginary" (ibid). At least two things are clear: these are deeply obscure remarks and, at the same time, they are of utmost importance for our understanding of Merleau-Ponty's phenomenology of imagination. What sense are we to make of them?

For Merleau-Ponty, the meaning of painting is to be located in the painter's own body. It is therefore crucial to ask: what does it mean to have a body? To have a body is to be open to the world by means of perception. But what does it mean to perceive the world? Resisting the tendency to construe the nature of perception as an activity of a disembodied mind, Merleau-Ponty emphasizes that perception is not a view *on* the world, but that it takes place *in* the world: "things and my body are made of the same stuff" (Merleau-Ponty 1964a, 164). This means, in effect, that perception is not a constitutive activity of an embodied subject, but, rather, that *the body is the medium through which the visible can see itself.* Far from being the correlate of the body, the world, taken together with the body, forms a single reality. The world and the body are made of one and the same *flesh* (*chair*), which, in effect, means that flesh is both subject and object, both the perceiving body and things perceived.[116]

The phenomenon of visibility rest upon the splitting of flesh into the seeing and the seen. Now, the seeing as such is not itself seen, which explains why Merleau-Ponty would claim that the visible has a layer of invisibility. As he puts it towards the end of the

---

[116]   Within Merleau-Ponty's late ontological monism, the concept of flesh (*chair*) is understood as the new element, which is designed to overcome the Cartesian dualism and its tendency to bifurcate all things into matter and spirit. See in this regard Moran 2013, 355.

essay, "the proper essence of the visible is to have a layer of invisibility in the strict sense, which it makes present as a certain absence" (Merleau-Ponty 1964a, 187). Being, which Merleau-Ponty speaks of here, reveals itself as an inwardly divided unity, that is, as visible-invisible. This inseparability of the visible and the invisible allows us further to understand why Merleau-Ponty would contend that "it is impossible to say that nature ends here and that man or expression starts here" (Merleau-Ponty 1964a, 188). Vision is what allows the embodied subjectivity to be absent from itself, or, in Paul Klee's words, "I cannot be caught in immanence."[117]

What, then, does a painting accomplish within this framework of ontological monism? Far from being a second order or a faded copy of the visible, a painting is to be thought of as nothing less than the manifestation of the world's own visibility. This means that, according to Merleau-Ponty, a painting performs a transcendental function in that it renders visible those very conditions that make visibility possible. The difference-in-unity of the world and the body is what comes to presence in a painting. "Manifest visibility must be repeated," and the painting repeats it by instituting "a secret visibility" (Merleau-Ponty 1964a, 164). This secret visibility strives to make visible the phenomenon of visibility itself. Yet how can a painting perform such a transcendental task? To do so, it cannot just copy things, but must rely on the resources provided by imagination. Only by going beyond the domain of actuality can a painting provide us with a diagram of the thing's life in my body. Thus, to be, as Merleau-Ponty claims, a second-order of the visible, a painting must become, as Gary B. Madison puts it, "a transcendental visible" (see Madison 1981, 100). When it fulfills such a transcendental task, a painting brings to light those very conditions that allow us to see things around us.

---

117 According to Merleau-Ponty's further elaboration of these words, which is inscribed on Klee's tomb, to be absent from oneself by means of vision ultimately means to be present at the inner separation of Being, and to be present not from the outside, but from the inside. Within such a framework, everything visual is to be understood as the result of a *"dehiscence* of Being (Merleau-Ponty 1964a, 187) or of a *"deflagration* of Being" (Merleau-Ponty 1964a, 180).

"Quality, light, color, depth" – they are all there in the painting because "the body welcomes them" (Merleau-Ponty 1964a, 164). The painting allows us to see and reflect upon the interplay of light, shadows and colors, which are the necessary conditions that render visibility possible. What comes to visibility in a painting is the "genesis of the visible," as Paul Klee puts it. This explains why, according to Merleau-Ponty, there is no progress in the history of painting: what *all* painting celebrates is the genesis of visibility and the phenomenon of its presence. Far from copying anything, the painting renders visibility itself visible – the coming of something into visibility. In "Eye and Mind," Merleau-Ponty conceptualizes this coming to visibility ontologically, as a perpetual outburst of Being, which he also interprets as the origin of meaning and rationality. This coming to visibility rests upon a distinct ontology, which one can qualify as ontological monism, and which Merleau-Ponty himself strives to elucidate in his late working notes and his last unfinished manuscript, *The Visible and the Invisible.*

"Eye and Mind" continues the project from Husserl of rethinking and broadening the meaning of the transcendental in phenomenology, a project which Husserl had reinterpreted through such seemingly empirical themes as the body and the intersubjective, thereby incorporating them into the field of transcendental phenomenology. In "Eye and Mind," we come across a further broadening of transcendental philosophy. In an unprecedented and, to this day, unsurpassed fashion, this text merges transcendental philosophy with the philosophy of painting.[118] Within such a framework, the transcendental no longer belongs to the absolute Subject,

---

[118]   To a certain extent, Merleau-Ponty's ontology of the imagination relies on Gaston Bachelard's phenomenologically-oriented analysis, which is strongly opposed to the reproductive model of imagination and aims to reconceptualize imagination in terms of pre-Socratic material elements. Merleau-Ponty acknowledges this debt to Bachelard especially in *The Visible and the Invisible*: "Being and the imaginary are for Sartre 'objects,' 'entities' – for me they are 'elements in Bachelard's sense" (Merleau-Ponty 1968, 267). By this we are to understand that the imaginary "is a presence of the immanent, the latent, or the hidden – something Bachelard understood when he said that each sense has its own imaginary" (Merleau-Ponty 1968, 245). For the significance of Bachelard's philosophy of material imagination in relation to Merleau-Ponty's ontology, see especially Mazis 2016, 255-270.

but rather, to embodied subjectivity as it finds itself in the world. Such a fusion of the mundane and the transcendental in its own way transforms the meaning of productive imagination. Much like Kant's *Einbildungskraft*, Merleau-Ponty's imagination also produces imageless schemas; however, the schemas Merleau-Ponty speaks of fundamentally reflect the manner in which things "touch" the *embodied* subjectivity. Productive imagination diagrams the manner in which bodily contact with the world gives rise to visibility. It discloses the life of the actual, "with all its pulp and carnal obverse [*son envers charnel*]" (Merleau-Ponty 1964a, 164-165), by bringing to light the play of lights, colors and shadows and thereby rendering visible the world's visibility.

Within the framework of ontological monism, it becomes understandable why Merleau-Ponty would contend that a painting is "the inside of the outside and the outside of the inside" (Merleau-Ponty 1964a, 164). It is the outside of the inside insofar as it brings to expression how the body is affected by the world's visibility; it is the inside of the outside insofar as it renders visible the origins of visibility. The ontological framework also enables us to understand why Merleau-Ponty would contend that "the imaginary is much nearer to, and much farther away from the actual" (Merleau-Ponty 1964a, 164). It is nearer, for when it is made manifest in a painting, the imaginary discloses how the world touches the body; yet for the same reason, it is also farther away, for a painting is a likeness not according to the mind, but "only according to the body" (Merleau-Ponty 1964a, 165). By disclosing the origins of visibility, the painting enables vision to follow up on its own inward traces, which Merleau-Ponty further qualifies as "the imaginary texture of the real" (Merleau-Ponty 1964a, 165). While the general goal of phenomenological analysis is to enable us to rediscover the world we live in, Merleau-Ponty contends that the perceptual world is shot through with imaginative characteristics. In a sense, it could be qualified as an imaginary world, although not because it is a world of illusions or projected phantasies. Rather, it is a real world that is always, and necessarily, textured by the imaginary.[119]

For Merleau-Ponty, the imaginary and the real join hands at the transcendental level, which a painting makes manifest. Merleau-Ponty's imaginary-real unity is a distinctly transcendental unity, which Annabelle Dufourcq quite appropriately calls the *imaginareal* (see Dufourcq 2018, 137). This unity expresses the ontological unity-in-difference of the body and the world. This unity is the enigma of visibility, which the painter strives to make visible by bringing into possession that which he himself sees. The real has an imaginary texture, for "our fleshly eyes are already much more than receptors for light rays, colors, and lines" (Merleau-Ponty 1964a, 165). According to Merleau-Ponty, a painting expresses a "prehuman way of seeing things" (Merleau-Ponty 1964a, 168): it brings to visibility mute meanings; it lays out an "oneiric universe of carnal essences" (Merleau-Ponty 1964a, 169). Essence and existence, the imaginary and the real, the visible and the invisible — in a painting that describes the prehuman vision of things, a clear distinction between these categories has not yet been drawn. This imaginary texture is the "texture of Being," in which the eye lives the way a human being lives in a house (see Merleau-Ponty 1964a, 166), that is, by no longer noticing its strangeness and by overlooking what it entails. To disclose the texture of Being, the painter must reach beyond the merely visual givens — he must render visible what profane vision believes to be invisible (light, lighting,

---

[119] As Kathleen Lennon puts it in *Imagination and the Imaginary* — a study that outlines what Merleau-Ponty calls "the imaginary texture of the real" — imagination gives the world its *"affective texture"* and "is at work in the everyday world that we perceive, the world as it is for us" (Lennon 2015, 3). This means that the perceptual world is "a world in which the imagination is at work, creating/disclosing forms, expressive of possibilities for living affectively and effectively within it" (Lennon 2015, 11). As she also puts it in a more recent study, "the invisible/imaginary texture of the perceived world is something that emerges from our corporeal immersion within it, a manifestation of the multiple possibilities of the real" (Lennon 2018, 122).

shadows, reflections, etc.) — thereby joining the visible with the invisible and disclosing the "imaginary texture of the real."[120]

The imaginary texture of the real is something to be disclosed within the given world and not arbitrarily projected onto it. Merleau-Ponty therefore emphasizes repeatedly that it is the things themselves that look at the painter, and not the other way round (see, for instance, Merleau-Ponty 1964a, 167); they reveal themselves as already *pregnant* with sense. Merleau-Ponty borrows the metaphor of pregnancy from Gestalt psychology and employs this metaphor repeatedly throughout his writings. As many commentators have acknowledged in their studies (Morley 2002, Lennon 2015, Mazis 2016, Dufourcq 2018), this metaphor implies that there is an intimate and inseparable relation between perception and imagination as well as between the real and the imaginary. Precisely because perceptual things are given to us as pregnant with sense, it falls upon the painter to disclose this sense by making it available to vision. Or, as Merleau-Ponty remarks, "the painter's vision is a continued birth" (Merleau-Ponty 1964a, 168). Here, we face a peculiar interrelation of receptivity and spontaneity, an interrelation which Merleau-Ponty himself describes in *The Visible and Invisible* with reference to painting by saying that Being, which is more than all painting, "appears as containing everything that will ever be said, and yet leaving us to create it" (Merleau-Ponty 1968, 170). As far as the ontology of painting is concerned, we can take this to mean that not only the visible, but also the invisible is given to the senses, yet one must creatively bring it to expression. The painter must "lend his body to the world" (Merleau-Ponty 1964a, 162) so that the pregnant sense ascribed to the visible can come to expression. As Merleau-Ponty shows in "Eye and Mind," a painter (through practice, of course) enables himself to participate in Being without restrictions. This self-opening to Being enables the painter to disclose the imaginary texture of the real.

---

[120] As Richard Kearney once put it, "imagination may, he [Merleau-Ponty — SG] believed, boast of a privileged access to the hidden dimensions of Being — what in his later writings he terms 'the invisible.' The invisible, he [Merleau-Ponty — SG] says, can be imagined, but it cannot be seen" (Kearney 1998, 121).

What, then, is productive imagination from the perspective of Merleau-Ponty's late phenomenology? It turns out to be distinctly transcendental in that it discloses the conditions of visibility; it also turns out to be ontological in that it brings to light the ontological unity-in-difference of the world and the body; and yet it is not spontaneous, nor is it rooted in transcendental subjectivity. For this reason, as Merleau-Ponty remarks in the "Working Notes" to *The Visible and the Invisible*, one should not think of productive imagination as a matter of performing syntheses.[121] As Kathleen Lennon puts it while addressing productive imagination in Merleau-Ponty, "the productive imagination here is bodily, and it does, not so much impose form, as take up form, as a consequence of its sensitivity to the world in which it is placed" (Lennon 2018, 123).[122] Taking this into account, one can speak of productive imagination in Merleau-Ponty's late work, in general, and in "Eye and Mind," in particular, as a concealed dimension of our intentional relation to the world, a dimension through which embodied subjectivity relates to what remains invisible in the visible. In turn, this opens up the further possibility of inquiring into how the imaginary is made possible by the very nature of things, and not by the apparently arbitrary faculty, identified as imagination (see Dufourcq 2018, 130). Productive imagination is not to be thought of as an exclusively spontaneous faculty; it does not produce anything *ex nihilo*, nor does it impose any kind of categorial form on presumably pregiven indeterminate data. Rather, it manifests itself as a disclosive/creative intentional

---

[121]   "If one starts from the visible and the vision, the sensible and the sensing, one acquires a wholly new idea of the 'subjectivity': there are no longer 'syntheses,' there is a contact with being through its modulations, or its reliefs" (Merleau-Ponty 1968, 269).

[122]   As Lennon puts it in her earlier study while focusing on Merleau-Ponty's philosophy of painting, a painting "is not expressive of an inner subjectivity, but of the world thinking itself through the painter" (Lennon 2015, 47). Indeed, as seen from the standpoint of Merleau-Ponty's ontological monism, it is a matter of confusion to suggest that the painter brings the world to expression. It is more accurate to describe the event of painting as the world coming to expression through the painter.

relation to the world. It is both *dialogical* and *dialectical*.[123] Being at the same time receptive and creative, it offers embodied subjectivity the possibility of grasping the shape of the world as it manifests itself in our embodied encounter with it. It would therefore be a mistake to think of productive imagination in the framework of Merleau-Ponty's phenomenology in terms of sense-constitution. Relying on the distinction that Merleau-Ponty draws between constitution and institution (see Merleau-Ponty 2010a), we can trace how imaginary dimensions are encountered in the sociohistorical field, which leads to the consequence that productive imagination is not only bodily, but also sociocultural. The imaginary is encountered as deposited. As Merleau-Ponty emphasizes in his *Lectures on Institution*, delivered at the *Collège de France* in 1954-1955, the intersubjective field is "our milieu, *our hinge*" (Merleau-Ponty 2010a, 123). The imaginaries that we encounter in the sociohistorical world are instituted imaginaries. They are the social residues that reflect the embodied encounters with the world. Productive imagination within such a framework turns out to be a matter of relating to such imaginary textures of the real, a matter of sense-releasement, or, more precisely, of the world disclosure that grasps what Merleau-Ponty identifies as the invisible dimension, understood as the inner framework and secret counterpart of the visible. We can take this to mean that productive imagination informs and animates all experience by binding embodied subjectivity to the imaginary texture of the real. Productive imagination is a *sui generis* mode of intentionality through which embodied subjectivity relates to what Merleau-Ponty, in *The Visible and the Invisible*, calls "an operative imaginary"—that imaginary, which forms the latent depth in the perceived world and which is "indispensable for the definition of Being itself" (Merleau-Ponty 1968, 85). Productive imagination enables us to relate to "the visible as in-visible" (Merleau-Ponty 1968,

---

123   In this regard, Merleau-Ponty's ontology of the imaginary manifests a close affinity to Bachelard's material imagination. As Richard Kearney (1998, 127) puts it, "Merleau-Ponty and Bachelard declared the primary function of the imagination to be a dialogue between inside and outside, between the being that is in the world and the world that being is in: a reciprocity rooted in a fundamental Being which is in both."

242), which in effect means that the invisible is not the nonvisible, but the "immense latent content" (Merleau-Ponty 1968, 114) that belongs to the visible. Borrowing a turn of phrase from Richard Kearney, one could say that while reproductive imagination renounces the visible, productive imagination redeems it by disclosing its in-visible genesis (see Kearney 1998, 125).

As Annabelle Dufourq insightfully shows in a recent contribution, Merleau-Ponty's late philosophy of the imagination enables us to "stretch the limits of productive imagination by investigating its ontological roots" (Dufourq 2018, 130). She goes on to claim that Merleau-Ponty's analysis is revolutionary, and for two fundamental reasons: it suggests that "the imaginary possesses a genuine flesh and is a particular mode of the being of things and persons themselves rather than a mere figment of a subjective faculty" and it "challenges the classical notion of reality in order to unveil the dimension of unreality, instability, faith, and indecisiveness that is an integral part of it" (Dufourq 2018, 130-131). Within such a framework, we are invited to rethink the nature of productive imagination as a disclosive form of intentionality, which is both transcendental and ontological. As a mode of an intentional relation to the world, productive imagination *responds* to the imaginary dimensions that are present in things themselves. With reference to the distinction between the "world side" and the "subject side" (see Merleau-Ponty 2010b, 124), one has good reasons to maintain that productive imagination is intentionally correlated with the imaginary, understood as an ontological and transcendental texture of reality, or, as Merleau-Ponty also puts it, as the invisible dimension of the visible. If phenomenality can be considered to be an integral part of the being of reality, then the imaginary, understood as the intentional correlate of productive imagination, is a no-less real dimension of things themselves. We face here a transcendental ontology of the imaginary brought to its highest pitch: if the visible necessarily entails the invisible dimension, then every being, without exception, must entail an imaginary texture, which, in turn, clarifies why in the concluding sentences of "Eye and Mind" Merleau-Ponty would so confidently maintain that "no painting comes to be the painting" and that paintings "have almost all their life still before them" (Merleau-Ponty 1964a, 190).

Conclusion

This chapter traced the development of Merleau-Ponty's phenomenology of imagination from his early to his late period. It offered a systematic and comprehensive account while paying close attention to the main features of Merleau-Ponty's phenomenology of imagination.[124] The analysis here offered made clear that even though Merleau-Ponty never aimed to offer a systematic and comprehensive account of the imagination, his phenomenological investigations provide us with deep, radical insights into the nature and structure of imagination. These insights are genuinely groundbreaking when we reflect on their ontological and transcendental meaning and significance. To this day, however, it is still uncommon to interpret Merleau-Ponty's phenomenology of imagination as a unique philosophy of productive imagination. This is unfortunate, for it is just not possible to speak of imagination in an unqualified way in the framework of Merleau-Ponty's thought. When, for instance, Richard Kearney writes that "Merleau-Ponty brings imagination back to life by demonstrating that imagination never left real life in the first place" (Kearney 1998, 135), his claim is correct insofar as productive imagination is concerned (although not reproductive imagination). Yet, we find reflections on both types of imagination in Merleau-Ponty's writings, and one must be attentive to these differences.[125]

---

[124] Needless to say, within the confines of a single chapter, it is not possible to be attentive to all of the details of Merleau-Ponty's conception. I would like to draw the readers' attention to a recent study by Glen Mazis (See Mazis 2016). Focused only on Merleau-Ponty, it provides a more detailed picture and pays special attention to virtually all of the relevant comments that Merleau-Ponty makes about imagination.

[125] To use but one example, when in the concluding paragraph of "Eye and Mind" Merleau-Ponty speaks about "spurious phantasy" (*faux imaginaire*), he clearly has in mind reproductive imagination, rather than productive imagination, that is, a kind of phantasy which is deprived of ontological significance.

My goal in this chapter was to show that it is possible to do justice to Merleau-Ponty's multifaceted account of imagination by interpreting it as a phenomenologically and ontologically oriented reflection on reproductive and productive imagination. Even though Merleau-Ponty does not speak explicitly about productive imagination—a clear conceptual distinction between different types of imagination is missing from his writings—his philosophy of the imagination is first and foremost a philosophy of productive imagination. According to the interpretation here proposed, in Merleau-Ponty's writings, productive imagination should no longer be conceptualized as a subjective faculty of syntheses that impose a categorial form on pregiven sensory materials, but it should be conceptualized, instead, as a disclosive and responsive— that is, dialogical and dialectical—intentional relation to the world that binds the embodied subjectivity to the transcendental and on-tological dimensions of the visible world—to the invisible dimension that lies at the heart of the visible.

CHAPTER VII
From Phenomenology to Hermeneutics: Paul Ricœur's Philosophy of Productive Imagination

Introduction

While Merleau-Ponty is the philosopher of perception, Ricœur is the philosopher of imagination, and more precisely, of productive imagination. As has been noted by a number of Ricœur scholars, the concept of productive imagination is a key concept of his philosophy and functions as the backbone of his entire work (for example, Taylor 2006, Almaric 2013, Dierckxsens 2018). When we reflect on his philosophy of imagination, we do not need to limit ourselves to an analysis of hidden clues; we do not need to follow the thread of implicit meaning, but can, instead, focus on his explicit reflections. While Chapter VII will focus on Ricœur's phenomenology of productive imagination as it appears in his published writings, Chapter VIII will supplement this analysis with a further investigation of Ricœur's so-far unpublished lectures on imagination, which Ricœur delivered at the University of Chicago in 1975, and which can, without any exaggeration, be considered to be one of his most important contributions to the phenomenologically-oriented philosophy of productive imagination.

Five tasks guide this chapter. First, I will begin by addressing imagination's seemingly paradoxical structure. I will argue that imagination opens a path that leads the subject in two opposite directions. On the one hand, it provides the subject with the freedom to flee the inhabited surroundings and thereby establishes a distance the subject can consciously take towards the world. On the other hand, imagination provides the subject with the powers to refashion its surroundings, that is, to constitute as well as reconstitute its socio-cultural world. Second, I will contend that most philosophical analyses of the imagination leave this apparent paradox unexplored and that insofar as this paradox remains unsettled, we are left with a truncated account of imagination. Third, I will contend that Ricœur is the only thinker to have addressed the paradoxical structure of imagination explicitly. In my analysis, I will focus on Ricœur's critique of the reproductive model of imagination and on his own alternative — the phenomenologico-hermeneutical account of productive imagination. Fourth, I will subject Ricœur's conception of productive imagination to a critique that relies upon the principles of classical phenomenology, which I have already presented in the earlier chapters. The goal of this critique is to open a path to a more comprehensive understanding of the paradox in question. Finally, I will conclude by spelling out some implications that follow from such a phenomenological engagement with Ricœur's philosophy of imagination.

The Paradox of Irreality

On the one hand, we can identify imagination as having an innocent capacity to intend either non-existent or absent objects, which remain cut off from our actual surroundings. Imagination enables us to escape from the confines of everyday reality, thereby freeing us from the bondage to our surroundings and transporting us into non-existent worlds, which are entirely cut off from actuality. Imagination has the capacity to empower the subject with a profound sense of freedom, which is strong enough to break the limits of what is actual and what is real. In what follows, I will call this element *the utopian tendency of imagination*: what is given in imagination remains without place within the horizon of actuality.

On the other hand, besides enabling the subject to escape the boundaries of actuality, imagination also empowers the subject to (re)constitute the surrounding world. If, following the first tendency, we were to liken an imaginative experience to a dream, then with the second tendency in mind, we could say, furthermore, that the dream in question does not contain content that merely remains in a dreamlike state — but, rather, that it strives to be realized. Imagination puts into question what presently exists. It provides the incentive to (re)constitute the subject's socio-historical reality. Imagination is thus by far not innocent. Rather, its tremendous force, and potentially its danger as well, lies in its capacity to (re)shape the very world that embraces our everyday actions, feelings and thoughts. I will call this tendency *the constitutive tendency of imagination*.

Imagination thus embodies both the tendency to flee the world and the tendency to shape it. Are these two tendencies compatible with each other? How can one and the same power enable us to escape and, at the same time, to build, to flee and, at the same time, to form, to suspend and, at the same time, to constitute? With these questions, we stumble against a paradox, which I will call *the paradox of irreality*: We cannot doubt that imaginary objects are irreal even though we simultaneously recognize imagination's capacity to transform reality.

How are we to understand this paradox? We do not face here a contradiction, whose resolution would come at the price of cancelling one of the above-mentioned tendencies. We face, instead, a paradox similar to what Husserl identifies as the paradox of subjectivity, which he addresses in §53 and §54 of the *Crisis of European Sciences and Transcendental Phenomenology*. Husserl writes:

> How can a component part of the world, its human subjectivity, constitute the whole world, namely, constitute it as its intentional formation, one which has always already become what it is and continues to develop, formed by the universal interconnection of intentionally accomplishing subjectivity, while the latter, the subjects accomplishing in cooperation, are themselves only a partial formation within the total accomplishment? The subjective part of the world swallows up, so to speak, the whole world and thus itself too. What an absurdity! (Husserl 1970, 179-180)

We face a similar dilemma: How can imagination place the subject outside of the world as well as in the world? What an absurdity! However, just as in the case of the paradox of subjectivity, the task is not to resolve the paradox, but to recognize that it is necessary and thus irremovable, so also, in the case of the paradox of irreality, the paradox is similarly not that type of paradox which gets resolved. More precisely, the task is to realize that these seemingly irreconcilable determinations belong to the very essence of the phenomenon under scrutiny. Thus, to invoke the paradox of irreality is not to suggest that it is impossible for imagination to perform two apparently contradictory roles. Rather, just as in the case of the paradox of subjectivity, in our case also the task is to interpret the apparent paradox as a transcendental clue, which can generate an insight into the essential structure of the phenomenon. What can the paradox in question tell us about imagination? What must imagination be like if it is to appear to us in such a seemingly paradoxical form? With these questions in mind, it becomes important to see how the paradox of irreality has been addressed in phenomenological accounts of imagination.

Utopian and Constitutive Tendencies: Sartre, Castoriadis and Ricœur

In the present chapter, I will limit myself to a set of reflections on some phenomenological approaches to imagination that were not addressed in the previous chapters. Nonetheless, let me remark in passing that one could read the whole historical development of these phenomenological accounts of imagination as the continuous shifting of attention from one tendency of imagination to another. While Husserl's (2005) and Sartre's (1962 and 2004) contributions highlight, in an unprecedented way, imagination's utopian tendency, Merleau-Ponty's (1993a and 1993b), Bachelard's (1994) and Castoriadis' (1997) accounts underscore the constitutive tendency of imagination.

Sartre's classical studies of imagination offer the most forceful representation of the utopian tendency. Yet, by conceptualizing imagination in terms of its capacity to reach out to non-existent, absent objects, as well as objects that exist elsewhere, or which have only a neutralized existence (Sartre 2004, 12), Sartre has, in effect, suppressed the constitutive tendency of imagination. Indeed, in *L'imagination* (1936) and *L'imaginaire: Psychologie phénoménologique de l'imagination* (1940) — his two early works, which are exclusively dedicated to an analysis of imagination — Sartre interprets imagination as an escapist tendency to flee from actual problems and from the need to resolve them. Imagination is, for Sartre, all too similar to his conception of bad faith, which initiates a flight from facticity and liberates one from responsibility. In Sartre's final work, *L'Idiot de la famille*, we come across such a notion of imagination in the figure of Flaubert, who, because he is incapable of modifying his worldly circumstances, falls back upon an imaginary solution to his difficulties.

As Thomas Busch points out in his analysis of Sartre's and Ricœur's philosophies of imagination, besides such an escapist notion of imagination, in such works as *Qu'est-ce que la littérature?* and *Plaidoyer pour les intellectuels*, Sartre presents a significantly different understanding of imagination, which intimates that even though there is no prose without imagination, prose does not fall victim to the escapist tendency that lies at the heart of other arts, such as poetry, painting and music. "Unlike the poet," Busch writes, "the prose writer employs words as signs directing the reader to clear meanings in the process of communicating a judgment about this world. Literature lifts life from the inchoate level of the lived to the thematic" (Busch 1997, 512).

Beata Stawarska corroborates such a view. She argues that Sartre's philosophy of the imagination relies upon two significantly different sources. Besides offering a pictorial theory of imagination, which draws its inspiration from Husserl's phenomenology, Sartre also conceptualizes imagination as spontaneous and self-determined. This second conception relies upon Pierre Janet's work on obsessive patients (See Stawarska 2005). So also, Lior Levy maintains that not just reproductive but also productive imagination plays a significant role in Sartre's work, notably in his account of aesthetic experience (See Levy 2014).[126] Last but not least, in a recent contribution, Kwok-ying Lau demonstrates that even in Sartre's

---

[126] Here Levy was led to the conclusion that Ricœur's critique of Sartre's philosophy of imagination, which focuses only on reproductive imagination, remains partial and unconvincing. In contrast to Ricœur's reading of Sartre, Levy proceeds to demonstrate that Sartre develops a notion of productive imagination. Furthermore, she also suggests that Sartre develops a notion of narrative identity well before Ricœur and that much like Ricœur, Sartre also conceives of selfhood as inseparable from imagination. See also Levy 2019, where she develops a new interpretation of Sartre's early works on imagination and argues that, as it appears especially in Sartre's account of impersonation, imagination enriches and augments perception, rather than suspends or replaces it with mental images.

early work, we come across an implicit account of productive imagination. According to Lau, the different examples Sartre employs in his analysis provide evidence that Sartre understood the different kinds of artworks implicit in his conceptualization of productive imagination (see Lau 2018).

These analyses provide the basis to suggest that Sartre develops two significantly different conceptions of imagination. Using the terminology I established above, let me further characterize these conceptions as utopian and constitutive. Yet, we are still left with a question: What exactly is the relation between these two significantly different notions of imagination? In Sartre's work, this question remains unexplored.

In contrast to Sartre, Castoriadis — one of the most forceful representatives of the constitutive tendency — thematizes imagination almost exclusively as a *vis formandi*, which underlies all other human activities, experiences and thoughts.[127] "To put it bluntly," writes Castoriadis, "it is because radical imagination exists that 'reality' exists *for us* – exists *tout court* – and exists *as* it exists" (Castoriadis 1997, 321). Castoriadis draws a distinction between two fundamental forms of radical imagination — the imagination of a singular human being and the social imaginary. Following two paths — a psychoanalytic and a philosophical path — he argues that what makes imagination radical is the very fact that it creates *ex nihilo*. Yet, just as Sartre's strong emphasis on utopian imagination comes along with the recognition of the constitutive powers of imagination, so, also, Castoriadis does not lose sight of reproductive imagination even as he focuses on radical imagination. Castoriadis

---

[127] In a recent contribution, Suzi Adams addresses Castoriadis' early writings on imagination against the background of the phenomenological tradition, and especially against the background of Merleau-Ponty's work. As Adams has it, "a return to Castoriadis's earlier work on the imaginary element (and other writings of that period) gives greater scope to extend his engagement with hermeneutic-phenomenology, not only in relation to the world and the interpretative aspect of meaning/the imaginary (via the symbolic and also through a greater elucidation of the meaning qua meaning as underdetermined), but also in furthering an elucidation of the third aspect of meaning that Castoriadis emphasized more explicitly in his earlier account of the imaginary element: the being of doing" (Adams 2018, 181).

explicitly opposes radical imagination to what he calls "secondary imagination" — a concept that encompasses imitative, reproductive and combinatory imagination.[128] Nonetheless, the question concerning the exact relation of these two types of imagination remains in Castoriadis' works unexplored. Just like Sartre, Castoriadis also leaves us to wonder whether we are justified in thinking of imagination as a unified concept. Shouldn't we, rather, concede that this term is a homonym which covers both creative and recreative capacities that manifest themselves at both the individual and at the social levels?

By focusing on one dimension of imagination, both Sartre and Castoriadis, although in diametrically opposite ways, have suppressed its other dimension. In this regard, they both represent a tendency which is deeply entrenched in diverse philosophies of imagination. It would hardly be an exaggeration to suggest that a large majority of available philosophical reflections on imagination tend to focus either on the utopian, or the constitutive, dimension. Because of such an exclusive focus, these accounts do not clarify the full-fledged phenomenon of imagination.

Within such a context, Ricœur's phenomenology of imagination occupies a special place. In this chapter, I will take three steps. First, I will sketch Ricœur's reasons why no successful resolution has been offered so far to the paradox of irreality. Second, I will turn to Ricœur's solution to the dilemma at hand, indicating what I consider to be both its compelling as well as its contentious aspects. Third, I will highlight what I take to be an unnecessary hermeneutical limitation that Ricœur has imposed upon his phenomenology of imagination.

The Reproductive Model of Imagination

According to Ricœur, the main reason why in the history of philosophy one cannot find explicit analyses of the paradox of irreality derives from a long-standing and deep-rooted prejudice, which

---

[128] According to Castoriadis, the distinction between these two forms of imagination can already be found in Aristotle's *De Anima*. See Castoriadis 1997, 319-320.

invites us to view imagination as the power to generate copies of a pregiven reality. The origins of this prejudice can be traced back not only to ancient philosophical sources, such as Aristotle's *De Anima*, but also to common sense.[129] Besides encountering objects in our perceptual surroundings, we also imagine them when they are no longer in our field of perceptual experience. Yet, how do we see others in portraits, pictures, caricatures or in mere phantasy? We see them as copies, as replicas of how they either have, or could have, appeared in actuality.

Are we then to say that all imaginary objects are copies of a pregiven reality? Typical counter-examples spring to mind: the imaginary presentations of a centaur, a siren or a chimera might not be uncommon, yet nobody has ever encountered them in the actual world. Where do these images and phantasy representations come from? These standard counter-examples are coupled with no-less-standard reservations concerning the productive capacities of imagination. Recall Descartes' well-known argument: the basic elements that compose these imaginary objects are replicas of what we have already encountered in the perceptual world. These basic elements are copies of reality, even though their configurations are new.

Should we then say that the capacity to create new forms out of pregiven material is the very origin that underlies the constitutive dimension of imagination? Ricœur resists such an answer. One can reconstruct two reasons for this resistance. First and foremost, in direct contrast to Sartre (See Sartre 1962, 1), Ricœur maintains that all experiences, including acoustic, visual and tactile experiences, are based on a selective enterprise. All experiences are, in one form or another, "creative," although they are not creative enough to reconstitute our everyday worlds in accordance with our

---

[129] This should not be taken to mean that we do not come across implicit accounts of productive imagination in Ancient philosophy. See, in this regard, Baracchi 2019 and Humphreys 2019—contributions which demonstrate that Plato and Aristotle provide us with accounts of imagination, which, contrary to the widespread view, cannot be subsumed under the category of reproductive imagination. These accounts, Baracchi and Humphreys suggest, in important ways complement and correct modern conceptions of productive imagination.

aspirations, desires and dreams. Second, imagination appears less suitable to perform the constitutive function. In contrast to perceptual objects, all imaginary objects are irreal. Everything that is creative about imagination unfolds within the confines of imaginary worlds. Thus, to return to Sartre's famous example, if I imagine my friend Peter getting hit by a car in Berlin, it will be irreal blood that will spill out of his irreal body — a sight accompanied by the irreal despair that will mark the irreal face of the irreal driver. These two reasons invite one to conclude that the reproductive model leaves the constitutive dimension of imagination unexplained.

According to Ricœur, the reproductive model can only justify the utopian tendency, not the constitutive tendency of imagination. Indeed, if imagination can only reproduce what the subject of experience has encountered in the actual world, then it lacks the resources needed to constitute and reconstitute reality. Presumably, if we think of images as copies of reality, then we will end up thinking of imagination as exclusively reproductive and lose all grounds to meaningfully speak of productive imagination.

At this point, let us turn to Ricœur's alternative — the conceptual framework designed to reconcile the utopian and the constitutive dimensions of imagination. As we will see, Ricœur's alternative will prove to be a necessary detour that will enable us to revisit Ricœur's critique of the reproductive model of imagination.

The Productive Model of Imagination

According to Ricœur, reproductive imagination forms an almost exhaustive horizon of reflections on imagination in the history of philosophy. Here the word "almost" is necessary, since as Ricœur himself points out on a few occasions, one cannot ignore either Aristotle's analysis of tragedy[130] or Kant's reflections on productive

---

130 Ricœur interprets Aristotle's portrayal of tragedy as the earliest account of productive imagination. As George H. Taylor insightfully remarks, "for Aristotle, the tragedy is not a copy or reduplication of human life but on the contrary has a 'power of disclosure concerning reality.' Aristotle's conception of imagination is thus directed against Plato's notion of imagination as a shadow" (Taylor 2006, 96).

imagination in the first and the third *Critiques*.[131] Yet, according to Ricœur, the subsequent philosophical reflections on imagination have overlooked the far-reaching significance of productive imagination in Aristotle's thought. Such a view is unjustifiable, as the analysis of productive imagination in the previous chapters of this study plainly demonstrates. Richard Kearney is right to observe that "the most decisive prelude to Ricœur's hermeneutic reformulation of imagining was surely Martin Heidegger's analysis of the Kantian conception of 'transcendental imagination' in *Kant and the Problem of Metaphysics* (1929)" (Kearney 1988, 143). Admittedly, as we have seen, Heidegger did not wish to develop a new hermeneutic of imagination *per se*. Rather, he spoke of imagination in the Kantian context and subsequently aimed to subsume the Kantian imagination under such new concepts as original temporality and *Dasein*. Nonetheless, one cannot help but be surprised by the lack of explicit analyses of Heidegger's hermeneutical phenomenology of imagination in Ricœur's own writings.

Limiting ourselves to Ricœur's own references, we should also note that as far as Kant's notion of productive imagination is concerned, Ricœur makes the surprising conclusion that it is not as far-reaching as Aristotle's notion of productive imagination. This is because while Kant's reflections on productive imagination in the first *Critique* were exclusively guided by questions concerning the possibility of cognition of empirical objects, in the third *Critique*, productive imagination was conceived as entirely subjective, merely tied to aesthetic judgment and thus without any effect on reality (See Taylor 2006, 97). Within the Kantian framework, imagination cannot augment the empirical reality that we already inhabit.

---

[131]   There are two different notions of productive imagination in Kant's work. In the first *Critique*, productive imagination is meant to synthesize concepts and intuitions. By contrast, in the third *Critique* productive imagination strives for the beyond, even though it fails to be adequate to it. George H. Taylor remarks that in the *Lectures on Imagination*, Ricœur addresses both notions of productive imagination in Kant. As Taylor goes on to say, "agreeing with Gadamer that cognition and aesthetics should not remain separated, Ricœur considers the task after Kant is to build a unified concept of imagination that brings the cognitive and aesthetic dimensions together" (Taylor 2013b, 6).

Following in Aristotle's and Kant's footsteps, Ricœur himself has sought to thematize a new alternative to the reproductive model of imagination within four frameworks: that of poetic imagination, epistemological imagination, socio-political imagination and religious imagination. Since Ricœur's analysis of poetic imagination constitutes the theoretical foundation that underlies his investigations of all of the other forms of imagination,[132] in my following reflections I will exclusively focus on poetic imagination.

Besides thinking of images as replicas of a pregiven reality, we can also think of them as fictions. One can clarify the difference between replicas and fiction by juxtaposing two forms of nothingness — the nothingness of *absence* and the nothingness of *non-existence* (See Ricœur 1979a, 126). To think of imaginary objects as replicas is to think of them as absent: they could be present, yet they are not. By contrast, to think of imaginary objects as fictions is to conceive of them as non-existent: for principle reasons, these objects could not manifest themselves in our actual experience.[133]

Although fictions do not refer to reality in a reproductive fashion, they do not lose all reference to reality. According to one of the central points of Ricœur's philosophy of imagination, fictions refer to reality in a productive, that is, constitutive way. This is what Ricœur calls "the paradox of fiction" (Ricœur 1979a, 127): "knowing how to abandon the real, fiction also 'knows' how to (re)constitute it."[134]

---

[132]   "Ricœur's main thesis in the *Lectures on Imagination*," George H. Taylor remarks, "is that the productive imagination can most prototypically be found in fiction" (Taylor 2013a, 6). Or, as Ricœur himself puts it in these lectures, "because fictions don't reproduce a previous reality, they may produce a new reality. They are not bound by an original that precedes them" (Quoted from Taylor 2013a).

[133]   One could of course argue that such a clarification remains imprecise: It invites one to think of such imaginary creatures as unicorns, sirens or the above-mentioned centaurs and chimaeras, as though they were fictive objects. However, purely imaginary beings are built out of the very same materials that we encounter in the perceptual world. In this expanded sense, they exemplify reproductive rather than productive imagination, which conceives of images as replicas of given reality.

[134]   Or, as George H. Taylor puts it: "productive imagination discloses new forms of reality; it augments reality…. [P]roductive imagination is the *manifestation* of new reality rather than simply *adequation* to existing reality" (Taylor 2013a, 5).

It is important to emphasize that, according to Ricœur, the dialectical structure of fiction is *language-based* (see, for instance, Ricœur 1979a, 127 and Ricœur 1991, 121). It is precisely this structure that accounts for the possibility of productive imagination. In Ricœur's view, to make sense of the paradox of fiction one needs to conceptualize imagination in a novel framework — not that of perception, but, rather, that of language. One needs to think of images not as pale copies of perceptions, but as intuitive fulfillments that can accompany the metaphorical use of language. Such, then, is Ricœur's thesis: a hermeneutical theory of metaphor can provide the fundamental clarification of the productive dimension of imagination (See Ricœur 1977, 173-216).

So as to understand the reasoning that underlies this claim, let us consider the metaphorical expression "time is a thief" as our guiding example. Although at the literal level, this expression is meaningless, the goal of the listener is to intend meaning where, literally, there is none. For this to take place, the listener must experience a clash between essentially different semantic fields. This is what Ricœur, building on Jean Cohen's analysis (See Ricœur 1977, 194), calls "predicative impertinence" — an experience of a shock, which, in turn, invites the subject to search for ways to liberate herself from it. We experience liberation from this shock as the endeavor to restructure our semantic field and to grasp meaning at the very core of immediate semantic meaninglessness. We understand metaphors only insofar as we overcome the original meaninglessness and reconstitute meaning on the basis of the restructured semantic field. On the basis of such a restructuring, we learn how to *see* time as a thief, an enemy as a wolf or sunrise as a new beginning. We learn how to interpret expressions as meaningful even though they are *literally* meaningless. Yet, what is this power that enables one to make sense of the metaphorical use of language? It is nothing other than productive imagination. As Ricœur maintains, "imagination is the apperception, the sudden insight, of a new predicative pertinence, specifically a pertinence within impertinence" (Ricœur 1979a, 131). We see here that for Ricœur, metaphor functions analogously to how the schema functions in Kant's writings. The schematism of metaphor gives rise to "the matrix of a new semantic pertinence that is born out of the dismantling of semantic networks caused by the shock of contradiction" (Ricœur 1977, 199). This schematism "turns imagination into the place where the figurative meaning emerges in the interplay of identity and difference" (Ricœur 1977, 199-200). In his *Time and Narrative*, Ricœur further develops such a conception of the schematism of imagination from the metaphorical act to the larger framework of a narrative act. We face here an extension of the same logic from the unit of the word (symbol), to that of a sentence (metaphor) to that of a text as a whole (narrative) (see, in this regard, Kearney 1998, 162).

To understand a metaphor, one needs to produce predicative compatibility on the grounds of a more primitive predicative incompatibility. This does not mean that the production of a novel predicative compatibility erases the former incompatibility. Rather, to understand a metaphor is to see meaning while still retaining the sense of a more original meaninglessness. This grounding of harmony in disharmony enables one to grasp the essential difference between metaphorical and literal uses of language. In contrast to metaphorical meaning, literal meaning invokes no tension between the substrate and the predicate, word and sentence, sentence and paragraph, etc.

Ricœur's hermeneutical account of the genesis of metaphor not only offers a highly significant contribution to our understanding of metaphor and imagination at large; it also introduces a deep-seated ambivalence. On the one hand, when Ricœur writes that "images are spoken before they are seen" (Ricœur 1979a, 129), or when he intimates that images are not derived from perception, but rather from language (ibid.), he invites one to interpret his hermeneutical approach as a suggestion that language constitutes the origin of all imagination, be it productive or reproductive.[135] On the other hand, Ricœur's admission that imagination resting upon the

---

[135] As Kearney remarks, "if images are *spoken* before they are *seen*, as Ricœur maintains, they can no longer be construed as quasi-material residues of perception (as empiricists believed), nor indeed as neutralizations or negations of perception (as eidetic phenomenology tended to believe)" (Kearney 1998, 147).

metaphorical use of language "is doubtlessly the productive, sche-matizing imagination" (Ricœur 1979a, 132), as well as his more re-served proclamation that "we *see* some images only to the extent that we first *hear* them" (Ricœur 1979a, 134), suggests something quite different, namely, that language constitutes the origin of pro-ductive, not reproductive, imagination. As the quoted passages show, one can derive textual evidence to support both readings. However, as far as the actual claims are concerned, the second read-ing is more compelling, if only because it does not deny the plain fact that imagination does not always and necessarily rely upon lan-guage.[136]

My following analysis will be grounded upon the conjecture that Ricœur sees the rootedness of imagination in metaphorical lan-guage as a peculiarity of productive imagination. While, for Kant, the function of productive imagination is to provide an image for a concept, for Ricœur the function is to generate images that accom-pany the metaphorical use of language.[137] Put in phenomenological terms, the task of productive imagination is that of bringing meta-phorical expressions to their intuitive fulfillment. Yet, that which is brought to fulfillment remains bound to language. So as to empha-size this founded nature of productive imagination, Ricœur draws a distinction between "free" and "bound" images (See Ricœur 1977,

---

[136]   At this point, one might object that Ricœur does not need to subscribe to such a narrow conception of language as the one I have attributed to him in my anal-ysis. Since not only Husserl's but also Heidegger's influence on Ricœur's thought is undeniable, should one not broaden the conception of language in a Heideggerian fashion by conceiving of language as the "house of Being," that is, as that which allows for meaningful being-in-the-world? Yet, as soon as lan-guage is conceived in such a broad way, Ricœur's conception of productive im-agination loses its *specificity* and *legitimacy*. It loses its specificity because it be-comes no longer clear how one is to distinguish productive imagination from reproductive imagination, for clearly, both forms of imaginations unfold within the horizon of Dasein's meaningful being-in-the-world. Another reason why it loses its legitimacy is because, as soon as language is conceived in a broad her-meneutical way, it no longer becomes clear why productive imagination is to be grounded in a theory of metaphor.

[137]   As Ricœur puts it in the context of his analysis of Paul Henle's theory of meta-phor, "if metaphor adds nothing to the description of the world, at least it adds to the way in which we perceive; and this is the poetic function of metaphor" (Ricœur 1977, 190).

211 and 1979a, 133), understanding the difference between them in a twofold way. First, while free images can be seen before they can be spoken, bound images must be spoken before they are seen. We can take this to mean that bound images are bound to language. Second, while free images are characteristic of reproductive imagination, bound images are typical of productive imagination.

What exactly does it mean to see the world as a stage or to drown in a sea of grief? First and foremost, this means to have bound images, which, in turn, means that these images are founded upon the metaphorical use of language. Moreover, to see an image as a bound image is not merely to see this or that thing, but rather to *see-something-as-something-other-than-it-is*. Within the horizon of perception, to see-something-as-something-other-than-it-is is to suffer from illusory consciousness. Yet, imaginary consciousness is not illusory. Imaginary consciousness neutralizes the reality of its object by lifting it out of the actual world. The imaginary seeing-something-*as-something-else* unfolds within an irreal world that is lifted above the actual one. Imagination is the power that enables the subject of experience to constitute such an irreal world. So as to highlight this irreal horizon of productive imagination, Ricœur speaks of "a sort of *epoché* of the real," of the "state of non-engagement" and of a "neutralized atmosphere" (Ricœur 1979a, 134). Within such a bracketed framework, the subject of experience obtains the freedom not only to devise new metaphors, but also to try out new ideas and values.

The *epoché* of the real constitutes only the first step that the metaphorical employment of language enables one to take. The second step, if taken, is far more important insofar as the full-fledged significance of productive imagination is concerned. Having escaped the confines of reality, productive imagination can also offer its re-description. With this second step in mind, we come to face the central thesis of Ricœur's hermeneutic phenomenology of imagination: "this positive function of fiction, of which the *epoché* is the negative condition, is only understood when the fecundity of the imagination is clearly linked to that of language, as exemplified by the metaphorical process" (Ricœur 1979a, 134). It thereby becomes understandable why Richard Kearney would maintain that "Ricœur's hermeneutic discussion of the imaginative function … represents the single most direct reorientation of a phenomenology of imagining towards a hermeneutics of imagining" (Kearney 1998, 145). According to the central thesis of Ricœur's philosophy of imagination, one must look beyond the first-order reference of empirical reality so as to disclose the second-order reference of possible worlds.

Pre-Predicative Imagination and the Genesis of Metaphors

Ricœur's emphasis on the primacy of language in the framework of his philosophy of imagination is meant to replace the primacy that classical phenomenology, from Husserl to Merleau-Ponty, has granted to pre-predicative experience. According to Ricœur, for as long as we refuse to recognize the primacy of language, we will continue to limit imagination to its reproductive function and thus fail to take productive imagination into account. For this very reason, the guiding question that underlies Ricœur's philosophy of imagination reads as follows: "if an image is not derived from perception, how can it be derived from language?" (Ricœur 1991, 121)

This shift from perception to language underlies Ricœur's understanding of the paradox of irreality. In the hermeneutical framework, the utopian tendency turns out to be a necessary detour that imagination takes so as to fulfill its constitutive function. The utopian tendency turns out to be a peculiar *epoché* of the real, without which a novel description of reality would not be possible. Such an understanding of the paradox in question relies upon the introduction of a new rupture at the heart of imagination, a rupture between reproductive and productive imagination.

Thus, one needs to ask, is it really true that perception and language constitute two irreconcilable origins of images? The answer appears self-evident insofar as productive imagination is identified with fiction and insofar as fiction is conceived as a language-based achievement. Yet besides being the ground that underlies our capacity to re-describe reality, is fiction not also an accomplishment that itself rests upon more rudimentary presuppositions, which ultimately reach back to what in classical phenomenology is identified as pre-predicative experience?[138]

In what follows, I would like to open up a conceptual space that allows for the reconciliation of the tension between Ricœur's philosophy of imagination, on the one hand, and classical phenomenology of imagination, on the other hand. With this in mind, I would like to supplement Ricœur's hermeneutical critique of phenomenology with a phenomenological critique of Ricœur's hermeneutics. Such a critique is geared toward the establishment of two closely related claims. First, I want to contend that metaphor is not the ultimate ground of productive imagination. Rather, the metaphorical employment of language itself relies upon more basic intuitive capacities, which antedate and motivate the genesis of metaphors. The second thesis directly springs from the first one: because it is not the ground of productive imagination, metaphor should be conceived as one particular modality of productive imagination. Since these two issues are closely related, I will address each alongside the other.

Ricœur's philosophy of imagination is built upon a theory of metaphor, which is focused upon how metaphors are read, heard and understood. By posing the question in such a manner, one presupposes the givenness of metaphors without inquiring into their generation. In a sense, such a strategy is understandable: we are all born into particular languages, which are not of our own making and which are metaphorical through and through. For this reason alone, we have always already come across metaphors and understood them before we have obtained the capacity to devise them. According to such an argument, our capacity to generate metaphors is reproductive of our more basic ability to understand them. Thus, it seems that, as Ricœur puts it, "images are spoken [or better, *heard*] before they are seen" (Ricœur 1991, 121). Or, as Ricœur puts it in his lectures on imagination, which we will address in greater detail in the next chapter,

---

[138]   For the most detailed account of pre-predicative experience in classical phenomenology, see Husserl 1973b.

> This is my argument: when we start from reproductive imagination, there is already an original, and therefore the main thrust of the analysis is on the negative side. I retreat from the original; all the spontaneity of imagination is exhausted in producing the nothingness alongside reality, in the margin of reality. The imaginary life is more or less described as a flight, as an escape. By contrast, if we start with an image without an original, then we may discover a kind of second ontology that is not the ontology of the original but the ontology displayed by the image itself, because it has no original (Ricœur, unpublished, 16:1).

Here we come across the most fundamental difference between classical Husserlian phenomenology and Ricœur's hermeneutical phenomenology. While the former heavily relies on the distinction between pre-predicative and predicative experience, the latter considers this distinction to be illegitimate. *The image itself has no original*, claims Ricœur, which in effect means that the second ontology is the only ontology there is. As George H. Taylor puts with reference to Ricœur's productive imagination, "the connection between language and experience goes all the way down" (Taylor 2018, 171).

Ricœur's view that language and experience are inseparable comes close to Hans-Georg Gadamer's account of the metaphorical process of concept formation as presented in the Third Part of *Truth and Method* (see Gadamer 2004, 427-433). According to Gadamer, concept formation is to be understood as a metaphorical rather than a logical process. Arguing against the view that the process of concept formation depends either on abstraction or on induction, Gadamer maintains that all concept formation relies on the "metaphoricity of language" (Gadamer 2004, 431). Ricœur refers to Gadamer's account of metaphorical concept formation with strong approval both in his *The Rule of Metaphor* (Ricœur 1975, 24) and *Lectures on Imagination* (Ricœur, unpublished, 16:12-13). According to Ricœur, the idea of an initial metaphorical impulse destroys the opposition between the "ordinary" and the "strange," as well as the "proper" and the "figurative" in language, by suggesting the idea that "order itself proceeds from the metaphorical constitution of semantic fields, which themselves give rise to genus and species" (Ricœur 1975, 24). Thus, for Ricœur, much like it is for Gadamer, the distinction between the predicative and the pre-predicative is unsustainable: it is metaphor all the way down.[139]

Nonetheless, even if one accepts this line of reasoning, one cannot avoid asking, what exactly is involved in the metaphorical process of concept formation? Clearly, it cannot be just a question of blindly introducing semantic impertinence with an empty hope that on this basis alone one will come to broaden one's semantic field and establish a new type of semantic pertinence. Clearly, there must be a certain guiding sense that underlies the generation of metaphors. Using phenomenological vocabulary, one could describe this guiding sense as a particular kind of intention, which can be either fulfilled or disappointed. The metaphorical process is born out of a specific kind of speechless intention, which strives to be fulfilled in language, even though no literal expression can bring it to fulfillment. In this context, it is helpful to recall Aristotle's observation at the end of the *Poetics*: "the greatest thing by far is to be a master of metaphor. It is the one thing that cannot be learnt from

---

[139] With reference to Gadamer's analysis, Ricœur poses the following hypothesis in *The Rule of Metaphor*: "Is there not, in Gadamer's terms, a 'metaphoric' at work at the origin of logical thought, at the root of all classification?" (Ricœur 1975, 24) In his recent contribution, George H. Taylor presents a compelling thesis by suggesting that Ricœur broadens his account of metaphor in his subsequent account of figuration in *Time and Narrative*. This, in turn, allows one to evaluate his philosophy of productive imagination by reading Ricœur backwards, as it were, from *Truth and Narrative* to his earlier works in the 1970s. Such an interpretive approach ultimately means that Ricœur's philosophy of productive imagination is in truth a philosophy of figuration, or more precisely, of pre-figuration, configuration and re-figuration. Within such an interpretive framework, Taylor suggests that, with regard to Ricœur's hypothetical question quoted above, we can substitute the term "figuration" for "metaphoric": "is there not a *figuration* at work at the origin of logical thought, at the root of all classification?" (Taylor 2018, 169) This transformation allows Taylor to argue that "figuration acts as a common root between the impression (the experiential and the conceptual (form) because the experiential, whether as impression or as human action, is always linguistically implicated and structured. It is figured" (Taylor 2018, 171). Although I find Taylor's interpretation of Ricœur's philosophy of productive imagination to be deeply compelling, in the present study I will not engage Ricœur's *Time and Narrative* at any great length or in any great depth. A detailed study of this work will have to wait for another occasion. My goal here is rather to pursue novel points of intersection between classical phenomenology of imagination, on the one hand, and hermeneutic phenomenology of imagination, on the other hand.

others; and it is also a sign of genius, since a good metaphor implies an *intuitive perception* of the similarity in dissimilars" (Aristotle 2001, 1459a 5-8 [my emphasis]).[140] For Aristotle, without intuitive perception, there would be no metaphors. In a good sense, and in direct contrast to Ricœur, *we see images before we speak them.*

While Ricœur's essays on the philosophy of imagination bypass the question concerning the genesis of metaphors, in *The Rule of Metaphor*, Ricœur turns to this question on a few occasions. First, in the context of his critique of Roman Jakobson (see Ricœur 1977, 174-180), Ricœur maintains that a semiotic theory, which conceives of metaphor as a substitution of one term for another, is incapable of taking into account the difference between newly invented metaphors and metaphors in common use. Jakobson understands the use of metaphors as a selection of a particular term from a pool of various terms, a substitution that is based on similarity. To this Ricœur responds: "in order that selection [of different terms] itself be free, it must result from an original combination created by the context and therefore distinct from pre-formed combinations within the code" (Ricœur 1977, 180). What is the combination of images to which Ricœur here refers and what is the context of which he here speaks? Ricœur's goal is not to return from a semiotic account of language to pre-predicative experience, but rather to offer reasons to supplement the semiotic account with a semantic account of discourse. It is the latter, not the former, that can account for newly invented metaphors. However, in the whole corpus of his works, Ricœur never provides a detailed account of how discourse can be conceived as the ground for the generation of metaphors.

In fact, one could argue that Ricœur himself provides good reasons to reject the claim that discourse constitutes the origin of metaphors. This brings us to the second occasion on which, in *The Rule of Metaphor*, Ricœur turns to the generation of metaphors. This time we are faced with Ricœur's argument that resemblance is both a cause and an effect of metaphor. According to Ricœur, one can only appreciate such an overwhelming role of resemblance if one

---

[140]   For Ricœur's analysis of this passage, see Ricœur 1977, 192, and Ricœur 1978, 144.

takes into account the inherently paradoxical nature of metaphor. To clarify the paradox in question, Ricœur maintains that, just as there is no metaphor without seeing the similar, so also no seeing of the similar is possible without its construction (See Ricœur 1977, 195). This coupling of seeing and constructing invites one to concede that the origin of metaphor lies in pre-predicative experience. One is invited to admit that a perceptual intuiting of the similar initiates the generation of metaphor: this perceptual intuiting lacks fullness and precision, which can only be derived from language. However, Ricœur is quick to dismiss such a possibility.[141] He maintains that if seeing and constructing are necessary elements of the generation of metaphor, then this generation must be inherently discursive. But, if this is so, then the metaphorical process must begin not with seeing but rather with constructing, which Ricœur ultimately understands as a poetic enterprise. Yet, this conclusion simply does not follow from the evidence Ricœur supplies, which leaves the reasoning for why one should favor this conclusion unexplained. Moreover, this conclusion undermines the very thesis that Ricœur wants to establish, namely, that resemblance is not only an effect, but also the cause that underlies the generation of metaphor.

Ricœur's arguments to the contrary notwithstanding, there are good reasons to maintain that not only language-based, but also pre-predicative imagination can be both reproductive and, at the same time, productive.[142] So as to provide this claim with further support, allow me to introduce three structural analogies between the two kinds of imagination. First, as we saw, to constitute a

---

[141]   In his "The Metaphorical Process as Cognition, Imagination, and Feeling," Ricœur calls such a possibility "bad psychology" (Ricœur 1978, 155), interpreting it in a Humean rather than in a phenomenological way.

[142]   In the present context, the concept of pre-predicative imagination refers to "sensory" imagination, that is, that kind of experience, which in a sensory mode (for example, visual or aural) intends an object that is not actually present. As Julia Jansen remarks, when phenomenologists turn to imagination, they mostly consider "sensory" imagination: "in order to emphasize its sensory and embodied dimension, they typically distinguish imagining something from entertaining its possibility merely in thought, which in other discourses is often referred to as 'propositional imagination', or 'imagining that'" (Jansen 2015).

metaphor, one must gather together the elements of language and assemble them in such a way that, at least at the literal level, appears to lack semantic justification. This capacity to assemble divergent elements of language parallels the capacity to assemble divergent elements of pre-predicative imagination. Here, I am alluding to the constitution of such imaginary objects as centaurs and chimeras. This constitution is based on imagination's capacity to assemble perceptual elements in a way that lacks "perceptual justification." Is it not one and the same power of imagination that manifests itself in diverse frameworks of experience? Moreover, is the unity that binds pre-predicative and language-based imagination obscured by Ricœur's sharp distinction between productive and reproductive imagination?

One might object that while pre-predicative imagination is only capable of constituting imaginary objects, language-based imagination constitutes fictive scenarios and scenes; and for this reason, the identification of pre-predicative imagination with reproductive imagination, as well as the identification of language-based imagination with productive imagination, is not only legitimate but also necessary. This objection brings us to the second analogy. It is important to stress that pre-predicative imagination is constitutive not only of irreal objects, but also of imaginary scenes. Basic examples should suffice: when I am exhausted, I can picture myself on the beach, enjoying the water, sand and sun; when I find my surroundings tedious, I can picture myself in an unfamiliar city, strolling through its beautiful streets, etc. The capacity to picture imaginary scenes is also built upon a peculiar *epoché*; it also presupposes a "state of non-engagement" and a "neutralized atmosphere," which Ricœur describes as a characteristic feature of productive imagination.

Third, not only language-based but also pre-predicative imagination can perform both utopian and constitute functions. Still, at the level of pre-predicative imagination, the *"epoché* of the real" now-and-again turns out to be the negative condition that underlies the productive role of imagination, which allows us to reconstitute our daily reality. Not only the utopian, but also the constitutive function of imagination can manifest itself at the level of pre-pre-dicative imagination that still lacks linguistic articulation. One is thereby invited to resist Ricœur's sharp distinction between pre-predicative and language-based imagination, and to contend, instead, that fiction is an elaborate and sophisticated form of productive imagination, whose roots can be traced back to the basic capacity to reconfigure the material that we borrow from our actual experience.

The Paradox of Irreality Revisited

Early on in this chapter, I asked how one is to understand the capacity of imagination to pull us out of the confines of the real and to transpose us into the irreal horizon that is cut off from actuality, alongside its other capacity to (re)constitute actuality. One cannot recognize the full force of imagination if one does not show how imagination can perform such seemingly contradictory functions. To the best of my knowledge, Ricœur is the only thinker to have addressed this paradox explicitly. According to Ricœur, the utopian element of imagination is a necessary negative condition that underlies its constitutive force. Without being utopian, imagination could not be constitutive.

Ricœur restores the unity of imagination that the paradox of irreality threatened to disrupt; however, at the same time, he disrupts this unity at a deeper level by introducing a seemingly irreconcilable breach between productive and reproductive imagination. Ricœur takes away with one hand what he has given with the other: he overcomes the dichotomy between utopian and constitutive tendencies of the imagination, yet only by introducing another, equally disruptive dichotomy between reproductive and productive imagination. In this regard, one is taken aback by the strange lack of parallelism between Ricœur's accounts of poetic imagination and socio-cultural imagination. In the framework of Ricœur's account of the socio-cultural imagination, utopia exemplifies productive imagination, while ideology represents reproductive imagination. As Ricœur argues in his *Lectures on Ideology and Utopia* (See Ricœur 1986), just as there is no ideology without utopia, so also there is no utopia without ideology. Yet, strangely, when it comes to poetic imagination, a similar kind of dialectic between productive and reproductive imagination is missing. Given this lack of parallelism, Ricœur's clarification of the paradox of irreality at the level of poetic imagination is regrettably restrictive. It enables one to make sense of the paradox in question, but it only enables this within a sphere that is strictly language-based. When it comes to dreams, daydreaming or non-language-based art – such as painting, dance and music – the hermeneutical justification appears to be ungrounded.[143]

My critical engagement in Ricœur's hermeneutical phenomenology of imagination is meant to broaden the horizon of hermeneutical reflections and thereby lend the hermeneutical insights greater significance. With this goal in mind, I argue that experience itself invites one to concede that the dialectic between the utopian and the constitutive tendencies is to be found not only at the level of language, but also at the level of pre-predicative imagination. Allow me to illustrate this by briefly turning to affective consciousness.[144] Spinoza, who recognized the affective significance of will and reason, famously maintained that "no affect can be restrained by the true knowledge of good and evil insofar as it is true, but only insofar as it is considered as an affect" (Spinoza 2002, 553). One can take this to mean that, according to Spinoza, if particular affects are

---

[143] To avoid confusion, I should note that Ricœur himself does recognize that productive imagination manifests itself outside of the language-based sphere. For instance, in his *Lectures on Imagination*, he refers to impressionism as a movement that embodies productive imagination. Impressionism creates "a new alphabet of colors capable of capturing the transient and fleeting with the magic of hidden correspondences. And once more reality was remade" (Ricœur, unpublished, 17:15). Yet, how exactly is one to reconcile this non-linguistic power of productive imagination with Ricœur's explicit emphasis that productive imagination is grounded in the metaphorical use of language? To the best of my knowledge, Ricœur does not answer this question.

[144] For Ricœur's own account of the affective dimensions of imagination, see especially Ricœur 1978, 155-158. Here, Ricœur distances himself from theories that ascribe a merely substitutive role to affection. According to these theories, imagination in general, and metaphor in particular, lack informative value, yet they cover up this lack with "informationless" imagery. In contrast to such a view, Ricœur argues that affection is irreducibly cognitive. To put the matter in the terms I have employed in this book, affection is *constitutive*.

to be overcome, they will be overcome not through pure will or pure reason, but rather through other affects, including intellectual joy (See Loydd 2008, 212). As Kathleen Lennon puts it in her brief commentary on this passage, "we cannot change people's way of looking at the world simply by offering them contrary facts. We need to offer them *alternative pictures* which make emotional and not just cognitive sense" (Lennon 2010, 387 [my emphasis]).

The expression "alternative pictures" is quite telling. Since pictures lack linguistic articulation, the expression suggests that the accomplishments of pre-predicative imagination have not just utopian, but also constitutive powers. By implication, if language-based imagination is constitutive as well (which it certainly is), then it entails the same powers that already lurk at the level of pre-predicative imagination.

Thus, within the framework of a phenomenological analysis of imagination, one can understand Spinoza's claim as follows: A pre-predicative presentation, which triggers one's passions and emotions in an immediate way, already entails affective and constitutive force. A pre-predicative presentation, which at first glance appears to be nothing more than a copy of a pregiven reality, has the affective power to (re)constitute our socio-cultural worlds. Isn't this the very thing one fears when one fears imagination? And does the tacit recognition of this state of affairs underlie one's unwillingness to salute the freedom of imagination as though it were nothing more than an innocent force, without any capacity to affect our actual worlds and actual experiences?

Not only language-based but also pre-predicative imagination has the power to lift the subject of experience out of the domain of everyday reality. One could metaphorically describe the back-and-forth movement between the utopian tendency of both pre-predicative and language-based imagination as the swinging movement of a pendulum. On the one hand, it is a retreat that can be followed by a return. On the other hand, the retreat in question can be interrupted mid-air: having transposed the subject into the irreal world, it need not manifest its effects upon reality. Yet, how could anyone know in advance if the constitutive element will follow the utopian one? Any answer to this question will have to rely upon prior knowledge of all the configurations of sense that the world could possibly take on. At least for the finite beings that we are, such knowledge is unattainable. Since this is the case, it becomes understandable how one and the same force can enable one to escape and, at the same time, to build, to flee and, at the same time, to form, to suspend and, at the same time, to constitute. Moreover, it becomes understandable how one and the same force can be seen as both innocent and threatening.

Conclusion

In place of a conclusion, I would like to touch upon two implications that follow from the foregoing analysis. The first implication concerns one of the most common claims made about Ricœur's philosophy in general. According to this claim, Ricœur is the philosopher who grafts hermeneutics onto phenomenology. I do not want to question the significance of such a philosophical endeavor. I do want to emphasize, however, that Ricœur's hermeneutic phenomenology presents us with an ongoing task and not with a finished accomplishment. Moreover, we are faced here with an endeavor, which in some frameworks has not been successfully carried out. My foregoing analysis shows that when it comes to the philosophy of imagination, Ricœur's analysis fluctuates between phenomenological and hermeneutical alternatives, without successfully resolving the tensions between them. Moreover, my analysis shows that in the framework of his philosophy of imagination, Ricœur does not graft hermeneutics onto phenomenology; it would be more accurate to claim the reverse, that, as far as his philosophy of the imagination is concerned, Ricœur grafts phenomenology onto hermeneutics. Thus, on the one hand, following hermeneutical principles, Ricœur dismisses the phenomenological claims regarding the primacy of pre-predicative experience: his philosophy of imagination presupposes the primacy of language. On the other hand, following phenomenological principles, Ricœur also maintains that philosophical accounts of imagination are accounts of different kinds of *seeing-as*, which Ricœur thematizes as the conceptual unity of the consciousness of sense and consciousness of images, and which he further qualifies as the sensible aspect of language itself (See Ricœur 1977, 212-213). One of my goals is to show that the tensions between these philosophical orientations continue to resonate in Ricœur's philosophy of imagination. These tensions leave us with the task of reconceptualizing the relation between phenomenology and hermeneutics. More precisely, one needs to rethink whether it is in fact possible to graft one tradition onto the other, or whether in some frameworks of analysis the traditions in question might not constitute two alternative paths, which now and again might lead in different directions.

The second implication concerns my contention that the origins of productive imagination already lurk at the level of pre-predicative experience, that is, at the level of perception's capacity to reconfigure pre-given material and thus to give rise to perceptual images of non-existent "things." As I emphasized in earlier chapters of this study, this realization motivates one to return to the very questions concerning perception and imagination that occupied a central place in classical phenomenological reflections. More precisely, we are once again led to ask, what exactly is pre-predicative experience and where exactly is one to locate its fundamental modes and limits, the recognition of which would enable one to distinguish perception from memory, anticipation, phantasy and image consciousness? And correlatively, what exactly is imagination, and what are its modes and limits, which make it possible to distinguish it from other related forms of intentional consciousness? Ricœur's repeated insistence that there is no such thing as pure perception (that is, that perception is always shot through with imagination[145]) provides a further impetus to address these questions.

"Thought does not like what is new," Ricœur remarks, "and does its best to reduce the new to the old" (Ricœur 1979a, 125). Let me conclude this chapter by saying that if one is to open up a fresh

---

[145]   As Ricœur puts it in his *Lectures on Imagination*, "[w]e can no longer oppose…imagining to seeing, if seeing is itself a way of imagining, interpreting, or thinking" (Ricœur, unpublished, 9:1).

dialogue between phenomenology and hermeneutics, one must do so by turning back to classical phenomenological problems, which in the purported grafting of hermeneutics onto phenomenology have remained either suppressed or overlooked. I will come back to this in the concluding chapter of this study. But, first, let us turn to Ricœur's unpublished lectures on imagination and address them against the background of Sartre's writings on the imagination.

CHAPTER VIII
From Jean-Paul Sartre to Paul Ricœur:
Ricœur's Lectures on Imagination Revisited

Introduction

While in Chapter VII I outlined the key features of Ricœur's hermeneutic philosophy of the imagination with reference to his published writings, in this chapter I will supplement the foregoing
analysis by turning to Ricœur's so far unpublished lectures on the
imagination, which he delivered at the University of Chicago in the
fall semester of 1975. Ricœur delivered nineteen lectures on the imagination during this semester, starting on September 30th and ending on December 4th. This set of lectures was titled "Imagination as
a Philosophical Problem" and it was divided into two unequal
parts. The first part was historical: it was composed of fourteen lectures that addressed a number of thinkers: ancient, modern and
contemporary. The second part was thematic and was designed to
present Ricœur's own theory of fiction. The first fourteen lectures
were based on Ricœur's analysis of Aristotle, Pascal and Spinoza,
Hume, Kant (two lectures, one each on the first and third *Critiques*),
Ryle, Ryle and Price, Wittgenstein, Husserl (two lectures) and Sartre (three lectures). And there were also five final lectures, which
were thematic and which focused on the analysis of fiction, a theme
Ricœur addressed while conceptualizing metaphor, pictorial aspect
of reference, models and poetry.

As this brief overview shows, in these lectures, Ricœur did not
treat any other philosophical tradition as extensively as phenomenology.[146] Moreover, in these lectures, Ricœur addressed Sartre far

---

[146] Admittedly, Ricœur's analysis of the phenomenological tradition is of a cursory
nature. His reflections on Husserl do not address the manuscripts that focused
on phantasy and image consciousness, which I addressed in Chapter II (that
Ricœur did not address these is understandable, given that Hua XXIII was only
published in 1980). Instead, Ricœur focused in his analysis on some key passages in the *Logical Investigations* and *Ideas I*. In these lectures, Ricœur did not

more comprehensively than any other philosopher[147] In fact, in none of his other published work has Ricœur presented his critique of Sartre in as great detail as in these lectures. In this chapter, I will supplement my foregoing analysis by turning to some central themes in Ricœur's lectures, which I will address by focusing on his critique of Sartre's phenomenology of imagination.

I will take five steps in my analysis. First, I will show how Ricœur's *Lectures* invite us to rethink the basis that underlies his critique of Sartre's philosophy of imagination. Ricœur has been commonly understood to hold the view that Sartre's chief limitation concerning imagination is that it exclusively focuses on reproductive imagination. However, Ricœur's *Lectures on the Imagination* make it clear that his view is somewhat different. Ricœur does not claim that Sartre so much ignores productive imagination in his work, but, rather, that he fails to properly set up a clear distinction between productive and reproductive imagination. Second, I will suggest that Ricœur's *Lectures* bring to light those philosophical commitments that separate Sartre and Ricœur from each other. While for Ricœur, a clear distinction between productive and reproductive imagination is indispensable, Sartre resists drawing up a sharp distinction between these forms of imagination. Third, in his *Lectures on Imagination*, Ricœur's critique of Sartre is not only hermeneutical, but is also phenomenological. Ricœur's phenomenology of painting, which we come across only in these *Lectures*, invites us to let go of our commitment that there is a sharp and central

---

address either Scheler's or Heidegger's writings on imagination (there were just a few references to Heidegger scattered throughout the text). Finally, as far as Sartre is concerned, Ricœur's analysis focused exclusively on Sartre's early writings on imagination and did not engage in the implicit phenomenology of imagination that we come across in his later writings. In these lectures, Ricœur aimed to substantiate a bold claim: he maintained that in the history of philosophy, we hardly come across any analyses of productive imagination. The analysis undertaken in the earlier chapters of this study must make clear that even if we limit ourselves to only the phenomenological tradition, this bold thesis does not stand. Nonetheless, even though this thesis is to be abandoned, Ricœur's own original contribution to the phenomenology of productive imagination cannot be ignored, nor should it be underestimated.

[147]   For critical engagements in Ricœur's reading of Sartre's philosophy of imagination, see Kearney 1998 and 2004, Busch 1997, Stawarska 2001, Flynn 2006, Erfani 2011, Levy 2014 and Lau 2018.

distinction between imagination and perception in Sartre's philosophy of imagination. Fourth, Ricœur's *Lectures* allow us to draw an alternative distinction between productive and reproductive imagination, a distinction which is different from the one that we come across in his published writings. Moreover, we can identify this alternative distinction as a phenomenological way that escapes Sartrean criticism. Finally, fifth, I will conclude with some reflections on the two fundamentally different ways in which Ricœur's *Lectures* lend themselves to interpretation.

Where is Pierre? The Paradigm of Absence and Reproductive Imagination

How does Ricœur read Sartre's early work on imagination? Ricœur singles out three levels that make up the core of Sartre's argument. At the first and most fundamental level, Sartre offers an account of the essential structure of the image (see Sartre 2004, 3-16). Sartre introduces a paradigmatic example of an absent object—Pierre, who is sometimes in Berlin, sometimes in London, and generally *appears to me as absent*—and subjects this example to the method of essential description. Citing this methodological basis, Sartre demonstrates that the image has four essential characteristics: (1) it is a consciousness (it is a unique type of intentionality); (2) it is marked by quasi-observation (although the imaged object is observable, one can only observe in it what one has put into it); (3) it is given as nothingness (the object of an image is not sensibly intuitive); and (4) the image consciousness is marked by spontaneity (this consciousness produces and conserves the object as imaged).

At the second level, along the lines of the initial inquiry, Sartre lays out the general field of imagination, what he calls the "image family" (see Sartre 2004, 17-53). Portraits, caricatures, imitations, schematic drawings as well as mental images are the most important members of this family. Ricœur is particularly impressed by this analysis. He is especially impressed by the following insight, which Sartre appropriates from the early Husserl and which makes up the core of Sartre's argument: in the case of both physical and mental images, we image something *in* something else, that is, *in* what Sartre calls the *analogon*.[148] "I must say that I am very much impressed by this analysis, because I don't see how we can put within the same framework a photograph and a mental image if there is not in common some equivalent, some representative of the real object that is overcome, that serves as a basis for a leap besides and beyond the material support" (Ricœur, unpublished, 13:7).

At the third level, Sartre offers an account of imaginary life (see Sartre 2004, 123-176). Here, questions concerning the status of the irreal object, the subject's conduct in the face of the irreal, as well as the role of belief and desire come to occupy the central place in Sartre's analysis. In short, "the three steps are first, the theory of absence; secondly, the family image; and then third, the imaginary life" (Ricœur, unpublished, 13:1). Thus, in Ricœur's interpretation, Sartre's analysis of "the probable" (that is, of the role that knowledge, affectivity, movements, words and the mode of appearance of things play in imagination) and of "the role of the image in psychic life" (that is, of the symbol, symbolic schemas and illustrations of thought, of the relation between the image and thought and of the image and perception) are not as central as the other parts of Sartre's analysis.

According to Ricœur, Sartre makes a strategic decision at the first stage of his analysis, a decision which drastically limits the scope and significance of Sartre's argument. "Sartre's choice of initial example is decisive .... I have an image of my friend Pierre who is now absent" (Ricœur, unpublished, 12:2). According to Ricœur, by regularly returning to this example in his reflections, Sartre transforms *absence* into the paradigm of nothingness. Yet, Sartre himself argues that nothingness can be understood in four fundamental ways: as absence, as existence elsewhere, as non-existence and as neutralization (see Sartre 2004, 12). Ricœur contends that the privileging of absence in Sartre's philosophy of imagination not only remains unclarified, but is, in fact, illegitimate. Sartre is the

---

[148]   Let us note in passing that Husserl subsequently discarded this view as illegitimate. Already in the second part of his lectures on phantasy and image consciousness from 1905, Husserl reached the conclusion that only in the case of image consciousness does one see something in something else. As far as phantasy is concerned, this duality is missing.

victim of his own example: he isolates absence as the paradigm of nothingness, even though his own taxonomy of nothingness does not justify this strategy.[149]

According to Ricœur, this illegitimate reduction of nothingness to absence disturbs Sartre's further treatment of imagination at the second and third levels of his analysis. Ricœur thus speaks of "the tyranny of the example" (Ricœur, unpublished, 12:19). He maintains that by building a philosophy of imagination on the paradigm of absence, Sartre is only able to offer an account of *reproductive imagination* – that is, that type of imagination which provides copies, or replicas, of the pregiven reality. According to Ricœur, because Sartre's conception of the image is an extension of his theory of absence, it does not cover the theory of fiction. Given this limitation, Sartre's accounts of both the field of imagination and the field of imaginary life remain illegitimately restrictive: the genuinely productive nature of imagination – its capacity to refashion and transform the world itself by enabling the subject to move beyond the established norms, structures and institutions – exceeds the scope of Sartre's philosophy of imagination.

---

[149]   In a recent contribution, Kwok-ying Lau brings this contention into question. According to Lau, if we focus not on the opening pages of Sartre's *The Imaginary*, but on the remarkably rich conclusion, we come to realize that Sartre relies, in some crucial points of his analysis, on examples that do not belong to the paradigm of absence, but rather, to the paradigm of non-existence. Thus, in his account of the freedom of consciousness, which he conceptualizes as the condition of image consciousness, Sartre develops his position not with reference to Pierre, but with reference to an example borrowed from Husserl's *Ideen I*, namely, the example of a flute-playing centaur (see Lau 2018, 152-153). As Sartre has it, "the arbitrary positing of the real as a world will not of itself make the centaur appear as an irreal object. For the centaur to arise as irreal, the world must be grasped precisely as world-where-the-centaur-is-not, and this can be produced only if different motivations lead consciousness to grasp the world as being exactly such that the centaur has no place in it" (Sartre 2004, 185). Commenting on this passage, as well as on Sartre's Conclusion to *The Imaginary* as a whole, Lau writes: "Sartre not only has not excluded image-fiction, thematized by Ricœur, as a family of image produced without any reference to an original in the order of reality; in addition, through the understanding of the act of imaginary consciousness as an act of nihilation of the world of reality, Sartre has given an ontological foundation to the creation and production of image-fiction through the description of the operation of the act of image consciousness" (Lau 2018, 153).

Ricœur as Sartre's Follower and Adversary

Although Ricœur presents the contours of this critique in his published essays on imagination (See especially Ricœur 1981, also 1979a and 1979b), nowhere else does he articulate this critique in as much detail as in the 12th, 13th and 14th *Lectures*, all of which are dedicated exclusively to the analysis of Sartre's philosophy of imagination. These lectures also enable one to see what Ricœur's published essays leave out of sight: Ricœur fully subscribes to the fourfold taxonomy of nothingness that Sartre maps out in *The Imaginary*.[150] In this regard, Ricœur is not merely Sartre's adversary, but also his follower.

When Ricœur's contribution is situated within the framework of the Sartrean legacy, one can further argue that Ricœur's philosophy of imagination is designed to fill a gap within the history of phenomenological studies of imagination. While Husserl's phenomenology of imagination focuses, first and foremost, on *neutralization*, and while Sartre's works transform *absence* and *existence elsewhere* into paradigms of nothingness,[151] Ricœur's philosophy of imagination focuses on the fourth figure of nothingness, namely, on *nonexistence*. In this regard, Ricœur's ambition is not to oppose Sartre's insights. Rather, one can conceive of his philosophy of imagination as an attempt to develop further, even to complete, the phenomenological project of conceptualizing the image as nothingness in the four fundamental senses of this term that we come across in Sartre's *The Imaginary*.

Ricœur is not only Sartre's follower, but also his critic. What exactly is Ricœur's critique of Sartre's philosophy of imagination based on? Supposedly, despite his ambition to give us a general theory of imagination, Sartre only gives us an account of reproductive imagination and passes it off as though it were a general theory

---

[150] As Ricœur remarks in the 12th *Lecture*, "it may be that the fundamental contribution of phenomenology is to have made of nothingness a phenomenological feature of the imaginary" (Ricœur, unpublished, 12:17).

[151] As Ricœur argues on various occasions in the *Lectures*, Sartre's example of Pierre, who is now and again in London, and now and again in Berlin, can be understood both as an example of absence and of existence elsewhere.

of imagination.[152] By contrast, Ricœur's own central ambition is to offer a hermeneutic phenomenology of productive imagination. It therefore seems that the difference between Sartre and Ricœur could not be greater. It seems that Sartre's writings on imagination represent the culmination of a tendency, which — Ricœur argues — is inscribed in the heart of Western philosophy of imagination, namely, the tendency to disregard productive imagination and focus exclusively on reproductive imagination.

It is hard to sustain this critique in light of Sartre's own writings. As I have already suggested in Chapter VII, with Ricœur's critique in mind, Thomas Busch, Beata Stawarska, Thomas Flynn, Farhang Erfani, Lior Levy and Kwok-ying Lau have demonstrated that productive imagination is by no means extraneous to Sartre's works.[153] Armed with this literature, one can single out at least three responses to Ricœur's critique. First, along with Thomas Busch and Farhang Erfani, one can argue that Sartre's philosophy of imagination cannot be reduced to what he states in *Imagination* and *The Imaginary*. It is precisely in Sartre's later works (such as *What is Literature?* and "A Plea for Intellectuals") that we come across a philosophy of imagination that takes into account the productivity of imagination and thereby demonstrates the limited scope of Ricœur's criticism.[154] Second, following Beata Stawarska, one can also argue that Sartre's *Imagination* and *The Imaginary* are highly ambiguous studies of imagination. Sartre's own ambition notwithstanding, these early works fail to offer a uniform theory of imagination because they are based on two competing sources of inspiration. On

---

[152]   Lior Levy recently suggested, for instance, that "commenting on Jean-Paul Sartre's theory of imagination, Paul Ricœur argues that Sartre fails to address the productive nature of imaginative acts" (Levy 2014, 43). "My aim in this paper," she went on to maintain, "is to offer an outline of Sartre's non-mimetic notion of imagination, and by so doing to rebut Ricœur's criticism" (Levy 2014, 45).

[153]   In this framework, Richard Kearney's defense of Ricœur's critique of Sartre constitutes an exception. See Kearney 1998 and 2004.

[154]   As Farhang Erfani argues, Ricœur is "partly right, but his argument is too partly limited to Sartre's early phenomenology of imagination. In the early phenomenology, only the escapist and impoverished attitude of imagination was considered, which of course was better fleshed out as bad faith later on…. Sartre's real productive imagination was not in his actual work on imagination" (Erfani 2011, 4).

the one hand, they presuppose Husserl's early account of imagination, which invites one to conceive of all imaginary acts as though they had the structure of a picture ("I see something *in* something else," that is, in what Sartre calls the *analogon*). Yet, on the other hand, they also presuppose Husserl's late account of imagination, which resists the conception of phantasy as a picture and invites one to claim that the image is *only* a relation.[155] While "the pictorial account" leads to the positing of what Ricœur calls "the primacy of the original," "the relational account" presents imagination as a free and creative activity.[156] Third, along with Lior Levy, one could further maintain that Sartre's account of reading, which we come across in *The Imaginary* and which conceptualizes reading as a hybrid consciousness ("half sign, half imagining," [Sartre 2004, 67]), shows how imagination can intend not merely replicas of pre-existent realities, but also can create non-existent worlds.

Thus, neither Sartre's early studies on imagination nor his later work reduces the image to its representational function. To reinforce this point, one can add two more observations. First, one should not disregard Sartre's anti-Humean claim: the image is not a reborn sensation (see Sartre 2004, 10). Arguably the strongest evidence for this lies in the dual insight that the imaged object obeys neither the principle of individuation nor the principle of identity (see Sartre 2004, 90-93). This means that even the most reproductive images distort the represented object: these images necessarily modify sensory givenness and render to consciousness what lies beyond the perceptual grasp. One must therefore admit that the image cannot be subsumed under the category of reproductive imagination. Second, one should not overlook Sartre's reflections on the symbol and symbolic schemas (see Sartre 2004, 97-122), which are essential to his account of the role of the image in psychic life.

---

[155]   With regard to the different accounts of imagination in Husserl's early and late works, see Jansen 2005, 121-132.

[156]   "[E]ven though Sartre's principal theory of imagination is that of pictorial representation, he also allows for a presentation of imaginary activity in terms of suspension of belief in the manner of the later Husserl. As such, he leaves room for theorizing imagination as a free and creative subjective activity; he also throws light on the internal division apparent within the life of the subject engaged in an imaginary scenario..." (Stawarska 2001, 100).

Sartre's contentions – that "the image plays neither the role of illustration nor that of support for thought" and that "the function of the image is *symbolic*" (Sartre 2004, 97) – suggest that images are types of pre-conceptual thought, which to a large degree determine one's worldview.

In this regard, it is crucial not to overlook the role that examples play in Sartre's writings. It is a common strategy in philosophy to use examples in general, and anecdotes in particular, with the aim of making one's arguments more comprehensible. In this regard, as Mary Warnock insightfully remarks, Sartre's philosophy might have been "the only philosophy to hold that the anecdote was enough, or rather that it was better than an argument" (Warnock 1978, 60). Thus, the images we come across in Sartre's writings take the place of arguments. They are meant to be productive; that is, they are designed to generate insights and transform the understanding of any phenomenon under consideration.

There are, thus, good reasons to resist Ricœur's contention that Sartre's *The Imaginary* is exclusively focused on reproductive imagination and that it disregards productive imagination entirely. If we are compelled by these reasons, we are also drawn to further questions: why would Ricœur make such a bold claim? How could Ricœur possibly think that Sartre, whose contributions to fiction are no less important than his contributions to philosophy, is entirely unaware of productive imagination? We can come to terms with these questions only if we keep in mind that Ricouer relies on a very specific conception of productive imagination. Ricœur takes over a concept with its own history, transforms the meaning of this concept, and subsequently proclaims that the concept, this time understood in accordance with its new meaning, is not to be found either in phenomenology or in any other philosophical tradition. For Ricœur, to claim that imagination is productive is to suggest that imagination can augment and transfigure the actual world. In this regard, one has to concede that we do not come across *such* a concept of concept of in Sartre's writings. The reason for this lies in Sartre's strategic bifurcation of perception and imagination, which, in turn, implies the corresponding bifurcation of the real and the imaginary.[157] This means that, as Kathleen Lennon puts it with reference to the examples Sartre employs in *The Imaginary*, "although the imagination is at work when we see Franconay as Chevalier, it is not at work, according to him [Sartre], when we see her as Franconay" (Lennon 2018, 118). This means that Ricœur's own conception of productive imagination is not to be found in Sartre's writings. This does *not* mean, however, that Sartre only speaks of reproductive imagination, in Ricœur's sense. The very distinction between productive and reproductive imagination that lies at the core of Ricœur's philosophy of the imagination has its own limits, and to a certain degree, is an instance of a fallacy of bifurcation. Sartre's account of the creation of fictional objects, which belong to the field of the imaginary, can be explained in accordance neither with the model of reproductive nor with productive imagination (in Ricœur's sense). Of decisive importance is the realization that, according to Sartre, the act of image consciousness is an irrealizing act, that is, an act that surpasses the world of reality and thereby enables image consciousness to create fictional entities that need not refer to objects within the real world. These fictional entities cannot be explained as products of reproductive imagination, yet, at the same time, they cannot be conceptualized as the accomplishments of productive imagination either (in Ricœur's sense of the term), since they do not augment or transfigure the world of reality. According to Sartre, the surpassing of the world of reality is in truth its nihilation, which means that by surpassing the world, image consciousness also constitutes the world as a world of reality (in the sense of defining its limits). Thus, in a curious way, Sartre's image consciousness constitutes nothing less than the world of reality, although without augmenting it or transfiguring it.[158]

---

[157]   As Sartre has it, "the image and the perception, far from being two elementary psychic factors of similar quality and that simply enter into different combinations, represent the two great irreducible attitudes of consciousness. It follows that they exclude one another" (Sartre 2004, 120).

[158]   As Kwok-ying Lau has it, "Sartre's explication of consciousness as imaginary consciousness, which constitutes the world as world by surpassing the world of reality in its act of nihilation towards the order of irreal, succeeds also in giving a transcendental status to consciousness, yet without the need to sacrifice the existence of the world of reality" (Lau 2018, 154).

At a Crossroads: Sartre and Ricœur Part Ways

Are we therefore to conclude that Ricœur's critique of Sartre is an instance of a misplaced criticism, and, thereby, are we to corroborate the prevailing view in the literature on Sartre's and Ricœur's philosophies of imagination? Such a conclusion would be premature. The reason for this brings us back to Ricœur's *Lectures on Imagination*. Towards the end of his 14th Lecture (which is the third and last lecture on Sartre), Ricœur writes: "I am convinced that Sartre has solved some of the difficulties of a theory of *productive imagination* by providing a general theory of the unreal on the basis of a limited phenomenology of the absent" (Ricœur, unpublished, 14:17, *emphasis added*). Thus, according to Ricœur, Sartre has something important to tell us about productive imagination. How, then, are we to understand Ricœur's critique of Sartre? Arguably, the problem is not that Sartre fails to address productive imagination, but rather that *he fails to draw a clear distinction between productive and reproductive imagination*. According to Ricœur, due to his failure to distinguish between these two forms of imagination, Sartre cannot give an accurate account of productive imagination.

Such a reformulation of Ricœur's critique of Sartre enables one to open a productive dialogue between these two philosophies of imagination. It is no longer possible just to point out that productive imagination has a place in Sartre's writings and, on this basis, consider Ricœur's critique futile and the debate closed. One rather needs to ask: *of what significance is the distinction between productive and reproductive imagination for a philosophy of imagination?*

It is in answering this question that Sartre and Ricœur part ways. What are the reasons that underlie their respective standpoints? As seen from Ricœur's perspective, if one fails to distinguish these forms of imagination, one will overlook productive imagination and limit oneself to reproductive imagination. Only a sharp distinction between these forms of imagination can counteract this deficiency. This is exactly what underlies the hermeneutical turn in Ricœur's phenomenology of imagination. According to Ricœur's central thesis, which was addressed in detail in Chapter

VII, while reproductive imagination is rooted in perception, productive imagination is rooted in language.

From the Sartrean perspective, such a sharp distinction between perception-based and language-based imagination lacks phenomenological justification. Sartre's claims that an image is not a reborn perception and that the function of the image is symbolic invite one to maintain that productive imagination cannot be circumscribed within the language-based sphere; we encounter it already in the field of pre-predicative experience. Yet, as soon as one draws a distinction between productive and reproductive imagination in the way that Ricœur does, one loses the capacity to explain how imagination could manifest its transformative force in dreams and day-dreaming, or in such forms of art as dance, music and painting. In response to Ricœur's objection that Sartre is a victim of his own example ("Pierre is not in Paris"), one could turn the tables on Ricœur and claim that it is actually Ricœur who is the victim of his own illustrations. When Ricœur introduces into his analysis such metaphorical expressions as "time is a beggar" or "old age is the close of the day" (Ricœur 1991, 122), he illegitimately transforms inexistence into the paradigmatic form of nothingness, and transforms language into the exhaustive horizon of productive imagination.[159] As seen from a Sartrean standpoint, Ricœur's aspiration to build an account of productive imagination on the basis of the theory of metaphor leads him to a truncated account of productive imagination. Such is the case because there are no legitimate reasons to exclude any sphere of experience beyond the reach of productive imagination. One could call this Sartre's phenomenological resistance to the hermeneutical turn in phenomenology of imagination.

---

[159]   Thus, in the 12th Lecture, Ricœur writes: "to what extent the object elsewhere is paradigmatic also for inexistent objects is perhaps one of the main difficulties of this [Sartre's] theory. Is it possible to build the concept of inexistence on that of absence, because in absence there is existence? There is an existent but elsewhere, whereas in fiction what will be the object?" (Ricœur, unpublished, 21:11) "This for me is the questionable aspect of Sartre's analysis;" Ricœur continues, "it is too much tied to the situation of absence… I should have preferred to start from the fiction…" (Ricœur, unpublished, 12:15).

Admittedly, what I have just identified as a Sartrean response to Ricœur is contentious: it implicitly presupposes that which it does not clarify explicitly. One claims that both productive and re-productive imagination unfold on the language-based and pre-predicative levels of experience, yet one does not clarify how these forms of imagination are to be distinguished from each other. In this regard, Ricœur's critique of Sartre is fully justified: Sartre does not explicitly conceptualize the distinction between productive and reproductive imagination, even though we come across examples of both in his writings. How, then, is one to conceptualize this distinction without introducing too sharp a dichotomy between language-based and pre-predicative imagination?

Ricœur's *Lectures* prove to be highly significant in light of this question. In what follows, I will try to show that this text provides the resources needed to draw an alternative distinction between productive and reproductive imagination. Language in general, and metaphor in particular, do not play as central a role in these lectures as they do in Ricœur's published essays on imagination. One must therefore emphasize that, as George H. Taylor has insightfully observed, the methodological orientation of Ricœur's *Lectures* is distinctly phenomenological.[160] Before articulating in detail how this phenomenological orientation might lead to an alternative and phenomenologically more legitimate distinction between productive and reproductive imagination, I will first address Ricœur's phenomenological critique of Sartre's philosophy of imagination.

Painting as a Form of Productive Imagination

In his *Lectures*, Ricœur offers a critique of Sartre that is not only hermeneutical, but also phenomenological. In this regard, the *Lectures on Imagination* significantly complement Ricœur's published work. Nonetheless, Ricœur does not articulate his phenomenological

---

[160] "It is additionally fascinating to me that at a time when, following *De l'interprétation* on Freud and *La métaphore vive*, Ricœur is said to have made the linguistic or hermeneutic turn, both his Lectures on Imagination and his Lectures on Ideology and Utopia are expressly phenomenological in orientation" (Taylor 2013a).

critique of Sartre from all possible angles, although he does provide all of the necessary elements for such a critique.

According to one of Sartre's central insights in *The Imaginary*, perception and the image represent two irreducible, heterogeneous and mutually exclusive attitudes of consciousness.[161] Sartre maintains that image consciousness does not contribute anything to perception, just as perception does not contribute anything to image consciousness. For Sartre, to be able to imagine, consciousness must be free,[162] which means that consciousness capable of imagination must meet two necessary conditions: it must be able to intend reality in its totality and it must also be able to deny it. Only the suspension of the world-horizon, conceived as the ultimate ground of reality as a whole, can enable consciousness to enter the "world" of imagination. The capacity to posit the thesis of irreality thereby turns out to be the essential condition that consciousness must meet if it is to be capable of imagination. Consciousness must be capable of positing objects that are affected by the character of nothingness, that is, objects that have no place in the totality of reality. Thus, imagination can only emerge on the basis of a "universal annihilation of the actual world," just as perception can only emerge on the basis of a "universal annihilation of the imaginary worlds."

Where does Ricœur stand in regard to this central conclusion that Sartre draws in his *The Imaginary*? According to Ricœur, Sartre's account of imaginary life is too formal—it unfolds within a framework that is too abstract—in that it fails to situate imagination within the full-fledged temporal horizon of subjective life. Sartre fails to see that the "universal annihilation of the actual world" can turn out to be the negative condition that underlies the "capacity to remake reality" (Ricœur, unpublished, 14:14). For Ricœur, it is precisely the coupling of annihilation with creation that renders imagination genuinely productive. When imagination is productive, "it produces a world of its own which enlarges our world" (Ricœur,

---

[161] "The formation of an imaging consciousness is accompanied ... by an annihilation of perceptional consciousness, and reciprocally" (Sartre 2004, 120).

[162] As Sartre famously contends in the Conclusion to *The Imaginary*, "the irreal is produced outside the world by a consciousness that *remains in the world* and it is because we are transcendentally free that we can imagine" (Sartre 2004, 186).

unpublished, 14:14). As Ricœur further observes, "I shall later use some of the modern theories of painting, which show that painting in fact adds to reality" (Ricœur, unpublished, 14:14). It is this reference to painting that underlies Ricœur's indirect and captivating phenomenological critique of Sartre's philosophy of imagination.

Towards the end of the 16th Lecture, Ricœur maintains that productive imagination unfolds in four domains. It unfolds in a poetic, epistemological, political and religious domain (Ricœur, unpublished, 16:17). Some of the most important critics of Ricœur's philosophy of imagination have come to the conclusion that Ricœur conceives of these four domains as exhaustive frameworks of productive imagination.[163] However, in the 17th Lecture, Ricœur further suggests that the transfiguration of experience and of reality that productive imagination makes possible can be studied "on the basis of a certain number of approaches borrowed from different aspects of experience" (Ricœur, unpublished, 17:1) — literary, artistic, scientific, religious and political. Where exactly is one to place what Ricœur here identifies as "the artistic approach?" It does not fit properly into any of the four classifications. It is closest to poetic imagination, and yet it does not need to take the form of linguistic expression. With Sartre's concept of "quasi-observation" in the back of one's mind, one could qualify the artistic approach as "quasi-poetic."

While in his published essays on imagination, Ricœur pays little attention to artistic imagination, in the 17th Lecture, he conceptualizes artistic imagination as the paradigm of productive imagination. Here, Ricœur singles out painting as the "paradigm for all kinds of transfigurations of reality through iconographic devices" (Ricœur, unpublished, 17:7) In its essence, this is an anti-Platonic claim. Whereas for the Plato of the *Phaedrus*, writing and pictures

---

[163]   George H. Taylor argues in his essay "Ricœur's Philosophy of Imagination" that "for Ricœur, three of the four domains of productive imagination — social and cultural imagination (the utopia), epistemological imagination, and poetic imagination — come under the rubric of being fictions" (Taylor 2006, 97) in the sense that precisely because they do not reproduce a previous reality, they can produce a new reality. As Taylor further observes, "the fourth domain of productive imagination — that of religious symbols — is excluded" (103) from this structural characterization.

impoverish reality, since they can offer only the shadows of real things, for Ricœur, in contrast, writing and pictures have the power to transform reality: they are figures of productive imagination.[164]

The 17th Lecture provides a number of examples from the history of painting. All of these examples are meant to demonstrate how, by breaking with reality, painting expresses reality. I will limit myself to two examples, both of which are connected to the color blue. The first example concerns Byzantine paintings. Although we perceive the sky as blue, in these paintings it is presented as gold. This brings out its value, which, in turn, transforms our subsequent perception. Supposedly, if these paintings were to have their comprehensive effect on us, we would no longer see the sky as blue: our vision would project onto the sky a value, and this value would become the inherent quality of the sky. With an eye to the role that the concept of *Einströmen* (*flowing in*) plays in Husserl's late writings,[165] one could say that we are here confronted with the realization that painting, conceived as a pre-linguistic reflection on the lifeworld, flows into and transforms our perceptual relation to the lifeworld.

The second example also concerns the same color blue, but this time as it appears in Picasso's blue period (1901-1904). Picasso's blue period portrays people who are living on the fringes of society — beggars, prostitutes, thieves and, more generally, the poor, the frail and the downtrodden. Ricœur pays particular attention to Picasso's "The Old Guitarist," which depicts a blind beggar in torn clothes, absorbed in the sounds of his guitar and oblivious to his loneliness and poverty. Picasso modeled "The Old Guitarist" after a blind artist he knew in Madrid and completed this painting in 1903, shortly after his close friend, Carlos Casagemas, strongly affected by a failed love affair, committed suicide. Around the time Ricœur was delivering his *Lectures*, this painting was hanging in the Art Institute of Chicago (it is still there today). According to his own

---

[164]　"Plato did not completely miss this point when he compared writing to painting, nor do we in comparing, in a reverse way, painting to writing" (Ricœur, unpublished, 17:11).

[165]　See especially Husserl 1970, §59, and Husserl 1993, 77-83. This concept is first and foremost meant to describe how any sustained reflection upon the world flows into and becomes part of the lifeworld.

admission, Ricœur returned almost every week to the Art Institute "to see the blue Picasso." In this painting, the anguish, isolation, poverty, melancholia and misery are expressed through the blue color.

Admittedly, in the history of painting, this is not an unprecedented occurrence. Picasso's predecessors, and especially the symbolist painters from France and Spain, used the color blue to convey the emotions of sadness and despair. Moreover, in a way that is quite reminiscent of El Greco, whom he was studying at the time, Picasso portrays these emotions by deforming the guitarist's body and stretching it out, as witnessed especially in the guitarist's face and fingers. Thus, because of "The Old Guitarist," we understand why Picasso has been credited with the expressions, "good artists borrow, great artists steal" and "when there's anything to steal, I steal." With Ricœur's distinction between productive and reproductive imagination in mind, one might be tempted to claim that Picasso's explicit admission that the background that underlies his art is not of his own making places his works within the confines of reproductive imagination. Yet, this is not the case. In this regard, Picasso's following observation calls for special attention:

> We all know that Art is not Truth. Art is a lie that makes us realize truth, at least the truth that is given us to understand. The artist must know the manner whereby to convince others of the truthfulness of his lies. If he only shows in his work that he has searched, and re-searched, for the way to put over lies, he would never accomplish anything. (Barr 1946, 270)

Picasso — the artist who, among other things, tells his critics that he cannot be explained — is also the artist who describes his paintings as a lie that enables his viewers to see the truth. One can interpret this turn of phrase as a suggestion that the artist can recognize his work as a successful accomplishment if and only if the viewer is transformed by it in such a way that she no longer sees the blue color as it appeared before. The blue color in this painting is meant to absorb human emotions; it is meant to become inseparable from the emotions it depicts; in the words of William James, it is meant to become flesh of their flesh and blood of their blood.

Although Ricœur does not explicitly reference Wallace Stevens's poem, "The Man with the Blue Guitar," this poem is supremely well suited to illustrate Ricœur's interpretation of this painting. Stevens composed this poem in 1937 and conceived of it as an imaginary conversation with Picasso's "The Old Guitarist." "They said, 'You have a blue guitar, / You do not play things as they are.' / The man replied, 'Things as they are / Are changed upon the blue guitar'" (Stevens 1990, 166). This is the same for Ricœur. By transporting the viewer into the imaginary world, "The Old Guitarist" transforms the viewer's perceptual relation into the actual world. We face here productive imagination in its full force, as it manifests itself in the pre-predicative field of experience.

One can conceive of Ricœur's reflections on painting as the basis of a phenomenological critique of Sartre's thesis that image and perception are two irreducible, heterogeneous and mutually exclusive attitudes of consciousness. If it is indeed true that painting transforms our perception of the world, then Sartre's thesis is unsustainable. What we actually see when we see colors or landscapes is to a large degree shot through with imagination: "Things as they are / Are changed upon the blue guitar."

Nonetheless, one cannot overlook the fact that Ricœur presents his phenomenology of painting in a severely underdeveloped form. What we come across in the *Lectures* is nothing more than a set of references coupled with underdeveloped insights, which, regrettably, are not articulated in any greater detail anywhere else. Why is this captivating phenomenology of painting so severely underdeveloped?

The reasons for this neglect are by no means accidental: Ricœur's phenomenology of painting is opposed not only to the central tenets of Sartre's early philosophy of the imagination, but also to Ricœur's own more mature hermeneutic of the imaginary. On the one hand, it is incompatible with Sartre's insistence that perception and the image constitute two irreconcilable attitudes of consciousness. On the other hand, it is just as incompatible with Ricœur's contention in his published work that productive imagination is language-based. This is the same problematic that I considered in my analysis of Ricœur's published writings in Chapter VII. However, we can now say: the phenomenological emphasis on the transformative nature of pre-predicative imagination stands opposed to the hermeneutic emphasis on the primacy of language. It thereby becomes understandable (although by no means justifiable) why a phenomenology of pre-predicative art in general, and of painting in particular, has no place in Ricœur's fourfold classification of productive imagination. It cannot be integrated, at least not in a straightforward way, into the language-based hermeneutics of imagination. This phenomenology of painting invites Ricœur to give up his claim that productive imagination is language-based and instead assert that language-based imagination constitutes an advanced form of productive imagination, a form whose roots can be traced back to pre-predicative experience. Here, we can recall Ricœur's subsequent observation in *Time and Narrative:* "We owe a large part of the enlarging of our horizon of existence to poetic works. Far from producing only weakened images of reality… literary works depict reality by *augmenting* it with meanings that themselves depend upon the virtues of abbreviation, saturation and culmination, so strikingly illustrated by emplotment" (Ricœur 1984, 80).

In *Time and Narrative*, Ricœur speaks of *iconic augmentation* within a hermeneutical framework: a new vision of the world emerges from the schematizing power of metaphorical language. Yet, as Ricœur's phenomenology of painting in the 17th Lecture makes clear, it is not only literary works, but also non-language-based artworks, that have the power to depict reality by augmenting it. This can be said not only of Picasso's works of art, but of other paintings, too; not only of other paintings, but, more broadly, of other forms of visual arts, too; not only of visual arts, but also of musical works, too. Ricœur's claims in his published writing notwithstanding, there is no need to limit the theme of augmentation to language-based augmentation, which, in effect, means that the project of grafting hermeneutics upon phenomenology has its limits, and that it needs to be supplemented with a reverse form of

grafting, namely, with the grafting of phenomenology upon hermeneutics.[166]

Towards a Phenomenology of Productive Imagination

Following Ricœur's own suggestions (see, for instance, Ricœur
1974, 3), one could qualify his philosophy of imagination as a hermeneutic phenomenology of imagination. On the basis of the analysis undertaken in the last two chapters, we can say that while
Ricœur's published essays on imagination are more hermeneutical
than phenomenological, his lectures on imagination are more phenomenological than hermeneutical. Ricœur's published essays are
hermeneutical insofar as they contend that productive imagination
is language-based. By contrast, his lectures present us with the insight that productive imagination manifests itself already at the
level of pre-predicative experience. Thus, in contrast to the published work, where he defends the hermeneutical standpoint une-
quivocally, in Ricœur's lectures we come across an unresolved ambiguity, an ambiguity which one could further depict as a tension
between the phenomenological and the hermeneutical conceptions
of productive imagination. We face here a tension because, while
the phenomenological conception is grounded in the primacy of
pre-predicative experience, the hermeneutical alternative is
grounded in the primacy of language.[167]

---

[166]　One must stress that such a supplementary move is not extraneous to Ricœur's
philosophical goals. Scott Davidson and Marc-Antoine Vallée make this point
in the Introduction to a recent volume: "Ricœur acknowledges that one could
legitimately speak also of a grafting of phenomenology onto hermeneutics. In
so doing, hermeneutics is able to establish a critical distance from the lived experience of belonging to a tradition. Phenomenology can thus lead hermeneutics beyond the mere acceptance of a tradition and bring about a deeper understanding of its meaning" (Davidson Vallée 2016, xiii). I will analyze this point
in more detail in the concluding chapter of this book.

[167]　Ricœur's reflections on painting represent the phenomenological standpoint
most forcefully. As far as his hermeneutical commitment is concerned, consider
Ricœur's reflections on Sartre's account of the distinction between perception
and imagination, which we come across in the 12th Lecture: "my problem here

While in his published essays Ricœur overcomes this tension by sacrificing the phenomenological tendency and endorsing the hermeneutical one, one might wonder if Ricœur's lectures do not provide the resources to distinguish productive and reproductive imagination in a reverse way, that is, by endorsing the phenomeno-logical primacy of pre-predicative experience? In light of this ques-tion, Ricœur's reflections on the impressionists' use of color in the 17th Lecture gain great significance (Ricœur, unpublished, 17:14). According to Ricœur, the history of color in Cézanne, Gauguin and Van Gogh is the demonstration of the conquest of how the value of color becomes re-expressed in the qualities of things. Baudelaire's critique of photography plays a central role in this context. It is im-portant to keep in mind that the medium of photography, which comes under attack in Baudelaire's *Salon* of 1859, is limited to that type of photography used almost exclusively for the purpose of copying fleeting realities and preserving memories. Since Baude-laire sees photography as a threat to art and its aspirations, his goal is to describe "a madness, an extraordinary fanaticism" that "took possession of all these new sun-worshippers" (Baudelaire 1955, 230):

> In matters of painting and sculpture, the present-day *Credo* of the sophisti-cated ... is this: "I believe in Nature, and I believe only in Nature.... I believe that Art is, and cannot be other than, the exact reproduction of Nature... Thus an industry that could give us a result identical to Nature would be the absolute of Art...." And now the faithful says to himself: "Since photog-raphy gives us every guarantee of exactitude that we could desire (they re-ally believe that, the mad fools!), then photography and Art are the same thing." (Baudelaire 1955, 230)

---

is whether we are not in fact dealing already with an account, because every-thing happens finally in language. When we say that we have perceived or that we have an image, we must rely on the capacity of sentences to have not only a sense but a reference" (Ricœur, unpublished, 12:12-13). Consider also Ricœur's remark in the 14th Lecture: "my claim is that this positive counterpart of the image can be seen only with fictions. Fictions may produce a new reality, be-cause they don't reproduce a previous reality" (Ricœur, unpublished, 14:16). Consider, in addition, Ricœur's methodological observation in the 15th Lecture: "it's only when we start from the fiction, which seems to be non-referential in the sense that it has no object, that a new kind of reference may be opened thanks to the absence of an original" (Ricœur, unpublished, 15:5).

Baudelaire has nothing to say about the photographer's choice of angles, shadows or the light of day. As Ricœur puts it, for Baudelaire "photography was a disaster" (Ricœur, unpublished, 17:14), first, because it described reality without introducing any break from it, and second, because it threatened to reduce art to the level of reproductive imagination. In other words, photography is marked by the complete suppression of productive imagination in that it only aims to transpose the objective dimensions of the exterior world. For Baudelaire, precisely because art introduces a break with reality, it accomplishes what photography fails to accomplish; it redescribes our perceptual relation to the world. This, indeed, is what is essential to art and to imagination: without breaking with reality, that is, without transposing ourselves into an imaginary world, we cannot establish reality's redescription in a way that would modify the perceptual world.

Baudelaire's critique of photography gives us the resources to draw an alternative distinction between productive and reproductive imagination. His critique offers an alternative to the distinction as it is drawn up in Ricœur's published essays on imagination. One can argue that while reproductive imagination is "photographic" in that it merely copies, or replicates, that reality, which we come across in the pre-given world, productive imagination is "artistic" in that by introducing a break with reality, it offers reality's redescription. One can further describe both forms of imagination as utopian if one understands utopia in the literal sense of the term: what is given in imagination remains without place in the horizon of actuality. To borrow Sartre's terminology to express an anti-Sartrean insight, one could say that while both forms of imagination are *isolating* and *annihilating*, only productive imagination is *constitutive* in the sense that it constitutes not only imaged objects, but also transforms our experience of the actual world as well. Moreover — and this point deserves special emphasis in the present context — there are no reasons to maintain that such a constitutive function can only be fulfilled in language-based imagination. On the contrary, as Baudelaire's critique of photography powerfully suggests, productive imagination, taken along with its constitutive functions, is essential not only to poetry and prose, but also to painting. Moreover, when we recall Picasso's "The Old Guitarist," we recognize that the constitutive function is essential not only to painting, but also to music, which augments and transforms our emotive relation to the world.[168]

Ricœur's *Lectures* provide us only with an underdeveloped outline of such a phenomenology of productive imagination. As I have argued, the hermeneutical distinction that Ricœur draws up between these forms of imagination lacks phenomenological justification simply because productive imagination is not reducible to language-based imagination. The fact that the proposed conception escapes this criticism constitutes one of its greatest advantages over the hermeneutical alternative.

Conclusion

In the *Lectures on Imagination*, Ricœur pursues various lines of analyses, which are subsequently excluded from his published essays on imagination. Here, we come across a richness of themes, which significantly exceeds what we encounter in Ricœur's published works. It is not that difficult to understand why some of these themes have no place in Ricœur's published writings: not all of these themes and lines of analyses are compatible with each other. As I have argued, the phenomenological and the hermeneutical tendencies are not easy to reconcile with each other. So also, it remains unclear whether in the *Lectures* language is conceived as the foundation of productive imagination or just as one specific sphere that exemplifies productive imagination. [169] Arguably, these

---

[168]   Consider in this regard Ricœur's observations in the 17th Lecture: "it's strange that Sartre was more ontological in his philosophy of emotions than in his philosophy of imagination, because for him we have only a kind of anti-world in imagination, whereas in fear, joy, and all the fundamental feelings, we are in the world" (Ricœur, unpublished, 17:16).

[169]   Thus, on the one hand, a number of comments in the Lectures leave one with the impression that Ricœur identifies productive imagination with language-based fiction. For instance, as Ricœur puts it in the 15th Lecture "imagination alone is nothing. Imagination is productive only in conjunction with a certain

apparent contradictions remain unresolved in Ricœur's work. As far as the tension between phenomenology and hermeneutics is concerned, despite the ambition to graft hermeneutics onto phenomenology, Ricœur's published essays on imagination suppress the phenomenological tendency while accentuating the hermeneutical one. The ambiguous status that language plays in this framework also remains without resolution.

One can therefore read Ricœur's *Lectures* in at least two fundamentally different ways. On the one hand, they provide alternative (and sometimes more compelling) solutions to the problems that occupy a central place in Ricœur's philosophy of imagination. My analysis of his phenomenology of painting illustrates such an interpretation. On the other hand, the *Lectures* can be read as a testament, clarifying the reasons why such a prolific writer as Ricœur, who considered imagination to be a central philosophical problem and theme, never published a book on imagination. In his commentary on Ricœur's *Lectures*, George H. Taylor remarks that "while it is clear at the end of the imagination lectures that Ricœur is beginning to think about themes that will change his orientation and lead to *Time and Narrative*, it still remains somewhat enigmatic to me that Ricœur did not himself publish a volume more directly on imagination" (Taylor 2013a). The tensions between the phenomenological and the hermeneutical commitments might provide an answer to this question. With an eye on Sartre's distinction between images in full bloom and images in the making (see Sartre 2004, 62), one could say that Ricœur's *Lectures* present us with the development

---

use of language. The verbal and the visual must be placed in a dialectical situation" (Ricœur, unpublished, 15:13). So also, as he suggests in the 16th Lecture, "it's in and through language that imagination may become creative" (Ricœur, unpublished, 16:1). Yet on the other hand, in the framework of his analysis of epistemological imagination, the theory of model replaces the theory of metaphor. In this framework, Ricœur observes that "we could have taken the reverse course and started from the theory of model and then applied it to metaphor. It's only for the pedagogical reasons ... that I did not proceed in that way" (Ricœur, unpublished, 15:14). Moreover, the analysis of painting in the 17th Lecture provides further reasons to maintain that for Ricœur, language-based imagination is by no means the only form of productive imagination and that in the framework of his philosophy of imagination, there is a space reserved for non-linguistic forms of productive imagination.

of extraordinary philosophical reflections *in their making*. No less importantly, they also highlight some of the fundamental tensions in various philosophies of imagination. Ricœur never resolved these tensions and, therefore, never published a volume on imagination. These tensions remain unresolved to this day. One can, therefore, conceive of Ricœur's *Lectures* as a highly significant impetus for the further development of phenomenological and hermeneutical studies of imagination. With regard to the hermeneutic phenomenology of imagination, one can say about Ricœur's *Lectures* what Sartre said about Husserl: he blazed the trail, and no study of imagination can ignore the wealth of insights he provides.

CHAPTER IX
Productive Imagination and Embodiment

Introduction

The analysis offered in the foregoing chapters makes it clear that the phenomenology of productive imagination constitutes an important, albeit often overlooked, part of a more general phenomenology of imagination. At this point, we can safely say that our understanding of the phenomenology of imagination remains deficient for as long as we continue to ignore phenomenological analyses of productive imagination. The very fact that, so far, no book-length studies have ever focused extensively on the phenomenology of productive imagination provides sufficient evidence for why such a study should be completed in full book-length form. It is not my goal in this study to address all of the phenomenologically-oriented thinkers who have devoted time and effort to the analysis of productive imagination. Such an undertaking would be an endless task. My goal, instead, is to open up, not to close off, a field of research. In the preceding chapters, I have focused on the central figures in the history of phenomenology alongside other, lesser known and underappreciated thinkers, who stand out in terms of their explicit analyses of productive imagination from a phenomenological point of view. Fortunately, there are many other thinkers to address under the heading of the phenomenology of productive imagination.

The thinkers I have focused on in this study have conceptualized productive imagination in a large variety of ways. This allows one to qualify productive imagination as an umbrella term that covers various forms and features of imagination and the imaginary. At the end of such a study, one cannot help but wonder: are there any good reasons to speak of the phenomenology of productive imagination in the singular, or should one rather speak of multiple phenomenologies of productive imagination in the plural? The foregoing analysis makes clear that, similar to phenomenology in general, the phenomenology of productive imagination in particular can also be addressed in many ways. The phenomenological tradition provides us with a plethora of theoretical approaches, which cannot be reduced to any one particular model. To paraphrase Ricœur's well-known observation (See Ricœur 1987, 9), the history of the phenomenology of productive imagination is the sum of the classical studies and the heresies issuing from them. Yet, all of this diversity and variability notwithstanding, one can nonetheless identify some common features characteristic of the phenomenological analyses of productive imagination.

In this concluding chapter, my analysis will unfold as follows. First, I will suggest that the goal of enriching our understanding of subjectivity consistently guides the phenomenological analyses of productive imagination. Such guidance comes about by thematizing the relation between imagination, on the one hand, and consciousness, language and the body, on the other hand. While the relations between imagination and consciousness, as well as imagination and language, have been studied in detail, we cannot say the same about the relation between imagination and the body. To fill in this gap in the literature, it makes sense to conclude this study with a chapter on the embodied nature of productive imagination. According to the view that I will present here, embodied subjectivity relates to the world not only perceptually and conceptually, but also imaginatively. This relation happens for two fundamental reasons: the first of which concerns the fact that insofar as we are embodied, we occupy the "zero point of orientation," while the second reason concerns the fact that our embodied relation to the world is shaped by drives, instincts and bodily needs. In short, for as long as subjectivity exists, it cannot help but be an embodied subjectivity; so also, for as long as subjectivity is embodied, it cannot help but shape its relation to the world not only perceptually and conceptually, but also imaginatively. My goal here is to endorse both claims, but also, and more importantly, to demonstrate that there is a deep relation between them. With this goal in mind, I will conclude this study with a series of reflections on social imaginaries and carnal hermeneutics.

Productive Imagination and the Subjectivity of the Subject

Ever since Kant, philosophical analyses of productive imagination were first and foremost concerned with enriching our understanding of subjectivity. Phenomenologically-oriented thinkers commonly aim to understand subjectivity by studying different modes and structures of intentionality. Within the phenomenological framework, productive imagination is commonly understood as a feature that permeates all of other basic intentional relations to the world: sensuous and conceptual, practical and theoretical, personal and social. Imagination is not just a specific modality of intentionality that provides the possibility of taking leave or even escaping from the world. Rather, it permeates all of the other modes of our intentional relations to the world; it colors and shines through those configurations of sense that we discover in the world.[170] Our ability to perceive and conceive can only be established within larger horizons of sense, and these horizons are always already shot through with imagination. Our mode of acting in the world unfolds within practical horizons, which are designed in terms of goals and objectives that are molded by productive imagination. How does human subjectivity inhabit the world? In what fundamental ways is the human mode of dwelling in the world already shaped by the powers of imagination? Is it possible to recognize and identify the fundamental ways that productive imagination permeates our basic modes of action, perception, knowledge and understanding? These are the kinds of questions that phenomenologically-oriented

---

[170] Following Richard Kearney (See Kearney 2015, 15-16), we can distinguish between three different types of sense. First, we discover sense at the embodied level of our existence: sense is *what is given through different sensations*. It is given to us as what we see, hear, etc. Second, we discover sense *as meaning* at the level of understanding. In terms of this type, we understand (or do not understand) what others tell us and through what others convey to us in books. Third, in terms of etymology, sense also refers to *direction* and concerns how we orient ourselves in time and space. In this regard, sense concerns *orientation*. According to the view defended in this study, imagination infiltrates sense in all three of these modalities. It thus affects both what we perceive and what we understand. And what is more, besides affecting sensibility and understanding, imagination also infiltrates the field of action.

thinkers aim to answer in their respective analyses of productive imagination.

Thus, to borrow an expression that Heidegger was fond of repeating in his lectures on Kant and in his *Kantbuch*: a phenomenological reflection on productive imagination is first and foremost concerned with the subjectivity of the subject (*Subjektivität des Subjektes*). But what exactly does this mean? My analysis in the earlier chapters of this study has clearly shown that the subjectivity of the subject is determined in many diverse ways through phenomenological reflections on productive imagination. Some thinkers, such as Husserl and followers of Husserl, were primarily concerned with the structures of consciousness. What must consciousness be like if it is to be capable of imagining, in general, and phantasizing, in particular? So runs the central question to which Husserl's voluminous reflections on phantasy and image consciousness provide an answer. Other thinkers, such as thinkers associated with the hermeneutical turn in phenomenology, were primarily concerned with the link that binds productive imagination to language. How does language, in general, and metaphor, in particular, provide the foundations for productive imagination? This is the central question that Ricœur and followers of Ricœur have attempted to answer. There is also a third group of thinkers who were primarily concerned with the link that binds productive imagination to the body. What must the body be like if an embodied being is to relate to the world not just perceptually and conceptually, but also imaginatively? This is the question that Scheler, Miki Kiyoshi and Merleau-Ponty have each, in their own way, attempted to answer.

We can thus single out three fundamental ways in which the phenomenology of productive imagination contributes to the more general phenomenological goal of enriching our understanding of the subjectivity of the subject. First, it advances our understanding by identifying those specific structures of consciousness and modes of intentionality, without which subjectivity could not relate to the world in terms of phantasy. Second, it shows how language can shape and reshape the human relation to the world. Third, it also demonstrates, how, due to its fundamentally embodied nature, subjectivity's perceptual and conceptual relation to things and to the world is co-determined imaginatively. In short, phenomenological analyses of productive imagination enrich our understanding of the subjectivity of the subject by thematising the conscious, linguistic and embodied nature of subjective life.

Both classical and contemporary research, especially in the Husserlian tradition, has addressed imagination in great detail. This research has understood imagination as a mode of intentionality that relies upon specific structures of consciousness. So also, numerous studies have addressed the question concerning the embeddedness of productive imagination in language, especially in phenomenological hermeneutics and other recent movements and traditions broadly grouped under the umbrella term of postmodernism. Yet, the question concerning the relation of productive imagination to embodiment has been hardly addressed in the literature. This is unfortunate, for a number of reasons. Some of these reasons concern the growing interest in embodiment in philosophy, in general, and other related fields, such as anthropology, biology, cognitive science, communication, education, gender studies, geology, kinesiology, performing arts, political science, psychology, sociology, etc. Other reasons why this topic has not been properly addressed include the growing interest in embodiment in philosophical hermeneutics, which has even given rise to what some thinkers identify as a new hermeneutical field, namely, carnal hermeneutics (See Hwa Yol Yung 2014 and Kearney and Treanor 2015). Taking these developments into account, I would like to conclude this study with some phenomenologically-oriented reflections on the relation between productive imagination and embodiment.

Phenomenology of Embodied Subjectivity

An embodied existence is the only existence available to us. From the moment of birth until the moment we die, we live in the flesh. No theory of perception, cognition or imagination should forget that before we can perceive, think or imagine, we are already embodied subjectivities. This ultimately means that all of the modes of intentionality are expressive of our embodied relations to the things around us and to the world at large. The traditional distinctions between materialism and idealism, as well as empiricism and transcendentalism need to be radically reconceptualized in light of this basic fact that concerns the embodied nature of our existence. This is very much the direction that contemporary philosophy and other related fields of research have taken in recent decades. However, while there is a clear recognition that only an embodied subject is capable of perceiving the world, and while this recognition is coupled with a growing interest in embodied cognition, we cannot say the same about imagination: its embodied nature has not yet been explored. This concerns all of its forms: reproductive and productive, psychological and ontological, empirical and transcendental, personal and social. Few other philosophical traditions have done more groundbreaking work in rehabilitating the body as phenomenology. Phenomenology provides us with some of the richest resources to explore the embodied nature of imagination, taken in its diverse forms.

What does it mean to be embodied? As seen from a phenomenological point of view, to claim that subjectivity is embodied is to contend that it has a material body (*Körper, la chose*) and that it is the lived-body (*Leib, la chair*). As Maxime Doyon and Maren Wehre have recently suggested, this essential two-sidedness of embodiment means that "one can perceive the body in a twofold way, namely from a personal (or first person) perspective, that is, as the subject of perception (*Leib*), or else from a naturalistic (or third-person) perspective, that is, as a physical thing (*Körper*)" (Doyon and Wehrle 2021, 124). The concept of the lived-body refers to the body, understood as the subject of *sensations, perceptions* and *movements*. This is the body that feels pains and pleasures, warmth and cold, tickles and irritations; this is the body that occupies the "absolute here" from which it perceives things around it; this is the body that freely moves from one location to another. Insofar as I conceive of my body as a lived-body, I cannot just say that I *have* a body; rather, insofar as I am embodied, *I am my body*, or rather, I am an embodied subjectivity. So as to emphasize the subjective dimension of embodiment, some have chosen to employ the concept of *subject-body* as the English rendition of the German concept *Leib* and the French concept *la chair*.

By contrast, to the extent that I conceive of my body as a material body, I understand it as an object extended in objective space and located in objective time. Admittedly, my material body is unlike any other object: in contrast to all other objects, *this* body is *mine*. Yet, the mineness (*Jemeinigkeit*) of my material body is of a different kind than the mineness of the lived-body. My material body is a physical entity that is placed in the nexus of biophysical causality. As a piece of material reality, it is subject to the same laws that guide physical nature. These laws are beyond my control. While the lived-body is unlike anything else I can possibly come across in my experience, the material body is very much like all other material bodies. As a material body, the body no longer has the sense of being the body that I am; understood as a mechanistic body, it is something that I *have*. So as to emphasize this objective dimension of embodiment, some have chosen to employ the concept of the object-body as the English equivalent of the German concept *Körper* and the French concept *la chose*.

While this double apprehension of the body constitutes an essential (that is, necessary and irreducible) two-sidedness, it is also important to stress that, as seen from a phenomenological point of view, the naturalistic apprehension of the body as a material body already presupposes the apprehension of the body as lived-body. Husserl expresses this in *Ideas II* by recognizing that the *personalistic* apprehension of the body is more fundamental than the *naturalistic* one (See Husserl 1989, 152). The lived-body, understood personalistically, is the essential precondition of our intentional relation to the world, taken in all its diverse modalities. As we will soon see, it forms the foundations of our perceptual and conceptual relations; so also, it lies at the basis of intersubjectivity and empathy.

If we want to learn the intricate details about the nature of the material body, we must turn not to phenomenology, but to other disciplines, such as anatomy and physiology. These disciplines, however, do not have much to contribute to our understanding of the lived-body. Phenomenology's contribution to the philosophy of embodiment relies, first and foremost, on the investigations of the lived-body.

Following Husserl, we can distinguish between four fundamental senses of the lived-body. (1) The lived-body is the *zero point of orientation*. It is the *absolute here*, which allows the relative *here* and *there* to relate (see Husserl 1989, §41a). (2) The lived-body is *the organ of my will and the seat of free movement*. While extra-bodily things can only be moved mechanically, the lived-body is "the *one and only Object* which, for the will of my pure Ego, is *moveable immediately and spontaneously*" (Husserl 1989, 159). (3) The lived-body is also *the expression of the spirit* (*Ausdruck des Geistes*). In Husserl's words, "the Body is not only in general a thing but is indeed expression of the spirit and *is at once organ of the spirit*" (Husserl 1989, 102). Thus, by limiting ourselves to some basic examples, we can say that our body language (facial expressions, gesticulations, etc.) and the way we dress our bodies up are expressions of different cultural worlds. What is more, the way we "see" the world and the way we sense various sensations is also marked by cultural characteristics. (4) Last but not least, the lived-body is also the *bearer of localized sensations* (See Husserl 1989, §§36, 40). It is a body that feels bodily pain and pleasure, senses heat and cold, feels itchings and ticklings, etc. In this sense, the lived-body is the *field of sensing*.

By further developing Husserl's phenomenology of the body, Merleau-Ponty explicitly and repeatedly contends that embodiment marks our most basic mode of existence and our most fundamental relation to the world. As he puts it in *Phenomenology of Perception*, "the subject that I am, understood concretely, is inseparable from this particular body and from this particular world" (Merleau-Ponty 2012a, 431). Because we are embodied, our consciousness is inseparably bound to the world. This does not only mean that we shape the contours of our relation to the world. It also means that we are situated in the world, not only naturally, but also culturally. As embodied beings, we always already have both an individual and a socio-cultural past that shapes our world-relation. Thus, while he qualifies perception as the primary mode of intentionality,

Merleau-Ponty also explicitly contends that our embodied relation to the world is largely shaped anonymously.

We can understand Merleau-Ponty's distinction between *body schema* and *body image* (Merleau-Ponty 2012a, 100ff) as a reinterpretation and further development of the Husserlian distinction between the lived-body and the material body. The concepts of *body schema* and *body image* have a long history, and the literature on Merleau-Ponty often indicates that this distinction has been misunderstood (see, for instance, Merleau-Ponty 2012a, xlix). In the present context, a basic clarification of the distinction between these concepts will have to suffice. The concept of the body image refers to the body, understood as an intentional object of (embodied) consciousness. It is the intentional correlate of a perceptual and conceptual relation that each of us attributes to his or her body. By contrast, the body schema refers to our pre-objective and pre-reflective awareness of the unity of our own bodies and their sensory-motor capacities. "I hold my body as an indivisible possession," Merleau-Ponty writes, "and I know the position of each of my limbs through a body schematism" (Merleau-Ponty 2012a, 100). Our awareness of our own body through the body schema enables us to judge whether we will fit through a door or on a chair, whether we can move or carry an object, whether we can reach a departing bus before it drives away, etc. Due to the body schema, the body is something more than a mere "zero point of orientation" (see Doyon and Wehrle 2021, 131). The analysis of the body schema enables Merleau-Ponty to transition from the spatiality of positions to a spatiality of situations: the body inhabits a field of action, which it structures according to practical tasks.

Merleau-Ponty's late ontologically-oriented reflections – which act like an umbilical cord tying together all of the perceptual and cognitive, actual and imaginary, theoretical and practical, personal and social activities to our bodies – were further reinterpreted as a bond that ties us to the flesh of the world (See Merleau-Ponty 1968, 107). This suggests another layer, a further reinterpretation of the Husserlian distinction between the lived-body and the material body: in Merleau-Ponty's phenomenological ontology, "the objective body [Husserl's *Körper* – SG] and the phenomenal body [Husserl's *Leib* – SG] turn about one another or encroach upon one another" (Merleau-Ponty 2012a, 117). Such mutual encroachment characterizes not only the relation between the lived-body and the material body, but also the relation between embodied subjectivity and the world: they are of the same *flesh* (*chair*). Such a radical way of developing a phenomenology of the body into an ontology of the flesh demonstrates that "the world and I are within one another" (Merleau-Ponty 1968, 123) and that our embodied relation to the world is a matter of encountering being from within.[171] This causes Merleau-Ponty to supplement his account of corporeality with reflections on "intercorporeality." In a mutual handshake, I experience the other's hand as an extension of my own: "he and I are like the organs of one single intercorporeality" (Merleau-Ponty 1964b, 168). Such intercorporeality is made possible by our mutual embodied belonging to one and the same world: our bodies are intertwined. Moreover, for Merleau-Ponty, such intercorporeality forms the foundations of social cognition. While in his early work, such as *Phenomenology of Perception*, Merleau-Ponty maintains that all forms of intentionality are at their core structures of our embodied relation to the world, in his late ontological writings, such as "The Intertwining – The Chiasm" and "Eye and Mind," he contends that all forms of intentionality are modes of *intertwining* and as such are inherent in being itself.

Embodied Subjectivity and Imagination

Let us turn back to the four determinations of the lived-body and let us ask, why are these determinations important for a phenomenology of productive imagination? Clearly, if it is possible to justify the claim that productive imagination is rooted in the body, we can

---

[171] "Before the essence as before the fact, all we must do is situate ourselves within the being we are dealing with, instead of looking at it from the outside – or, *what amounts to the same thing*, what we have to do is put it back into the fabric of our life, attend from within to the dehiscence (analogous to that of my own body) which opens it to itself and opens us upon it, and which, in the case of the essence, is the dehiscence of the speaking and the thinking" (Merleau-Ponty 1968, 117-118).

only demonstrate this by showing how the body, when it is understood phenomenologically, grounds the possibility of productive
imagination. Let me remark in passing that all four determinations
are important in this respect. However, in the present context, I will
limit myself to the elaboration of the first determination, since this
first determination is, arguably, more fundamental than the other
determinations in terms of establishing a phenomenology of imagination in general, and a phenomenology of productive imagination in particular.

For the most part, when phenomenologists explore imagination, they direct their attention at sensory imagination, rather than
propositional imagination ("imagining what" rather than "imagining that"). More so than with other modes of imagination, sensory
imagination reproduces the general structures of our embodied existence within the imaginary field. When I imagine in the sensory
mode, it is *as if* I see, *as if* I hear, etc. Sensory imagination is necessarily an embodied imagination, although, obviously, not because
the subject of experience necessarily imagines *himself* or *herself*. I can
imagine that I am a different being from the one that I am. Nonetheless, as far as sensory imagination is concerned, it is not possible
to imagine myself as anything other than an *embodied* being. I can,
for example, imagine that I am King Tutankhamun descending into
the underworld, yet when I do this, I cannot help but still "see"
things above and below, to the right and to the left, at a greater or
smaller distance, etc. This means that I cannot help but apperceive
my imaginary lived-body as the zero point of orientation. In this
fundamental sense, imagination reproduces the structure that
grounds my embodied existence, and only because of this reproduction of my subjectivity am I capable of sensory imagination. To
return to the earlier example, when "I" — that is, King Tutankhamun — descend into the underworld, I cannot help but see things at
a distance from my imaginary body. In order to imagine in a sensory mode, I must replicate at the imaginary level the structures of
my actual embodied existence.

One might object that when it comes to sensory imagination,
there is no need for me to imagine myself, or imagine myself as

someone else. I can, for instance, imagine the zebras and the crocodiles roaming in Serengeti national park without at the same time placing myself, or any other imaginary subject, for that matter, into the imaginary field. This is undeniable. Nonetheless, even in such cases, sensory imagination replicates the fundamental structures of my embodied existence. The wild animals I imagine in the Seregeti national park cannot but appear at a shorter or greater distance from the co-posited "zero point of orientation." They must appear to the left or to the right, from this or that perspective, etc. No matter whether I thematically imagine myself (as myself, or as someone else) in the imaginary scene, this does not change the fact that sensory imagination is fundamentally embodied in the sense that it is made possible only by the imaginary duplication of the zero point of orientation, that is, by its transference into the imaginary field.

One might be willing to raise a different objection, which goes like this: even if it makes sense to claim that these observations are relevant for the general structures of *reproductive imagination*, since they concern the manner in which objects appear in the mode of the *as if*, it is nonetheless questionable whether there are good reasons to maintain that this zero point of orientation is truly important to the constitution of *productive imagination*. Is it the case that productive imagination must always be embodied? After all, productive imagination has often has been qualified as transcendental and ontological, rather than empirical and ontic. Could it be the case that, although some form of embodiment must always come along with reproductive imagination, productive imagination, to the contrary, can appear disembodied?

Productive Imagination and Embodiment

According to the view defended by many phenomenologists (admittedly, different thinkers have employed different terms to express this insight), productive imagination is the common root of both sensibility and understanding. This leads to two points: (1) To claim that imagination lies at the root of sensibility is to recognize that our perceptual relation to the world is soaked in imagination. And (2) to claim that it lies at the root of understanding is to complement the foregoing thesis with the further suggestion that our conceptual relation to the world is also imaginative through and through. Let us address these two points in greater detail.

We are beings in the world. This is due to the embodied nature of our existence. Since we are embodied, we stand in relation to things in our surrounding world. The five senses constitute the basic modalities of our sensory relation to the world. They are the original modes of intentionality. Because of these modes, at the most basic level, our intentional relation to the world is fundamentally embodied. However—and this is the point I wish to emphasize in the present context—the embodied nature of our existence does not only provide us with access to the world, but also imposes a limitation on how we relate to things around us. To be embodied is to be situated here and now and to relate to things around us from this zero point of orientation. We cannot help but see things from a certain point of view, which, to put it paradoxically, means that we simultaneously see things and do not see them. We see them because they are given to us; we do not see them, however, because they are given as transcendent, that is, as irreducible to the mode of their givenness. No visible thing can be accounted for as the sum of sense data. This, in effect, means that each visible thing has to harbor within itself the invisible. According to the phenomenological wager (defended especially strongly by Merleau-Ponty, although also by other phenomenologists, such as Scheler and Miki Kiyoshi), productive imagination is what enables us to supplement the visible sides of the thing with its invisible dimensions. In this regard, productive imagination is not a distinguishing feature of human existence, but a dimension of experience that is characteristic of many other forms of life. The possibility cannot be excluded that any embodied being whatsoever—understanding this in the phenomenological sense of term, as an inseparable, intertwining unity of both lived-body and material body—supplements the visible dimensions of things with their invisible dimensions and thus relates to the world not just perceptually, but also imaginatively.

Thus, due to our embodment, we cannot help but relate to things around us both directly and indirectly. What is more, insofar as we are capable of reflection, we are beings who recognize the natural limitations imposed upon our intentional relation to the world: we see our own blindness. This capacity to reflect and see ourselves from without ultimately means that we are both in the world and against the world, as Helmuth Plessner puts it (See Plessner 2019, 283). In other words, as Husserl formulates it (See Husserl 1970, 181), we are both in the world and for the world. This dual, or, as Plessner puts it, *excentric* nature of our existence both enables us to recognize the role played by productive imagination in our world experience and places the further demand on us that we shape our world imaginatively. We see more than is given to sight and, more generally, we experience more than we sense. With the help of productive imagination, we stretch the limits of our experience. Moreover, what holds at the sensible level is also true at the conceptual level.

What has just been said constitutes only *one* of many reasons why phenomenologists have consistently maintained that our embodied relation to things and to the world is soaked in imagination. An embodied being is a being whose relation to the world is shaped by instincts, drives, desires and bodily needs.[172] In the phenomenological tradition, Husserl was the first to characterize "inborn instincts as an intentionality that belongs to the original essential structure of psychic being" (Husserl 2006, 169). Virtually all other phenomenologists have followed him in this regard.[173] Instinct is

---

[172]   In this regard, Nam-in Lee draws an important distinction between instinct, understood as instinctive behavior, and instinct, understood as an innate drive, specific to a species (See Nam-in Lee 2021, 241ff). While there are indeed good reasons to speak of "instinct reduction" in human life, *insofar as instincts are understood as instinctual behavior* (for example, nest building), when it comes to instincts understood as innate drives, we need to replace all talk of instinct reduction with instinct enlargement. Nam-in Lee also adequately describes the bond that ties all instincts to embodiment when he writes: "instinct as innate drive manifests itself through the organism's behavior. In this respect, there is no essential difference between humans and animals. The difference between them simply lies in the kind of behavior through which each respective type of instinct is manifested" (Lee 2021, 242).

[173]   For a different view, see Nam-in Lee 2021. Although Nam-in Lee's various studies of instinct in the framework of Husserlian phenomenology are outstanding, I nonetheless cannot agree with his contention that "the different types of post-

the genetic origin of various kinds of consciousness, which further suggests that a phenomenology of instinct lies at the bottom of various fields of genetic phenomenology (see Nam-in Lee 2021, 245). All of our basic instincts — for example, nourishment, sexual desire, the maternal and paternal drives, social intuitions, self-preservation, curiosity, the inclination to objectify, etc. — are rooted in our bodies. Insofar as an embodied being is driven instinctually, it can be characterized as a being that has basic needs and that is never content with what it receives. This is one of the most important reasons why its relation to the world is shot through with imagination. Because it is driven by instinct intentionality, embodied subjectivity

---

Husserlian phenomenology do not address the issue of the phenomenology of instinct" (Lee 2021, 247). I do not think it is accurate to contend that Scheler "does not deal with the phenomenological concept of instinct as a basic concept of his philosophy" (ibid). Nam-in Lee explains this in the following way: "this is due to the fact that in his analysis of instinct he [Max Scheler — SG] is guided by the concept of instinct as instinctive behavior" (Lee 2021, 247). Yet this is hard to accept. I argue in Chapter III that the concept of instinct plays a central role in Scheler's phenomenology of phantasy. The following passage from Scheler's *Cognition and Work* speaks for itself: "there is in all kinds of living beings an inborn system of antagonistic drives and instincts which are ordered according to their intensity, the urgency of satisfying the need, and above all according to originally given, dynamic directions: drives and instincts directed toward a particular value sphere and its accompanying course of feelings; drives and instincts that are originally goal-directed, holistic, lasting, and also effective in respect to rhythmic change of more intensive movement, and are genetically the point of departure for chosen and willful actions as well of for the so-called reflexes. Only if one accepts that the drives themselves originally bring forth the representational images relative to them, can one understand the phantasy world as a form of primitive, childish, and ailing emotional life — but never if one thinks of them as combined afterward from pieces of perceptions" (Scheler 2021, 150). Similarly, I find it difficult to accept Nam-in Lee's further assertion that Merleau-Ponty, much like Scheler before him, is also guided by the non-phenomenological concept of instinctive behavior rather than by the phenomenological concept of instinctive drive that is specific to a species. Consider, for instance, Merleau-Ponty's observation in his account of the phenomenal field in *Phenomenology of Perception*: "we will attempt to reveal the instinctual infrastructure of perception and, simultaneously, the superstructures that are built upon it through the exercise of intelligence. As Cassirer says, by distorting perception from above, empiricism also distorts it from below: the impression lacks instinctive and affective sense as much as it lacks ideal signification" (Merleau-Ponty 2012a, 53). Arguably, according to Merleau-Ponty, impressions are infused with an instinctive and affective sense precisely because they are largely shaped by instinctive drives. In the present context, these observations will have to suffice.

always and necessarily finds itself inwardly compelled to supplement whatever it receives with the constant drive for what it has not received. Its most basic sensations are already infused with values, desires, aspirations, withholdings and yearnings. Embodied subjectivity cannot find itself at rest or be satisfied by what is given because it is *absolutely needy*: without supplementation, it would perish.[174] Since needs pervade its relation to the world, being as such does not satisfy it. This is why it is destined to search for ways to enrich what is given to it, and this is why it constantly aims to overcome what it lacks in a myriad of ways. Our relation to the world is imaginative through and through because the power of imagination arises out of drives, instincts and needs that flicker at the basic level of our existence. As Plessner observes in his discussion of lower animals, "an earthworm is surrounded only by earthworm things, a dragonfly only by dragonfly things" (Plessner 2019, 229). Despite the important differences that distinguish human existence from the life of lower and higher animals, which Plessner addresses so powerfully, and especially in his account of the power of the negative, of which, he maintained, all animals are incapable (See Plessner 2019, 270), in a different and no-less important sense *human beings are also surrounded only by human things*. Resisting what some authors have recently called "hegemonic human exceptionalism" (Dess 2021, xvi), one can say that, much like other non-human animals, human beings are also absolutely needy beings, and therefore, that the human experience of the world is also shaped by instincts, drives and needs.[175] A human being cannot help but

---

[174] So as to avoid any misunderstanding, it must be stressed that to qualify embodied subjectivity as absolutely needy does not mean that embodied subjectivity is absolutely controlled by its needs. Rather, as Ricœur emphasized forcefully in his account of the intentionality of needs (See Ricœur 1950, 88ff), needs incline without compelling, they constitute one set of motives among others, and thus, "there are men who prefer to die of hunger rather than betray their friends" (Ricœur 1950, 93). That being said, human beings can choose not to eat, yet they cannot choose not to be hungry, and in this sense, they are beings of absolute need.

[175] As Ricœur maintains in *Freedom and Nature*, "our needs, in all senses of the word, are the material of which our motives are made. Now our needs are opaque not only to reasoning which would deduce them from the ability to

supplement what is given with what is not given, and the mode in which the human discerns the invisible within and behind the visible cannot help but be distinctly human. As Terence famously puts it, *homo sum, humani nihil a me alienum puto.*

In his early writings, Ricœur highlights the link that binds bodily needs to imagination more forcefully than any other phenomenologists. In *Freedom and Nature*, he argues that *needs* are characterized by a specific lack and a directed urge. Thus, when I am hungry, I am both aware of a specific absence as well as driven towards its overcoming, and even in the absence of any image, I am still driven beyond myself. Needs thus manifest themselves both as a certain consciousness (of absence) and as a certain action, or rather pre-action, which precedes all sensations of fulfillment and satisfaction. Needs compel, but do not coerce: embodied subjectivity is free either to fulfill needs or to sacrifice them in the name of other motives, "as Ghandi chose not to eat in order to affect his adversary" (Ricœur 1966, 93). Yet, how exactly are we to account for this link that binds needs to action? Clearly, in order to act, I must know what I am seeking. Yet, according to Ricœur, needs are blind at the basic level of their existence. Ricœur's answer to this question is especially important in the present context: "we are led to seek the crossroads of need and willing in imagination — imagination of the missing thing and of action aimed towards the thing" (Ricœur 1966, 95).

We can reconstruct Ricœur's argument in the following way: embodied subjectivity can only be in need of what it does not have, which in effect motivates it to search for other, that is, non-perceptual, ways to intend the object whose appropriation would satisfy the need in question. Imagination thereby comes to the rescue: it assumes the place of perception in the absence of the thing. It represents an absent object at a distance; it intends it without giving it; it makes a promise of enjoyment as if this non-given object were able to be given and as if this distance were able to be overcome, that is, as if the non-actual object were to become actual. In short,

---

think, but even to the light of reflection. To experience is always more than to understand" (Ricœur 1950, 86).

"the alluring qualities of need appear through the imaginary" (Ricœur 1966, 97). Embodied subjectivity is no longer merely driven outward from within by needs, but also attracted outward by the imaginary. When supplemented by imagination, our needs obtain their possible objects of satisfaction and embodied subjectivity thus knows how to act. From this moment onward, one can no longer distinguish between the affective and sensible in one's perception. In such a way, imagination provides us with a telos of action, which clarifies why Ricœur speaks of "a central role of imagination in this juncture of need and willing by starting from the intermingling of perception and need" (Ricœur 1966, 97). With these considerations, Ricœur confirms the same point I make here: embodied subjectivity is a creature of needs, who turns to imagination to understand these needs, to satisfy them, and yet, also, to distance oneself from them.

One would be right to observe that, in *Freedom and Nature*, Ricœur conceptualizes imagination and the imaginary in a heavily Sartrean way. Yet, at the same time, we witness in this text a new configuration of meaning that Ricœur is projecting upon the imagination and the imaginary. Ricœur explicitly maintains that imagination cannot be reduced to the function of evasion and denial. He contends that "imagination is also, and perhaps primarily, a militant power in the service of a diffuse sense of the future by which we anticipate the actual-to-be, as an absent actual at the basis of the world" (Ricœur 1966, 97). As we know from Chapter VII, in his later writings and lectures, Ricœur conceptualized this dimension of imagination under the heading of utopia, understood as one particular modality of productive imagination. As Ricœur further suggests, reproductive imagination, understood in the Sartrean sense, as a consciousness of absence, is "a luxury won from an imagination beset by concerns" (Ricœur 1966, 98), that is, by what in his later writings, Ricœur calls productive imagination. Yet, in contrast to these later writings, here, in *Freedom and Nature*, Ricœur emphasizes the corporeal dimension of this original form of the imaginary. In short, for Ricœur, without the imagination, need would not propel us to action.

When need is coupled with the imaginatively given object of its potential satisfaction, it transforms into desire. As Ricœur has it, "desire is the present experience of need as lack and as urge, extended by the representation of the absent object and by anticipation of pleasure" (Ricœur 1966, 101). One could say that while the intentionality of need calls for an imaginatively given object that could serve the function of satisfaction, the intentionality of desire calls for imaginatively given pleasure that would fulfill the desire. It is the anticipation of pleasure that gives the imagined object its full affective force.

As I mentioned earlier, in his account of imagination in *Freedom and Nature*, Ricœur often employs Sartrean vocabulary and conceptualizes the imaginary as absence and quasi-presence. However, by linking imagination with need and desire, Ricœur comes to terms with a conception of imagination that is more originary than the Sartrean one. "The power of imagination to fascinate, to dupe, and to deceive … has to be understood by starting from this function of affective anticipation and of latent valuation" (Ricœur 1966, 102). More precisely, "imaginary pleasure can be uprooted from need and pursued for itself" (Ricœur 1966, 102-103), and precisely therefore, "it is more important to understand how imagination *mediates* between need and willing before breaking the pact by false fascination" (Ricœur 1966, 103). Only when abstracted from the anticipatory function does imagination manifest itself as a consciousness of nothingness, understood as an absence that simultaneously seduces and deceives. In short, for the early Ricœur of *Freedom and Nature*, reproductive imagination, understood as a consciousness fascinated by nothingness, is derived from productive imagination, understood as an affective anticipation of fulfillment.

As embodied beings whose lives are guided by drives, instincts and needs, we cannot help but supplement what is given with what is not given. As Scheler, Merleau-Ponty, Miki Kiyoshi, Ricœur and other phenomenologists have maintained, the human way of discerning the invisible within and behind the visible is largely shaped by the power of imagination. We can take this to mean that in the lives of higher animals, as well as humans, it is drives, instincts and needs which call for the help of imagination in their search for fulfilment. Such a broadening of perspective beyond the boundaries of philosophical anthropology motivates one to further ask: is there anything distinctive about the role that productive imagination plays in human existence? The answer has to be that there is something distinctive. Only in the framework of human existence does productive imagination shape not only our sensible, but also our conceptual relation to things around us and to the world at large. This brings us to the second claim singled out above: productive imagination lies not only at the root of sensibility, but also at the root of understanding.

The fundamental reason for this concerns what in phenomenology is called the founded nature of our cognitive relation to the world. Ever since Husserl, phenomenologists have consistently maintained that our predicative relation to the world is founded in pre-predicative experience. To take genetic phenomenology seriously is to accept that our embodied relation to things around us and to the world at large genetically underlies all of our cognitive activities. This carries far-reaching epistemological consequences: from the start, phenomenology finds itself compelled to give up a century-long epistemological dualism between consciousness and the body, on the one hand, and consciousness and the world, on the other hand. From Husserl onwards, phenomenology distances itself from that kind of epistemology, which, to borrow Thomas Nagel's celebrated turn of phrase, can be characterized as "the view from nowhere." Phenomenological epistemology is grounded in our embodiment, which ultimately means that, as James Mensch forcefully emphasizes, the commonality of meanings must come from our bodily "I can."[176] The very fact that all of our understanding is grounded in our embodiment further means that "there is no possibility of ever achieving a 'pure,' uncontaminated stance" (Mensch 2009, 8).

---

[176]   As James Mensch suggests, the basis of the commonality of meanings is the fact that "we have similar bodies and, by virtue of our social nature, similar body-dependent projects.... It is the gift of those others from whom we learned our body-projects.... The "realm of the ideas" — rather than being timeless — is that of our parents, caregivers, friends, and teachers" (Mensch 2009, 8).

Thus, our perceptual and our conceptual relations to the world are both centered in our bodies. This should be understood in the two senses singled out above: (1) just as with our perceptual relation, so also our conceptual relation to things and to the world is necessarily perspectival; (2) just as with our perceptual relation, so also our conceptual relation to the world is suffused in our instinctual drives, desires and needs. This double rootedness of our conceptual relation to the world in the lived body hints at the double function that productive imagination plays within this framework. First, just as in the case of sensibility, so also in the case of understanding, we need to supplement what is given with what is non-given, or to borrow Merleau-Ponty's expression; in other words, we need to recognize the invisible at the heart of the visible. Only by means of such a supplementation can we make sense of states of affairs within their more general horizons. Therefore, just as we experience more than we sense, so also we understand more than we conceive. This is one of the central reasons, although not the only reason, why the sphere of human understanding is soaked in imagination. Second, not only the perceptual relation, but also the conceptual relation to the surrounding world is of a selective nature. Just as the earthworm is surrounded by earthworm things, and just as the dragonfly is surrounded by dragonfly things, so, also, the human is also surrounded by humanlike things. However, in contrast to dragonflies and earthworms, the human relates to the world *conceptually*, although also in a distinctly human way. As Nietzsche puts it, "we behold all things through the human head and cannot cut off this head" (Nietzsche 1984, 15). This rootedness of human cognition in instincts, drives and needs constitutes the second reason why the sphere of human cognition is shot through with imagination.

Embodiment and Social Imaginaries

According to the view I have here presented, the productivity of imagination is rooted in our embodiment: it is derived from the body's situatedness in the zero point of orientation as well as from its rootedness in instincts, drives and needs. As a productive force, imagination colors our perceptual and conceptual relations to things around us and to the world at large. Yet, we do not only inhabit the world as perceiving and conceiving agents. Rather, as Miki Kiyoshi stresses, we inhabit the world as acting agents and our world is given to us as a field of action.

As acting agents, we inhabit a sociocultural world, which can never be fully accounted for in terms of its perceptually and conceptually intended characteristics. The sociocultural world we are part of is characterized by the way its inhabitants imagine their social existence, that is, by the set of what Miki Kiyoshi calls myths (histories, customs, traditions, symbols, values) and institutions through which members of a social community imagine the social whole. The social bonds that tie human beings to each other are their own accomplishments. More precisely, they are the constitutive achievements of productive imagination. The form of imagination I am here referring to is of a fundamentally social nature and the texture of meaning intended by this kind of imagination is addressed in the literature under the heading of *social imaginary*.

The social imaginary is a concept that refers to the symbolic dimensions of the social world, those dimensions that bind human beings to each other within a shared collective life. We can further qualify social imaginaries as the general background understanding that members of the same community all share. Charles Taylor employs this concept to refer to "largely unstructured and inarticulate understanding of our whole situation, within which particular features of our world show up for us in the sense they have" (Taylor 2004, 25). This shared background understanding cannot be clarified conceptually with reference to any specific intellectual schemes that one might possess while reflecting on social reality in a detached manner. It goes without saying that human beings were bound to each other by the social imaginary well before they started reflecting on themselves in a theoretical fashion. In this regard, what holds true at the individual level proves also to be true at the social level: our conceptual relation to the world arises as a modification of preconceptual modes of intentionality.[177]

The concept of social imaginaries is thus designed to explain the way that members of a community implicitly make sense of their social existence pre-theoretically, and also to delineate how they appropriate the normative images and concepts that guide them in their daily actions and expectations. In his *Modern Social Imaginaries*, Taylor clarifies his choice of the concept of social imaginaries over social theory in the following way:

> (i) Because my focus is on the way ordinary people 'imagine' their social surroundings, and this is often not expressed in theoretical terms, but is carried in images, stories, and legends. It is also the case that (ii) theory is often the possession of a small minority, whereas what is interesting in the social imaginary is that it is shared by large groups of people, if not the whole society. Which leads to a third difference: (iii) the social imaginary is that common understanding that makes possible common practices and a widely shared sense of legitimacy. (Taylor 2004, 23)

The very fact that this common understanding can never be adequately clarified in any kind of explicit concept or doctrine, that is, the fact that this background understanding is of an essentially indefinite nature, constitutes yet another reason for qualifying this shared inarticulate understanding as social imaginary (See Taylor 2004, 25).

For our purposes, the foregoing clarification of the concept of social imaginaries will have to suffice. In the present context, I especially wish to stress the following: the founding bond that brings about human communities cannot be clarified either perceptually or conceptually; rather, its founding rests on the establishment of a common pre-theoretical understanding, which is an accomplishment of a shared productive imagination. As Miki argues in his *The Logic of the Imagination*, the twentieth century has its own myths; and we can certainly say the same about the twenty-first century.

---

177   Admittedly, the relation between theory and the imaginary is not one-sided. As Taylor has it, "if the understanding makes the practice possible it is also true that it is the practice that largely carries the understanding" (Taylor 2004, 25). In Husserlian phenomenology, this dual relation is commonly addressed under the heading of *Einströmmen*.

These myths, understood as social imaginaries, bind humans to each other as well as separate human communities from each other.

While it is obvious that research undertaken in this area significantly enriches our understanding of the social world, it is also undeniable that this research is haunted by the specter of idealism. The claim that social reality is grounded in social imaginaries appears to carry the unfortunate implication that reality has little, if anything, to do with any kind of materiality. One might even wonder how one can in full seriousness maintain the notion that the real is the imaginary. By identifying the social world with the social imaginaries, do we not end up lifting the social field above the one and only domain, which can be rightfully qualified as real? It is not my wish in this present context to engage in the standard controversy between materialism and idealism as it has been carried out in the field.[178] Rather, I wish to stress that what to this day remains missing in the literature on social imaginaries is a clear recognition that because the subject is capable of social imaginaries, the subject is an *embodied* subjectivity. The theoretical discussions that we come across in the field of social imaginaries rest on unclarified presuppositions, which ultimately concern the way we relate to other subjectivities. These presuppositions were addressed in Chapter II: they ultimately concern our embodied relation to other subjectivities. According to Husserlian phenomenology and its subsequent, although slightly modified, defense by many other phenomenologists, it is our embodied nature that renders our relation to others possible. Moreover, as Nam-in Lee remarks, "the different kinds of instincts and the different kinds of intentionality founded on them are the constitutive origin of the different types of world such as the world of meals, the aesthetic world, the religious world, and the moral world as partial worlds within the pre-scientific lifeworld" (Lee 2021, 246). We are therefore in the right to maintain that just as it is with personal forms, so it also is with interpersonal forms of productive imagination: they are all rooted in the human body. By

---

[178] See in this regard Chapter III of Charles Taylor's *Modern Social Imaginaries*, which is titled "The Specter of Idealism" and which focuses on the controversy between idealism and materialism in the framework of social imaginaries.

exposing phenomenological presuppositions that underlie the field of social imaginaries, one can find a compelling response both to reductive idealism and to the no-less reductive materialism. Social imaginaries emerge from and depend on our embodiment. We can imagine only insofar as we are embodied, which does not mean, of course, that the content of our imagination — both personal and social — lends itself to be explained in materialistic terms. Yet. it does mean that social imaginaries retain the dual aspect that characterizes the manner in which productive imagination affects sensibility and understanding. First, as we saw, both at the sensible and the conceptual level, our intentional relation to the world is irreducibly perspectival, which in effect means that we cannot help but "fill in the gaps" and recognize the invisible behind and within the visible. Something similar is to be said about social imaginaries. They are also situated within a certain history; they reflect the community's customs, traditions and values; they schematize the way phenomena appear to the members of the community; being of essentially indefinite nature, social imaginaries constitute the invisible dimensions that color everything visible; as modes of pre-theoretical understanding, they shape the look of things and prefigure the forms in which they appear. Second, as we also saw, our perceptual and conceptual relation to the world is affected by instincts, drives and needs, and in this sense also, everything that we perceive or conceive is affected by our embodied existence. In this sense, also, we have the right to speak of embodied social imaginaries, for they also reflect the drives, instincts and needs that originate at the level of embodied existence. It is the satisfaction and dissatisfaction with how the social imaginaries enable the members of the community to fulfill their multifaceted needs that provide the motivation either to enforce or replace the existing social imaginaries.

In short, social imaginaries are always and necessarily situated socioculturally and historically; the values that they embody are expressive of the drives, instincts and needs that are dominant in a particular community. While the structure of social imaginaries replicates on the social level the structure of our embodied existence (situatedness, perspectivism, horizon), their genesis replicates the rootedness of all other forms of imagination and the imaginary in our embodied existence (drives, instincts, needs). In this dual sense, social imaginaries must remain bound to human embodiment because they must replicate at the social level the two fundamental features of this embodiment.

Phenomenology of Embodiment and Carnal Hermeneutics: A New Ground for the Philosophy of Imagination?

My decision to conclude this study with a set of reflections on the bond that ties productive imagination to embodiment might strike one as deeply unfashionable and anachronistic. Hasn't the hermeneutical turn in phenomenology taught us to respect the freedom of imagination from our merely embodied existence? Isn't imagination that very power that allows us to forget the here and now to which our bodies keep us bound? Last but not least, is it not language — that very thing that separates the human from the animal! — that lies at the basis of productive imagination?

Yet, the widespread interest in embodiment that characterizes the present-day philosophical landscape is to a large degree a reaction against some of the adverse effects that were brought about by the linguistic turn in philosophy. This reaction has been largely motivated by the suspicion that language does not constitute the exhaustive horizon of philosophical reflections and that a revamped philosophy of the body can provide fresh resources to resist the dangers of linguistic idealism.[179] In the present context, I especially wish to stress that in contemporary philosophical hermeneutics we come across a clear recognition of the danger brought about by the idealistic tendency that has characterized many hermeneutical analyses for more than half a century. Consider, in this regard, Richard Kearney's telling observations:

---

[179]   This should not be taken to mean that philosophical hermeneutics is linguistic idealism. Such a critique would be too reductive. It means, however, that the central doctrines of philosophical hermeneutics can easily degenerate into linguistic idealism, which happens when language is conceptualized as the exhaustive horizon of hermeneutical reflections.

[P]henomenological inquiries opened new doors to a hermeneutics of flesh. And yet when the explicit "hermeneutic turn" occurred in the 1960s — with the publication of Ricœur's *Conflict of Interpretations* and Gadamer's *Truth and Method* (inspired by Heidegger and Dilthey) — we witnessed an embrace of language at the expense of body. The journey from flesh to text often forgot a return ticket. And so we find the "linguistic turn" of hermeneutics parting from the carnal as a site of meaning, replacing body with book, feeling with reading, sensing with writing. As if the two could be separated. (Kearney 2015, 16-17)

There was a time when things were different. Ricœur's analysis of the body in *Freedom and Nature: The Voluntary and the Involuntary*, which appeared in print in 1950, provides a powerful counter-example to his own hermeneutical turn. As we saw, throughout this early study, Ricœur speaks of an embodied subjectivity, which he calls the *incarnate cogito*. Here, Ricœur reinterprets the Husserlian distinction between the lived-body and the material body as a distinction between the personal body and the object-body. The personal body creates an inseparable bond between consciousness and the body. Ricœur contends that the link between them is experienced at the very core of subjective life.[180] He interprets this bond as the unbreakable union between affectivity and thought and as the permanent connection between the voluntary and the involuntary.[181]

As Kearney writes, "there is no denying that the linguistic *turn to the text* was often construed as a *turning away from the flesh* — in practice if not in principle" (Kearney 2015, 17). Reacting against these unfortunate and unnecessary limitations imposed on

---

[180] With an eye on the personal body, Ricœur writes: "it is my body which introduces this existential note; it is the initial existent, underivable, *involuntary*. Suddenly the entire abstract relation of willing to its motives comes to life; the brackets which shielded pure description are removed; the 'I am' or 'I exist' infinitely overwhelms the 'I think' (Ricœur 1966, 85).

[181] As Geoffrey Dierckxsens notes in a recent study, Ricœur "builds his entire hermeneutical phenomenology on a conception of embodied subjectivity. This is especially apparent in his first major work: *Freedom and Nature*" (Dierckxsens 2018, 42). As far as imagination is concerned, consider Dierckxsens' further remark, which he makes still with reference to Ricœur's *Freedom and Nature*: "Our embodied relation with the world is thus imaginative and narrative through and through – creating types of cognition that go from basic to more complex forms — and 'imagination' is in that sense 'carnal' (Dierckxsens 2018, 47).

philosophical hermeneutics, Richard Kearney, Brian Treanor, Hwa Yol Yung and others have initiated a discussion of what they call *carnal hermeneutics,* a version of hermeneutics that emerges out of a desire to return hermeneutics to material reality (See Treanor 2015, 71). Carnal hermeneutics is a kind of hermeneutics that "begins in the flesh" and "goes all the way down, from head to foot" (Kearney 2015, 16). What is at stake here is a broadening of the hermeneutical field of research. This broadening ultimately relies on the realization that bodily sensations entail what Heidegger calls "the hermeneutic as-structure." This amounts to the insight that our most basic embodied relation to the world is interpretive through and through. In short, sensations comprise interpretations. But if this is true, then just like all of the other interpretive practices, our embodied relation to the world also depends upon carnal hermeneutics.

The carnal turn in hermeneutics is both a step back and a step forward. It is a step back because it requires the rediscovery of already available philosophical accounts that demonstrate the presence of meaning at the basic level of carnal existence. For Kearney, this means that carnal hermeneutics must begin with reflections on Aristotle and then turn to Husserl, then to reflections on Stein, Scheler, Sartre and Levinas, and then come to recognize how Merleau-Ponty has radically revised the Husserlian line of analysis and how this line was further developed in the writings from Ricœur that precede the "turn to the text" (especially *Freedom and Nature*) as well as some of his later writings (such as *Oneself as Another*). Thus, much like Ricœur's hermeneutics, carnal hermeneutics is a philosophy of detours: it is a philosophy that develops its insights in conversation with others. Besides being a step back, it is also a step forward because it requires that one demonstrate how a hermeneutical turn to the flesh pairs with and enriches the hermeneutical turn to the text. It needs to demonstrate how meaning that originates at the level of sensations is retained and further developed at the level of textuality; it also needs to show how meaning that is developed at the textual level is reabsorbed into our basic carnal relation to things and to the world at large. In short, carnal hermeneutics must demonstrate how flesh becomes text and how text becomes flesh.

One might wonder whether carnal hermeneutics is a new name for an old thing. As Kearney remarks, "my aim throughout is to show how carnal phenomenology is intimately and ultimately carnal hermeneutics" (Kearney 2015, 19). Not surprisingly, therefore, even the authors Kearney points to as spokespersons of carnal hermeneutics are in fact the same thinkers who are usually characterized as phenomenologists (Husserl, Merleau-Ponty, Ricœur, etc.). What, then, is the difference between carnal hermeneutics and the phenomenology of the body? The difference appears to be one of emphasis: just like all other forms of hermeneutics, carnal hermeneutics is also first and foremost concerned with interpretation. The fundamental question of carnal hermeneutics concerns how we interpret the world through our senses. What is at issue in carnal hermeneutics is, then, the distillation of the interpretive dimension from our embodied relation to the world, the extraction of the hermeneutical element from all other components that characterize our embodied existence, its condensation as well as a further investigation into what binds it to all other interpretive practices. We face here a dialectical approach, designed to show how the phenomenology of the body flows into carnal hermeneutics. Ultimately, the differences between the fundamental goals of phenomenology and hermeneutics turn out to be what differentiates the two.

There are two main reasons why, in the context of this study, it is important to address carnal hermeneutics. The first concerns hermeneutics and its relation to the philosophy of the body. At this point we can safely say: there is nothing anachronistic about the proposal to complement hermeneutical reflections on productive imagination with a renewed inquiry into the embodied nature of productive imagination. Such a research direction resonates well alongside the present-day tendency in philosophical hermeneutics to turn back from text to flesh. The main inadequacy that we identified in hermeneutical reflections on productive imagination is the same inadequacy that some of the spokespersons of carnal hermeneutics have identified in the recent philosophical hermeneutics in general: this inadequacy comes from embracing language at the expense of the flesh. The second reason has to do with carnal hermeneutics and its relation to the philosophy of productive imagination. So far, the carnal hermeneutics of imagination is nowhere to be found. The general tendency to move (back) from text to flesh has not been undertaken in the field of imagination. This is surprising, for Richard Kearney stands out not only as one of the main spokespersons for carnal hermeneutics, but also as a thinker who over the last thirty years has contributed more to hermeneutical analyses of imagination than anyone else. It is my hope that *Phenomenology of Productive Imagination* will provide a foothold for the further developments of a carnal hermeneutics of productive imagination. Just as phenomenology of imagination must begin in the flesh, so also hermeneutics of imagination must begin in the flesh.

Conclusion

In the *Critique of Pure Reason*, while addressing productive imagination under the heading of schematism, Kant is conspicuously vague in his account of the nature and operation of productive imagination. As he famously puts it, "this schematism of our understanding with regard to appearances and their form is a hidden art in the depths of the human soul, whose real modes of activity nature is hardly likely ever to allow us to discover" (Kant 2007, A141/B180). As we reflect on the contribution of those phenomenologists, whose implicit and explicit reflections on productive imagination were addressed in this study, we are invited to consider a different hypothesis. The transcendental imagination which Kant discusses is no less embodied than the empirical imagination. If it is indeed a secret power hidden in the human soul, then the soul of which we here speak is fundamentally embodied. In other words, the phenomenological alternative to the Kantian approach suggests that imagination is a power that is not rooted in the human soul, but is, rather, rooted in the lived body. It is a secret power. Husserl remarks on this in *Ideas II* when he writes that "the 'turning point' which lies in the Body, the point of the transformation from causal to conditional process, is hidden from me" (Husserl 1989, 168). More precisely, it is a transcendental power that is embedded in instincts, drives, desires and bodily needs, which in various ways shapes the human experience of the surrounding world by forming the contours of action, intuition, knowledge and understanding. We find support for this view especially in Scheler's, Merleau-Ponty's and Miki Kiyoshi's work. At this point, there is no further need to rehearse the claims that these thinkers present in their writings, since their ideas have already been addressed in sufficient detail in the earlier chapters of this study.

Thus, phenomenology both rehabilitates and radically reinterprets the Kantian insight that productive imagination is the hidden root of both sensibility and understanding. In a phenomenological framework, what is at stake is not the transcendental power of *Einbildungskraft*, understood in a distinctly Kantian fashion (as thematized in the Introduction to this study), but, instead, productive phantasy, understood as a constitutive power and as a form of intentionality rooted in the body (instincts, drives, desires, needs) that shapes the human experience of the surrounding world by forming the contours of action, intuition, knowledge and understanding.

Here we can recall Heidegger's provocative interpretation of Kant and his twofold claim that productive imagination is both the "hidden stem" of sensibility and understanding as well as the intermediary midpoint between them. In the present context, let us leave aside the question of whether such a twofold claim accurately represents Kant's view, as presented in the *Critique of Pure Reason*. In this concluding chapter, I would simply like to stress that, *mutatis mutandis*, such a twofold claim is well-suited to characterize both the phenomenological approaches to productive imagination and the phenomenological accounts of the relation between productive imagination, on the one hand, and sensibility and understanding, on the other hand. As seen from a phenomenological point of view, both sensibility and understanding are rooted in productive imagination. Moreover — and this is also something we have already seen — the genetic account of the relation between sensibility and understanding establishes a mediating role for productive imagination in the genetic project of grounding judgment in experience.

Thus, in a curious way – and in a significantly different context from the one that Heidegger had explicitly in mind when conceptualizing productive imagination in his writings and lectures on Kant – productive imagination proves to be both the hidden root and the intermediary midpoint between sensibility and understanding. However, in contrast to Heidegger, the phenomenological perspective that I here defend suggests that productive imagination is not the original power, which can ultimately be identified with and reinterpreted as original temporality, but is itself rooted in the lived body. Subjectivity never exists in a vacuum. It is not that we are embodied because we imagine, but, on the contrary, it is because we are embodied that we imagine. Our own embodied existence is the cradle of sensibility, understanding and imagination, taken in all of their diverse forms.

Here, we can recall James Mensch's observations in *Embodiments*: "to take our embodiment seriously is to accept that it affects the totality of our understanding" (Mensch 2009, 4). It affects not only the totality of our understanding, one might add, but all of the fundamental ways we inhabit the world. Indeed, "to be embodied is to be in the world," for "we disclose the world through our bodily abilities — our bodily 'I can'" (Mensch 2009, 6). The central place that phenomenologically-oriented thinkers from Husserl onwards have reserved for the body ultimately means that, at least in this regard, phenomenology takes on the opposite view from the one that most Western philosophers, starting with Plato, have defended. As Mensch has it, "it is not the case that if we wish to grasp the reality of the world as it is 'in itself,' we must abstract ourselves from our bodies. It is, in fact, through our bodies that we can grasp the world outside of ourselves *from within*" (Mensch 2009, 7). Yet, how exactly do we grasp the world *from within* our bodies? According to the view presented in this study, we grasp the world in a way that is always already shaped by productive imagination.

References

Abraham, Anna, ed. 2020. *The Cambridge Handbook of Imagination*. Cambridge, UK: Cambridge University Press.

Adams, Suzi. 2018. "On Castoriadis and the Social Imaginary Institution of the Real: Hermeneutic-Phenomenological Affinities and Critiques via His Dialogue with Merleau-Ponty." In *Stretching the Limits of Productive Imagination: Studies in Kantianism, Phenomenology and Hermeneutics*, edited by Saulius Geniusas, 163-186. London and New York: Rowman and Littlefield.

Alais, David and Burr, David. 2004. "The Ventriloquist Effect Results Form Near-Optimal Bimodal Integration." *Current Biology* 14: 257-262.

Aldea, Andreea Smaranda. 2019. "Imagination and Its Critical Dimension: Lived Possibilities and Another Kind of Otherwise." *The New Yearbook of Phenomenology and Phenomenological Philosophy*, Vol. XVII: 204-224.

Almaric, Jean-Luc. 2013. *L'imagination vive: une genèse de la philosophie Ricœurienne de l'imagination*. Paris, Éditions Hermann.

Andrea, Andreea Smaranda. 2019. "Imagination and Its Critical Dimension: Lived Possibilities and an Other Kind of Otherwise." *The New Yearbook of Phenomenology and Phenomenological Philosophy*, Vol. XVII: 204-224.

Aristotle, 2001. *Poetics*. In *The Basic Works of Aristotle*. Edited by Richard McKeon. New York: The Modern Library.

Armitage, Duane. "Imagination as Groundless Ground: Reconsidering Heidegger's Kantbuch." *Epoché: A Journal for the History of Philosophy* 2 (6): 477-496.

Bachelard, Gaston. 1994. *The Poetics of Space*. Translated by Maria Jolas. Boston, MA: Beacon Press.

Baiasu, Roxana. 2020. "Heidegger's Interpretation of Kant's Transcendental Schematism." In *Kant and the Continental Tradition: Sensibility, Nature, and Religion*, edited by Sorin Baiasu and Alberto Vanzo, 61-78. New York: Routledge.

Baracchi, Claudia. 2019. "The Cosmos of Imagination." *Social Imaginaries* 5 (1): 19-36.

Barash, Jeffrey Andrew. 2012. "Ernst Cassirer, Martin Heidegger, and the Legacy of Davos." *History and Theory* 51: 436-450.

Barr, Alfred. 1946. *Picasso: Fifty Years of His Art*. New York: Simon & Schuster.

Baudelaire, Charles. 1955. *The Mirror of Art: Critical Studies*. Translated and edited by Jonathan Mayne. London: Phaidon Press.

Baudrillard, Jean. 1994. *Simulations and Simulacra*. Translated by Sheila Faria Glaser. Ann Arbor, MI: University of Michigan Press.

Bello, Angela Alos. 1991. "Phenomenology as Archeology vs. Contemporary Hermeneutics." In *The Yearbook of Phenomenological Research*, Vol. XXXVI: *Husserl's Legacy in Phenomenological Philosophies*, edited by Anna-Teresa Tymnieniecka, 3-16. Dordrecht: Springer.

Berger, Christopher C. and Ehrsson, H. Henrik. 2013. "Mental Imagery Changes Multisensory Perception." *Current Biology*, 23 (14): 1367-1372.

Bernet, Rudolf. 2003. "Unconscious Consciousness in Husserl and Freud." In *The New Husserl: A Critical Reader*, edited by Donn Welton, 199-222. Bloomington, IND: Indiana University Press.

Bernet, Rudolf. 2010. "The Hermeneutics of Perception in Cassirer, Heidegger, and Husserl." In *Neo-Kantianism in Contemporary Philosophy*, edited by Rudolf Makkreel and Sebastian Luft, 41-58. Bloomington: Indiana University Press.

Biceaga, Viktor. 2010. *The Concept of Passivity in Husserl's Phenomenology*. Dordrecht: Springer.

Blumenberg, Hans. 2000. *Die Verführbarkeit des Philosophen*. Suhrkamp: Frankfurt am Main.

Boehme, Hartmut, and Boehme, Gernot. 1996. *Das Andere der Vernunft: Zur Entwicklung von Rationalitätsstrukturen am Beispiel Kants*. Frankfurt am Main: Suhrkamp Verlag.

Bourdieu, Pierre. 1991. *The Political Ontology of Martin Heidegger*. Stanford: Stanford University Press.

Busch, Thomas. 1997. "Sartre and Ricœur on Imagination." *American Catholic Philosophical Quarterly*, LXX (4): 507-518.

Casey, Edward, S. 1976. *Imagining: A Phenomenological Study*. Bloomington, IND: Indiana University Press.

Cassirer, Ernst. 1931. "Kant und das Problem der Metaphysik. Bemerkungen zu Martin Heideggers Kantinterpretation." *Kant-Studien* 36: 1-16.

Cassirer, Ernst. 1965. *The Philosophy of Symbolic Forms. Volume 3: The Phenomenology of Knowledge*. Translated by Ralph Manheim. New Haven and London: Yale University Press.

Cassirer, Ernst. 1974. *Myth of the State*. New Haven and London: Yale University Press.

Castoriadis, Cornelius. 1997. "Radical Imagination and the Social Instituting Imaginary." In *The Castoriadis Reader*, edited by David Curtis, 319-337. Oxford: Blackwell Publishers.

Curley, Melissa Anne-Marie. 2019. "Miki Kiyoshi: Marxism, Humanism, and the Power of Imagination." In *The Oxford Handbook of Japanese Philosophy*, edited by Bret W. Davis, 447-464.

Depraz, Natalie. 1998. "Imagination and Passivity. Husserl and Kant: a Cross-Relationship." In *Alterity and Facticity: New Perspectives on Husserl*, edited by Natalie Depraz and Dan Zahavi, 29-56. Dordrecht: Kluwer.

De Santis, Daniele. 2019. "'Das Wunder hier ist die Rationalität': Remarks on Husserl on Kant's *Einbildungskraft* and the Idea of Transcendental Philosophy (With a Note on Kurd Laßwitz)." *The New Yearbook of Phenomenology and Phenomenological Philosophy*, Vol. XVII: 268-287.

Dess, Nancy, ed. 2021. *A Multidisciplinary Approach to Embodiment: Understanding Human Being*. New York and London: Routledge.

Dierckxsens, Geoffrey. 2018. "Imagination, Narrativity and Embodied Cognition: Exploring the Possibilities of Paul Ricœur's Hermeneutical Phenomenology for Enactivism." *Unisino Journal of Philosophy* 19 (1): 41-49.

Dilthey, Wilhelm. 2002. *The Formation of the Historical World in the Human Sciences*. Edited by Rudolf A. Makkreel and Frithjof Rodi (Selected Works, Vol. III). Princeton: Princeton University Press.

Doyon, Maxime. 2019. "Kant and Husserl on the (Alleged) Function of Imagination in Perception." *The New Yearbook of Phenomenology and Phenomenological Philosophy*, Vol. XVII: 180-203.

Doyon, Maxime and Wehrle, Maren. 2021. "Body." In *The Routledge Handbook of Phenomenology and Phenomenological Philosophy*, edited by Daniele De Santis, Burt Hopkins and Claudio Majolino, 123-137. London and New York: Routledge.

Drost, Mark P. 1990. "The Primacy of Perception in Husserl's Theory of Imagining." *Philosophy and Phenomenological Research*, L (3): 569-582.

Dufourcq, Annabelle. 2010. *La dimension imaginaire du réel dans la philosophie de Husserl*. Dordrecht: Springer.

Dufourcq, Annabelle. 2011. *Merleau-Ponty: une ontologie de l'imaginaire*. Dordrecht: Springer.

Dufourcq, Annabelle. 2018. "The Imaginary Texture of Beings and Its Ethical Implications: Rethinking Realism with Husserl and Merleau-Ponty." In *Stretching the Limits of Productive Imagination: Studies in Kantianism, Phenomenology and Hermeneutics*, edited by Saulius Geniusas, 129-146. London: Rowman & Littlefield.

Dumont, Augustin. 2019. "Imagination and Indeterminacy: The Problematic Object in Kant and Husserl." *The New Yearbook of Phenomenology and Phenomenological Philosophy*, Vol. XVII: 288-305.

Erfani, Farhang. 2011. *Aesthetics of Autonomy: Ricœur and Sartre on Emancipation, Authenticity, and Selfhood Lanham*, MD: Lexington Books.

Evans-Pritchard, E.E. 1970. "Lévy-Bruhl's Theory of Primitive Mentality." *JASO*, 1 (2): 9-60.

Ferencz-Flatz, Christian. 2009. "Gibt es Perzeptive Phantasie? Als-ob-Bewusstsein, Widerstreit und Neutralität in Husserls Aufzeichnungen zur Bildbetrachtung." *Husserl Studies* 25: 235-253.

Ferrarin, Alfredo. 2018. "Productive and Practical Imagination: What Does Productive Imagination Produce?" In *Productive Imagination: Its History, Meaning, and Significance*, edited by Saulius Geniusas and Dmitri Nikulin, 29-46. London and New York: Rowman & Littlefield.

Flynn, Thomas. 2006. "Sartre as a Philosopher of Imagination." *Philosophy Today* 50: 106-112.

Freud, Sigmund. 1959. "Creative Writers and Day-Dreaming." In *The Standard Edition of the Complete Psychological Works of Sigmund Freud, Vol. IX (1906-1908)*, edited by James Strachey, 143-153. London, UK: Hogarth Press.

Friedman, Michael. 2000. *A Parting of the Ways: Carnap, Cassirer, and Heidegger*. Chicago and La Salle: Open Court Publishing.

Frings, Manfred S. 2001. *The Mind of Max Scheler*. Milwaukee: Marquette University Press.

Fujita, Masakatsu. 2011. "*Logos* and *Pathos*: Miki Kiyoshi's Logic of the Imagination." In *Japanese and Continental Philosophy: Conversations with the Kyoto School*, edited by Bret W. Davis, Brian Schroeder, and Jason M. Wirth, 305-318. Bloomington & Indianapolis: Indiana University Press.

Gadamer, Hans-Georg. 2004. *Truth and Method*. Translated by Joel Weinsheimer and Donald G. Marshall. London and New York: Continuum.

Geniusas, Saulius, ed. 2018. *Stretching the Limits of Productive Imagination: Studies in Kantianism, Phenomenology and Hermeneutics*. London: Rowman & Littlefield.

Geniusas, Saulius and Nikulin, Dmitri, eds. 2018. *Productive Imagination: Its History, Meaning and Significance*. London: Rowman & Littlefield.

Geniusas Saulius, ed. 2019. *Varieties of Creative Imagination*. Special Issue of *Social Imaginaries* 5 (1).

Geniusas, Saulius. 2020a. "Husserl's Concepts of *Apperzeption* and *Weltapperzeption*." In *Die Welt und das Reale / The World and the Real / Le Monde et le reel*, edited by Karel Novotny and Cathryn Nielsen, 187-204. Nordhausen: Traugott Bautz.

Geniusas, Saulius. 2020b. "What is Productive Imagination? The Hidden Resources of Husserl's Phenomenology of Phantasy." In *The Subject(s) of Phenomenology*, edited by I. Apostolescu, 135-153. Dordrecht: Springer.

Golob, Sacha. 2013. "Heidegger on Kant, Time and the 'Form' of Intentionality." *British Journal for the History of Philosophy* 21 (2): 345-367.

Gordon, Peter E. 2004. "Continental Divide: Ernst Cassirer and Martin Heidegger at Davos, 1929 — An Allegory of Intellectual History." *Modern Intellectual History* 1 (2): 219-248.

Gordon, Peter E. 2010. *Continental Divide: Heidegger, Cassirer, Davos*. Cambridge: Harvard University Press.

Habermas, Jürgen. 2001. "The Liberating Power of Symbols: Ernst Cassirer's Humanistic Legacy and the Warburg Library." In *The Liberating Power of Symbols: Philosophical Essays*, translated by Peter Dews, 1-29. Cambridge, MA: MIT Press.

Heidegger, Martin. 1996. *Being and Time. A Translation of* Sein und Zeit. Translated by Joan Stambaugh. Albany: SUNY Press.

Heidegger, Martin. 1997(a). *Kant and the Problem of Metaphysics*. Fifth Edition, enlarged. Translated by Richard Taft. Bloomington, IND: Indiana University Press.

Heidegger, Martin. 1997(b). *Phenomenological Interpretation of Kant's Critique of Pure Reason*. Translated by Parvis Emad and Kenneth Maly. Bloomington, IND: Indiana University Press.

Heidegger, Martin. 2001. *The Fundamental Concepts of Metaphysics: World, Finitude, Solitude*. Translated by William McNeill and Nicholas Walker. Bloomington, IND: Indiana University Press.

Heidegger, Martin. 2010a. *Logic: The Question of Truth*. Translated by Thomas Sheehan. Bloomington, IND: Indiana University Press.

Heidegger, Martin. 2010b. *Kant und das Problem der Metaphysik* (*Martin Heidegger Gesamtausgabe, Band 3*). Frankfurt am Main: Verlag Vittorio Klostermann.

Humphreys, Justin. 2019. "Aristotelian Imagination and Decaying Sense." *Social Imaginaries* 5 (1): 37-56.

Husserl, Edmund. 1960. *Cartesian Meditations: An Introduction to Phenomenology*. Translated by Dorion Cairns. The Hague: Martinus Nijhoff Publishers.

Husserl, Edmund. 1970. *The Crisis of European Sciences and Transcendental Phenomenology*. Translated by David Carr. Evanston: Northwestern University Press.

Husserl, Edmund. 1973. *Experience and Judgment*. Translated by James Spencer Churchill and Karl Ameriks. Evanston, Ill: Northwestern University Press.

Husserl, Edmund. 1980. *Phantasie, Bildbewusstsein, Erinnerung*. Den Haag: M. Nijhoff. Quoted as *Hua XXIII*.

Husserl, Edmund. 1983. *Ideas Pertaining to a Pure Phenomenology and to a Phenomenological Philosophy. First Book: General Introduction to a Pure Phenomenology*. Translated by Fred Kersten. The Hague: Martinus Nijhoff.

Husserl, E. 1989. *Ideas Pertaining to a Pure Phenomenology and to a Phenomenological Philosophy. Second Book: Studies in the Phenomenology of Constitution*. Translated by Richard Rojcewicz and André Schuwer. Dordrecht: Springer.

Husserl, Edmund. 1993. *Die Krisis der europäischen Wissenschaften und die transzendentale Phänomenologie. Ergänzungsband. Texte aus dem Nachlass 1934-1937*. Edited by Reinhold N. Smid. Dordrecht: Kluwer.

Husserl, E. 2001. *Analyses Concerning Active and Passive Synthesis. Lectures on Transcendental Logic*. Translated by Anthony J. Steinbeck. Dordrecht: Kluwer Academic Publishers.

Husserl, Edmund. 2005. *Phantasy, Image Consciousness, and Memory (1898-1925)*. Translated by John B. Brough. Dordrecht: Springer.

Husserl, Edmund. 2006. *Späte Texte uber Zeitkonstitution (1924-1934). Die C-Manuskripte*. Edited by Dieter Lohmar. Dordrecht: Springer.

James, William. 1950. *The Principles of Psychology. Volumes I & 2*. New York: Dover Publications, Inc.

Jansen, Julia. 2005. "On the Development of Husserl's Transcendental Phenomenology of Imagination and Its Use for Interdisciplinary Research." *Phenomenology and the Cognitive Sciences* 4: 121-132.

Jansen, Julia. 2010. "Phenomenology, Imagination and Interdisciplinary Research." In *Handbook of Phenomenology and Cognitive Science*, edited by Daniel Schmicking and Shaun Gallagher, 141-158. Dordrecht: Springer.

Jansen, Julia. 2015. "Imagination – Phenomenological Approaches." In *Routledge Online Encyclopedia of Philosophy*. https://www.rep.routledge.com/articles/thematic/imagination-phenomenological-approaches/v-1/sections/the-role-of-imagination-in-perception-and-thought.

Kaegi, Dominic. 2002. "Davos und davor — Zur Auseinandersetzung zwischen Heidegger und Cassirer." In *Cassirer-Heidegger: 70 Hahre Davoser Debatte*, edited by Dominic Kaegi and Enno Rudolph, 67-105. Hamburg: Felix Meiner Verlag.

Kant, Immanuel. 2000. *Critique of the Power of Judgment*. Translated by Paul Guyer. Cambridge, UK: Cambridge University Press.

Kant, Immanuel. 2007. *Critique of Pure Reason*. Translated by Norman Kemp Smith. Palgrave Macmillan.

Kaufmann, Fritz. 1949. "Cassirer, Neo-Kantianism, and Phenomenology." In *The Philosophy of Ernst Cassirer*, edited by Paul Arthur Schilpp, 799-853. Evanston, Ill: The Library of Living Philosophers.

Kearney, Richard. 1988. *The Wake of Imagination*. London: Routledge.

Kearney, Richard. 1998. *Poetics of Imagining: Modern to Post-Modern*. New York: Fordham University Press.

Kearney, Richard. 2004. *On Paul Ricœur — The Owl of Minerva*. Aldershot, UK: Ashgate Publishing.

Kearney, Richard. 2015. "The Wager of Carnal Hermeneutics." In *Carnal Hermeneutics*, edited by Richard Kearney and Brian Treanor, 15-56. New York: Fordham University Press.

Kearney, Richard. 2018. "Exploring Imagination with Paul Ricœur." In *Stretching the Limits of Productive Imagination: Studies in Kantianism, Phenomenology and Hermeneutics*, edited by Saulius Geniusas, 187-204. London and New York: Rowman and Littlefield.

Kern, Iso. 1964. *Husserl und Kant. Eine Untersuchung über Husserls Verhältnis zu Kant und Neukantianismus*. Den Haag: Martinus Nijhoff.

Kind, Amy. 2016. *The Routledge Handbook of Philosophy of Imagination*. New York: Routledge.

Krois, John. 2002 "Warum fand keine Davoser Debatte statt?" In *Cassirer-Heidegger: 70 Hahre Davoser Debatte*, edited by Dominic Kaegi and Enno Rudolph, 234-242. Hamburg: Felix Meiner Verlag.

Krummel, W.M. John. 2017. "Creative Imagination, *Sensus Communis*, and the Social Imaginary: Miki Kiyoshi, and Nakamura Yujiro in Dialogue with Contemporary Western Philosophy." In *The Bloomsbury Research Handbook of Contemporary Japanese Philosophy*, edited by Michiko Yusa, 255-284.

Lau, Kwok-ying. 2018. "Image-Picture vs. Image-Fiction: Is Sartre Ignorant of Productive Imagination?" In *Stretching the Limits of Productive Imagination: Studies in Kantianism, Phenomenology and Hermeneutics*, edited by Saulius Geniusas, 147-162. London and New York: Rowman and Littlefield.

Lee, Nam-in. 2021. "Instinct." In *The Routledge Handbook of Phenomenology and Phenomenological Philosophy*, edited by Daniele De Santis, Burt Hopkins, and Claudio Majolino. London and New York: Routledge, 241-249.

Lengyel, Zsuzsanna M. 2015. "Questioning Beyond Subjectivity—Cassirer and Heidegger. A Case Study: on the Davos Dispute." *Transylvanian Journal of Multidisciplinary Research*, 20 (2): 296-318.

Lennon, Kathleen. 2010. "Re-Enchanting the World: The Role of Imagination in Perception." *Philosophy*, 85 (3): 375-389.

Lennon, Kathleen. 2015. *Imagination and the Imaginary*. London and New York: Routledge.

Lennon, Kathleen. 2018. "Unpacking 'the Imaginary Texture of the Real' with Kant, Sartre and Merleau-Ponty." In *Stretching the Limits of Productive Imagination: Studies in Kantianism, Phenomenology and Hermeneutics*, edited by Saulius Geniusas, 113-128. London and New York: Rowman & Littlefield.

Lévy-Bruhl, Lucien. 1985. *How Natives Think*. Translated by Lilian A. Clare, 3rd Edition. Princeton: Princeton University Press.

Levy, Lior. 2014. "Sartre and Ricœur on Productive Imagination." *The Southern Journal of Philosophy*, 52 (1): 43-60.

Levy, Lior. 2019. "Ways of Imagining: A New Interpretation of Sartre's Notion of Imagination." *The British Journal of Aesthetics* 59 (2): 129-146.

Lofts, Steve G. 2015. "Cassirer and Heidegger: The Cultural-Event. The *Auseinandersetzung* of Thinking and Being." In *The Philosophy of Ernst Cassirer: A Novel Assessment*, edited by J. Tyler Friedman and Sebastian Luft, 233-258. Berlin: De Gruyter.

Lohmar, Dieter. 2003. "Husserl's Type and Kant's Schemata: Systematic Reasons for Their Correlation or Identity." In *The New Husserl: A Critical Reader*, edited by Donn Welton and translated by Julia Jansen and Gina Zavota. Bloomington, IND: Indiana University Press.

Lohmar, Dieter. 2005. "On the Function of Weak Phantasmata in Perception: Phenomenological, Psychological and Neurological Clues for the Transcendental Function of Imagination in Perception." *Phenomenology and the Cognitive Sciences* 4: 155-167.

Lohmar, Dieter. 2008. *Phänomenologie der schwachen Phantasie: Untersuchungen der Psychologie, Cognitive Science, Neurologie und Phänomenologie zur Funktion der Phantasie in der Wahrnehmung*. Dordrecht: Springer.

Lloydd, Genevieve. 2008. *Providence Lost*. Cambridge, MA: Harvard University Press.

Luft, Sebastian. 2004. "A Hermeneutic Phenomenology of Subjective and Objective Spirit: Husserl, Natorp, and Cassirer." *New Yearbook for Phenomenology and Phenomenological Philosophy IV*: 209-248.

Madison, Gary B. 1981. *The Phenomenology of Merleau-Ponty: A Search for the Limits of Consciousness*. Athens, OH: Ohio University Press.

Mazis, Glen A. 2016. *Merleau-Ponty and the Face of the World: Silence, Ethics, Imagination, and Poetic Ontology*. New York: SUNY Press.

Mensch, James R. 2009. *Embodiments: From the Body to the Body Politic*. Evanston, Ill: Northwestern University Press.

Merleau-Ponty, Maurice. 1964a. *The Primacy of Perception*. Translated by Carleton Dallery. Evanston, Ill: Northwestern University Press.

Merleau-Ponty, Maurice. 1964b. *Signs*. Translated by Richard C. McCleary. Evanston, Ill: Northwestern University Press.

Merleau-Ponty, Maurice. 1968. *The Visible and the Invisible*. Translated by Alphonso Lingis. Evanston, Ill: Northwestern University Press.

Merleau-Ponty, Maurice. 1993. *The Merleau-Ponty Aesthetics Reader: Philosophy and Painting*. Edited by Michael B. Smith. Evanston, Illinois: Northwestern University Press.

Merleau-Ponty, Maurice. 2010a. *Child Psychology and Pedagogy. The Sorbonne Lectures (1949-1952)*. Translated by Talia Welsh. Evanston, Ill: Northwestern University Press.

Merleau-Ponty, Maurice. 2010b. *Institution and Passivity. Course Notes from the Collège de France (1954-55)*. Translated by Leonard Lawlor and Heath Massey. Evanston, Ill: Northwestern University Press.

Merleau-Ponty, Maurice. 2012a. *Phenomenology of Perception*. Translated by Donald A. Landes. London and New York: Routledge.

Merleau-Ponty, Maurice. 2012b. "Review of *L'Imagination*." In Jean-Paul Sartre, *The Imagination*. Translated by Kenneth Williford and David Rudrauf. London and New York: Routledge.

Meyer, Thomas. 2006. *Ernst Cassirer*. Hamburg: Ellert and Richter.

Miki, Kiyoshi. 2011. "Towards a Logic of Imagination." In *Japanese Philosophy: A Sourcebook*, edited by James W. Heisig, Thomas P. Kasulis, John C. Maraldo, 705-707. Honolulu: University of Hawaii Press.

Miki, Kiyoshi. 2016. "Myth." Translated by John W.M. Krummel. *Social Imaginaries* 2 (1): 25-69.

Miki, Kiyoshi. 2021. "Institution/s." Translated by John W.M. Krummel. Unpublished manuscript.

Möckel, Christian. 1992. "Symbolische Prägnanz—ein phänomenologischer Begriff?" *Deutsche Zeitschrift für Philosophie* 40 (9): 1050-1063.

Moran, Dermot. 2013. "'There is No Brute World, Only an Elaborated World': Merleau-Ponty on the Intersubjective Constitution of the World." *South African Journal of Philosophy* 32 (4): 355-371.

Morley, James. 1998. "The Private Theater: A Phenomenological Investigation of Daydreaming." *Journal of Phenomenological Psychology* 29 (1): 116-134.

Morley, James. 2002. "The Imaginary Texture of the Real: Merleau-Ponty on Imagination and Psychopathology." In *Imagination and Its Pathologies*, edited by James Phillips and James Morley, 87-102. Cambridge, MA: The MIT Press.

Mousalimas, S.A. 1990. "The Concept of Participation in Lévy-Bruhl's 'Primitive Mentality." *JASO* 21 (1): 33-46.

Muramoto, Shoji. 2010. "Kiyoshi Miki (1897-1945): Age, Life, Works and Implications for Jungian Psychology." *Journal of Foreign Studies* 61, 7-29.

Nagatomo, Shigenori. 1995. *A Philosophical Foundation of Miki Kiyoshi's Concept of Humanism* (Studies in Asian Thought and Religion, Vol. 15). Lewiston/Queenston/Lampeter: The Edwin Mellen Press.

Nanay, Bence. 2010. "Perception and Imagination: Amodal Perception as Mental Imagery." *Philosophical Studies* 150: 239-254.

Nelson, Eric S. 2018. "Wilhelm Dilthey and the Formative-Generative Imagination." In *Stretching the Limits of Productive Imagination: Studies in Kantianism, Phenomenology and Hermeneutics*, edited by Saulius Geniusas, 23-46. London and New York: Rowman and Littlefield.

Nicholas, Craig M. 2000. "Primordial Freedom: The Authentic Truth of Dasein in Heidegger's Being and Time." In *Thinking Fundamentals, IWM Junior Visiting Fellows Conferences, Vol. 9*, edited by David Shikiar, 1-14. Vienna: IWM.

Nietzsche, Friedrich. 1986. *Human, All Too Human: a Book for Free Spirits.* Translated by Reginald John Hollingdale. Cambridge, UK: Cambridge University Press.

McGurk, Harry and MacDonald, John. 1976. "Hearing lips and seeing voices." *Nature* 264 (5588): 746-748.

Nikulin, Dmitri. 2018. "What is Productive Imagination?" In *Productive Imagination: Its History, Meaning and Significance*, edited by Saulius Geniusas and Dmitri Nikulin, 1-28. London and New York: Rowman & Littlefield.

Nuzzo, Angelica. 2018. "The Productive Imagination in Hegel and Classical German Philosophy." In *Productive Imagination: Its History, Meaning, and Significance*, edited by Saulius Geniusas and Dmitri Nikulin, 63-84. London and New York: Rowman & Littlefield.

Plessner, Helmuth. 2019. *Levels of Organic Life and the Human: An Introduction to Philosophical Hermeneutics*. Translated by Millay Hyatt. New York: Fordham University Press.

Ribot, Théodule-Armand. 1906. *Essay on the Creative Imagination*. Translated by Albert Baron. Chicago: The Open Court Publishing Company.

Ricœur, Paul. 1966. *Freedom and Nature: The Voluntary and the Involuntary*. Translated by Erazim Kohak. Evanston, Ill: Northwestern University Press.

Ricœur, Paul. 1967. *Husserl: An Analysis of His Phenomenology*. Translated by Edward G. Ballard and Lester E. Embree. Evanston, Ill: Northwestern University Press.

Ricœur, Paul. 1974. *The Conflict of Interpretations: Essays in Hermeneutics*. Translated by Kathleen Blamey. Evanston, IL: Northwestern University Press.

Ricœur, Paul. 1975. *Lectures on Imagination*. Edited by George H. Taylor and Patrick Crosby. Unpublished manuscript.

Ricœur, Paul. 1977. *The Rule of Metaphor*. Translated by Robert Czerny. Toronto: University of Toronto Press.

Ricœur, Paul. 1978. "The Metaphorical Process as Cognition, Imagination and Feeling." *Critical Inquiry* 5 (1): 143-159.

Ricœur, Paul. 1979a. "The Function of Fiction in Shaping Reality." *Man and World*, 12 (2): 123-141.

Ricœur, Paul. 1979b. "The Metaphorical Process as Cognition, Imagination, and Feeling." In *On Metaphor*, edited Sheldon. Sacks, 141-157. Chicago: University of Chicago Press.

Ricœur, Paul. 1981. "Sartre and Ryle on the Imagination." In *The Philosophy of Jean-Paul Sartre*. Edited by Paul A. Schilpp, 167-178. LaSalle, IL: Open Court.

Ricœur, Paul. 1986. *Lectures on Ideology and Utopia*. Edited by George H. Taylor. New York: Columbia University Press.

Ricœur, Paul. 1987. *A l'école de la phénoménologie*. Paris: Vrin.

Ricœur, Paul. 1991. *From Text to Action*. Translated by Kathleen Blamey and John B. Thompson. Evanston, IL: Northwestern University Press.

Rockmore, Tom. 2018. "Hegel on Cognition as Phenomenological, Hermeneutical and Historical." In *Hermeneutics and Phenomenology: Figures and Themes*, edited by Saulius Geniusas and Paul Fairfield, 7-18. New York: Bloomsbury.

Sabolius, Kristupas. 2019. "Traversing Life and Thought: Gilbert Simondon's Theory of Cyclic Imagination." Social Imaginaries 5 (2): 37-57.

Sallis, John. 1990. *Echoes: After Heidegger*. Bloomington: Indiana University Press.

Sallis, John. 1992. "Spacing Imagination: Husserl and the Phenomenology of Imagination." In *Eros and Eris*, edited by Paul van Tongeren et al., 201-215. Dordrecht: Kluwer Academic Publishers.

Sartre, Jean-Paul. 1936. *L'Imagination*. Paris: Presses Universitaires de France.

Sartre, Jean-Paul. 1962. *The Imagination*. Translated by F. Williams. Ann Arbot: The University of Michigan Press.

Sartre, Jean-Paul. 1964. *Situations, IV*. Paris: Gallimard.

Sartre, Jean-Paul. 1981. "Interview with Jean-Paul Sartre." In *The Philosophy of Jean-Paul Sartre*, edited by Paul A. Schilpp, 5-51. La Salle, Ill: Open Court.

Sartre, Jean-Paul. 1986. *L'Imaginaire*. Paris: Gallimard.

Sartre, Jean-Paul. 2004. *The Imaginary: A Phenomenological Psychology of the Imagination*. Translated by Jonathan Webber. London and New York: Routledge.

Schalow, Frank. 1994. "The Unique Role of Logic in the Development of Heidegger's Dialogue with Kant." *Journal of the History of Philosophy*, 32 (1): 103-125.

Schrag, Calvin. 1967. "Heidegger and Cassirer on Kant." *Kant-Studien* 58: 87-100.

Scheler, Max. 1961. *Man's Place in Nature*. Translated by Hans Meyerhoff. Boston, MA: Beacon Press.

Scheler, Max. 1977. *Erkenntnis und Arbeit*. Frankfurt am Main: Vittorio Klostermann.

Scheler, Max. 1979. *Schriften aus dem Nachlass, II. Erkenntnislehre und Metaphysik*. Edited by Manfred S. Frings. Bern: Francke Verlag.

Scheler, Max. 2012. "Metaphysics and Art." In *Max Scheler (1874-1928): Centennial Essays*, edited by Manfred S. Frings, 101-121. Dordrecht: Springer.

Scheler, Max. 2021. *Cognition and Work*. Translated by Zachary Davis. Evanston, Ill: Northwestern University Press.

Sekuler, Robert, Allison B. Sekuler, and Lau Renee. 1997. "Sound alters visual motion perception." *Nature* 385: 308.

Skidelsky, Edward. 2008. *Ernst Cassirer: The Last Philosopher of Culture*. Princeton and Oxford: Princeton University Press.

Sorel, Georges. 2004. *Reflections on Violence*. Edited by Jeremy Jennings. Cambridge and New York: Cambridge University Press.

Spinoza, Baruch. 2002. *Complete Works*. Translated by Samuel Shirley. Edited by Michael L. Morgan. Indianapolis, IND: Hackett.

Stawarska, Beata. 2001. "Pictorial Representation or Subjective Scenario? Sartre on Imagination," *Sartre Studies International* 7 (2): 87-111.

Stawarska, Beata. 2005. "Defining Imagination: Sartre Between Husserl and Janet." *Phenomenology and the Cognitive Sciences* 4: 133-153.

Stevens, Wallace. 1990. *The Collected Poems of Wallace Stevens*. New York: Vintage Books Edition.

Steeves, James B. 2004. *Imagining Bodies: Merleau-Ponty's Philosophy of Imagination*. Pittsburgh, PA: Duquesne University Press.

Storck, Joachim W., ed. 1989. *Martin Heidegger und Elisabeth Blochmann, Briefwechsel, 1918-1969*. Marbach am Neckar: Deutsche Schillergesellschaft.

Strawson, Peter F. 1974. *Freedom and Resentment and Other Essays*. London: Methuen.

Taylor, Charles. 2004. *Modern Social Imaginaries*. Durham and London: Duke University Press.

Taylor, George H. 2006. "Ricœur's Philosophy of Imagination." *Journal of French Philosophy*, 16 (1): 93-104.

Taylor, George H. 2013a. "Ricœur's Lectures on Imagination," Keynote Presentation at the conference, *Paul Ricœur et la philosophie contemporaine de langue anglaise*, Paris, November 20.

Taylor, George H. 2013b. "Identidadde Perspektiva." In *Ética, Identidade e Reconhecimento Na Obra de Paul Ricœur*, edited by Fernando Nascimento and Walter Salles, 122-147. Rio de Janeiro, Brazil: Editora PUC-Rio and Ediçoes Loyola.

Taylor, George, H. 2018. "The Deeper Significance of Ricœur's Philosophy of Productive Imagination: The Role of Figuration." In *Productive Imagination: Its History, Meaning, and Significance*, edited by Saulius Geniusas and Dmitri Nikulin, 157-181. London and New York: Rowman & Littlefield.

Townsend, Susan C. 2009. *Miki Kiyoshi 1897 – 1945. Japan's Itinerant Philosopher*. Brill's Japanese Studies Library, Vol. 32. Leiden/Boston: Brill.

Treanor, Brian. 2015. "Mind the Gap: The Challenge of Matter." In *Carnal Hermeneutics*, edited by Richard Kearney and Brian Treanor, 57-76. New York: Fordham University Press.

Wang, Qingjie James. 2018. "Two Starting Points in Heidegger's Critical Interpretation of Kant's Transcendental Imagination." In *Stretching the Limits of Productive Imagination: Studies in Kantianism, Phenomenology and Hermeneutics*, edited by Saulius Geniusas, 77-90. London and New York: Rowman & Littlefield.

Warnock, Mary. 1978. *Imagination*. University of California Press.

Warnock, Mary. 1994. *Imagination and Time*. Oxford: Blackwell Publishers.

Wittgenstein, Ludwig. 1986. *Philosophical Investigations*. Translated by Gertrude E. M. Anscombe. Oxford: Basil Blackwell Ltd.

Yung, Hwa Yol. 2014. *Prolegomena to Carnal Hermeneutics*. Lanham, MA: Lexington Books.

Yusa, Michiko. 1998. "Philosophy and Inflation. Miki Kiyoshi in Weimar Germany, 1922-1924." *Monumenta Nipponica* 53 (1): 45-71.

Zöller, Günter. 2018. "The Productive Power of the Imagination: Kant on the Schematism of the Understanding and the Symbolism of Reason." In *Stretching the Limits of Productive Imagination: Studies in Kantianism, Phenomenology and Hermeneutics*, edited by Saulius Geniusas, 1-22. London and New York: Rowman & Littlefield.

Index